EDUCATING LAWYERS

JB JOSSEY-BASS

EDUCATING LAWYERS

Preparation for the Profession of Law

William M. Sullivan, Anne Colby,
Judith Welch Wegner, Lloyd Bond,
Lee S. Shulman

 THE CARNEGIE FOUNDATION FOR THE ADVANCEMENT OF TEACHING

John Wiley & Sons, Inc.

Published by Jossey-Bass
A Wiley Imprint
989 Market Street, San Francisco, CA 94103-1741   www.josseybass.com

Jossey-Bass books and products are available through most bookstores. To contact Jossey-Bass directly call our Customer Care Department within the U.S. at 800-956-7739, outside the U.S. at 317-572-3986, or fax 317-572-4002.

Jossey-Bass also publishes its books in a variety of electronic formats. Some content that appears in print may not be available in electronic books.

Library of Congress Cataloging-in-Publication Data

Educating lawyers : preparation for the profession of law / William M. Sullivan ... [et al.].
    p. cm.
Includes bibliographical references and index.
ISBN-13: 978-0-7879-8261-4 (cloth)
ISBN-10: 0-7879-8261-X (cloth)
    1. Law—Study and teaching—United States. I. Sullivan, William M.
KF272.E38 2007
340.071'173—dc22   2006037964

Printed in the United States of America
FIRST EDITION
HB Printing   10 9 8 7 6 5 4 3 2 1

The Preparation for the Professions Series

The Preparation for the Professions Series reports the results of The Carnegie Foundation for the Advancement of Teaching's Preparation for the Professions Program, a comparative study of professional education in medicine, nursing, law, engineering, and the preparation of the clergy.

CONTENTS

ABOUT THE AUTHORS

William M. Sullivan is co-director of the Carnegie Foundation's Preparation for the Professions Program. He is formulating a research design for the comparative aspects of the studies, drawing out common themes and identifying distinct practices in professional education. The author of *Work and Integrity: The Crisis and Promise of Professionalism in America* (2005) and a coauthor of *Habits of the Heart: Individualism and Commitment in American Life* (1996), Sullivan examined the link between formal training and practical reflection in effective education. Prior to coming to Carnegie, Sullivan was a philosophy professor at La Salle University. He earned a Ph.D. in philosophy at Fordham University.

Anne Colby is a senior scholar at The Carnegie Foundation for the Advancement of Teaching, where she co-directs the Political Engagement Project and the Preparation for the Professions Program. Prior to joining the Carnegie Foundation in 1997, she was director of the Henry Murray Research Center at Harvard University. She is coauthor of five books: *A Longitudinal Study of Moral Judgment* (1983), *The Measurement of Moral Judgment* (1987), *Some Do Care: Contemporary Lives of Moral Commitment* (1992), *Educating Citizens: Preparing America's Undergraduates for Lives of Moral and Civic Responsibility* (2003), and *Educating for Democracy: Preparing Undergraduates for Responsible Political Engagement* (2007). She is co-editor of *Ethnography and Human Development: Context and Meaning in Human Inquiry* (1995), *Competence and Character Through Life* (1998), and *Looking at Lives: American Longitudinal Studies of the Twentieth Century* (2002). She holds a B.A. from McGill University and a Ph.D. in psychology from Columbia University.

Judith Welch Wegner received her B.A. from the University of Wisconsin-Madison and her J.D. from UCLA. Before joining the faculty of the University of North Carolina School of Law in 1981, she was a special assistant to United States Secretary of Education Shirley M. Hufstedler. Wegner was dean of the University of North Carolina School of Law from 1989 to 1999 and served as the chair of the campus-wide faculty from 2003 to 2006. Wegner has been active in the Association of American Law Schools and served as the association's president in 1995. She was a senior scholar with The Carnegie Foundation for the Advancement of Teaching from 1999 to 2001.

Lloyd Bond received his Ph.D. in psychology from Johns Hopkins University. He is a senior scholar at The Carnegie Foundation for the Advancement of Teaching and professor emeritus of educational research methodology at the University of North Carolina, Greensboro. Dr. Bond has been an associate editor and member of the editorial boards of the leading journals in educational and psychological measurement, and consults regularly with school districts, state departments of education, testing organizations, R & D Centers, and other organizations on assessment issues. He has published widely in the major psychological and measurement journals and has made fundamental contributions to many areas of test theory and applied assessment. A fellow of the American Psychological Association, he served on both the 1985 and 1999 committees to revise the Standards for Educational and Psychological Testing, and from 1997 to 2002 was Senior Advisor to the National Board for Professional Teaching Standards. Dr. Bond is the recipient of numerous honors and awards including the AERA Presidential Award for Contributions to the Field of Educational Measurement.

Lee S. Shulman is the eighth president of The Carnegie Foundation for the Advancement of Teaching. Shulman became the first Charles E. Ducommun Professor of Education Emeritus at Stanford University after being professor of educational psychology and medical education at Michigan State University. He is a past president of the American Educational Research Association (AERA) and a fellow of the American Academy of Arts and Sciences. Shulman's research and writings have dealt with the study of teaching and teacher education, assessment, the central role of a "scholarship of teaching and learning" in supporting change in the cultures of higher education, and signature pedagogies in the professions. Shulman received the 2006 Grawemeyer Prize in Education for his volume of collected essays on teaching, *The Wisdom of Practice.*

EDUCATING LAWYERS

INTRODUCTION

LAWYERS HAVE LONG HELD PROMINENT POSITIONS in American soci-
ety. Indeed, it was clear from early in the nation's history, as Alexis de Tocqueville famously observed, that lawyers would play a leading part in
ordering its life, in government, business, political, and civil affairs. And
the United States, in fact, continues to lead the world in the number of
lawyers per capita, with approximately one million lawyers in practice
today. Since 1970, the legal profession has increased its ranks three times
faster than have the professions as a whole, for the first time outstripping
the number of medical doctors in ratio to the population (Sander and
Williams, 1989; Putnam, 2000). Although mostly drawn from relatively
privileged socioeconomic strata, lawyers entering practice today are more
diverse in gender and race than their peers a generation earlier (Dinovitzer
and others, 2004). Law is, of course, a particularly public profession.
Besides representing private clients, lawyers have official standing as officers of the court, charged with making the legal system function. In addition to their more conspicuous roles as champions in courtroom conflicts,
lawyers have become indispensable suppliers of what an observer has
called "artificial trust"—the enforceable agreements and contracts that
formalize social relationships and seem increasingly necessary to hold
together a turbulent and litigious society (Galanter, 1998).

The causes of these trends are no doubt complex, but it is clear that in
important respects, American society has become more dependent on the
legal profession for its functioning than ever before. Americans, therefore,
have ever more reason to take an interest in the legal profession and, we
believe, in how lawyers are prepared for their important public responsibilities. Thus the focus of this book is on the preparation of lawyers, more
particularly on their preparation in law school—the crucial portal to the
practice of law.

We adopted an unusual angle of vision during the study that informed
this volume. We tried to understand legal education, as well as its implications for the profession it serves, by focusing on the daily practices of

1

teaching and learning through which future legal professionals are formed. We compared these practices with those in other professions. We also looked at them through the lens of contemporary understanding of how learning occurs. It is our hope that the insights this approach affords will be of interest to legal educators, to professional educators more generally, and to the concerned public as well.

In many ways, the value of taking the educational practices of law school as the starting point for our investigation is obvious. Law school provides the single experience that virtually all legal professionals share. It forms minds and shapes identities. And nearly everyone is familiar with the common perception of what it is like to study law—to spend three years in law school pursuing the juris doctor (JD) degree. In particular, it is the experience in the classroom, in the required first-year experience of the Socratic case dialogue, which has become fixed in the popular imagination through *The Paper Chase* (a novel, a film, and a television show) and memoirs such as *One L.*

Each day, several times a day, seventy to eighty law students gather in a lecture theater, where a professor stands at the center of the class, closely questioning students chosen at random about a legal case assigned for analysis. The instructor demands answers: What are the facts of the case? What are the legal points at issue? How has the court reasoned in justifying its decision? What underlying principles or legal doctrines are involved? How might changing the pattern of facts have altered the judgment? What analogies can be drawn between this and other cases?

Students in these classes know that they will have to present more than memorized formulas: they will face detailed questioning in a situation of intense and public competition with fellow students. Along with the pressure to keep up or excel, there is often excitement, as students put aside their instinctive reactions and their laypersons' reasoning about cases, to try in earnest to "think like a lawyer." Although generations of disgruntled students (and some observers) have noted that the case-dialogue method easily degenerates into a game of "hide the ball"—a sort of Twenty Questions without clear pedagogical point—there is no denying that these practices carry a profound mystique.[1] They also produce lasting results. Unlike medical schools, which demand a specific set of "pre-med" college courses, students enter law school from any number of paths. But by the end of their first year, most have developed a clear ability to reason and argue in ways distinctive to the American legal profession.

For all its prominence during the critical first year of law school, however, the case-dialogue method is only a part of the typical student's experience. The American Bar Association accredits 193 law schools, with somewhat more than half of these described as private; the rest are public. In 2004, these schools enrolled over 148,000 students, with 48,000 in the first year. Of these students, 52.5 percent identified themselves as male, 47.5 percent as female, and 22.3 percent as nonwhite. The curriculum at most schools follows a fairly standard pattern. The JD degree is the typical credential offered, requiring three years of full-time or four years of part-time study. The degree is required in most states for admission to practice, but a separate bar examination is also required (American Bar Association, 2005a).

The typical law school curriculum is described this way by the U.S. Bureau of Labor Statistics:

> During the first year or year and a half of law school, students usually study core courses, such as constitutional law, contracts, property law, torts, civil procedure, and legal writing. In the remaining time, they may elect specialized courses in fields such as tax, labor, or corporate law. Law students often acquire practical experience by participating in school-sponsored legal clinic activities; in the school's moot court competitions, in which students conduct appellate arguments; in practice trials under the supervision of experienced lawyers and judges; and through research and writing on legal issues for the school's law journal (U.S. Bureau of Labor Statistics, 2006).

Law schools use Socratic case-dialogue instruction in the first phase of their students' legal education. During the second two years, most schools continue to teach, by the same method, a number of elective courses in legal doctrine. In addition, many also offer a variety of elective courses in seminar format, taught in ways that resemble graduate courses in the arts and sciences. What sets these courses apart from the arts-and-sciences experience is precisely their context: law school as apprenticeship to the profession of law.

This volume concentrates on the dramatic way that law schools are able to develop legal understanding and form professional identity. In particular, we explore the modes of teaching and learning that law schools use to accomplish the common aim of all professional education: specialized knowledge and professional identity. Although our discussion ranges considerably beyond the first-year experience, because that experience is so significant in shaping the whole of legal education, it is our emphasis.

The academic institutions in which most professionals, such as lawyers, clergy, nurses, physicians, and engineers, begin their apprenticeships have become essential to the professional enterprise. Professional schools are an institutional context in which the organized profession can exert significant control. They are perhaps the sole site where the professions' standards of good work set the agenda for learning. Professional schools are not only where expert knowledge and judgment are communicated from advanced practitioner to beginner; they are also the place where the profession puts its defining values and exemplars on display, where future practitioners can begin both to assume and critically examine their future identities. This is a complex educational process, however, and its value depends, in large part, on how well the several aspects of professional training are understood and woven into a whole. That is the challenge of professional preparation for the law: linking the interests of educators with the needs of practitioners and the members of the public the profession is pledged to serve—in other words, participating in civic professionalism. How well the challenge of linking these interests and needs is met is, in large part, determined by how clearly civic professionalism is understood (Sullivan, 2005). The aim of this book is to contribute to that understanding.

Law School: Hybrid Institution, Contested Agenda

Like other professional schools, law schools are hybrid institutions. One parent is the historic community of practitioners, deeply immersed in the common law and carrying on traditions of craft, judgment, and public responsibility. The other heritage is that of the modern research university. These two strands of inheritance were blended by the inventors of the modern American law school, starting at Harvard in the 1870s. The blend, however, was uneven. Factors beyond inheritance—the pressures and opportunities of the surrounding environment, for example—have been very important in what might be called the epigenesis of legal education. But as American law schools have developed, their academic genes have become dominant.

At the time of the law school's invention, the American research university was itself still in gestation, but its essential "DNA" had already been synthesized. The American inventors, especially Harvard's president, Charles Eliot, and his law dean, Christopher Columbus Langdell, were drawn to a somewhat idealized model of the German university, then at the apex of its worldwide influence. Their model was an institution largely shaped by academic intellectuals, not simply teachers but scholars and researchers. As the Americans understood it, the university embodied an advanced epistemology—a modern understanding of what knowledge is, how it is created, and how it can be used to underwrite progress. This conception of knowledge would have enormous influence on the organization and operation of the new kind of law school.

The new university's commitment to science drew cultural support from an ideal of knowledge for which reason was identified with procedures for testing—and correcting—claims to truth. The new university education would not be about shaping the self, as the earlier American college had been. Instead, the updated university curriculum emphasized testing and criticizing beliefs in order to build up a body of well-established "facts" that are supported by a true understanding of the principles according to which things work. The emphasis was on objective, quantitative measurement. This put a premium on formal knowledge, abstracted from context. It also provided an unquestioned canon, according to which intellectual disciplines came to be established, then to be distinguished from, what were considered more primitive claims to knowledge.

In the form of philosophical positivism, the new viewpoint became a militant movement intent on remaking modern education and culture, one that claimed to have superseded all previous forms of knowledge and insight. In style, it cultivated a distinctly cool stance of detached criticism. As a correlate, it denigrated older traditions of practice as too subjective, too uncritical toward the assumptions embedded in inherited ways of doing. Instead, the new model stressed the value of importing or applying scientifically generated knowledge as technical instruments for managing events in more rational ways. The new and reinvented disciplines of the sciences and social sciences produced great cognitive gains. The ideology that so often went with them, however, narrowed their focus and undermined the academic legitimacy of practical knowledge.

In the world of legal theory, this new spirit was exemplified in the efforts of legal positivists, who viewed law as an instrument of rational policymaking—a set of rules and techniques rather than a craft of interpretation and adaptation embedded in the common law. All this spelled the eclipse of traditional forms of practitioner-directed apprenticeship by academic instruction given by scholar-teachers. Law entered the American university at a time when attempts to blend academic and practitioner traditions of legal training resulted in what was, in some respects, less a reciprocal enrichment than a protracted hostile takeover.

Law School as Legal Analysis: The Triumph of Formal Knowledge

Langdell's new law school embraced the emphasis on formal knowledge by presenting law as a science in the making. Judicial decisions were analyzed in a scientific spirit as specimens from which general principles and doctrines could be abstracted. Once formulated, these doctrines would be used to classify the fast-expanding mass of American legal decisions, forming the body of law into fields such as contract law, tort law, and criminal law. Students taught from Langdell's case books were being introduced by their professors to legal research, much as a laboratory or seminar professor in the arts and sciences of those days would have led students to grasp the principles organizing the particular domain. Once discovered, these principles were to be "applied" to existing law, to make legal practice a more rational pursuit. Through this new procedure, Langdell updated a central tradition of classical jurisprudence: American law was now to be analyzed by academic specialists and criticized in the light of general ideas and principles.

In the first place, up-to-date legal scholarship was to turn the jumble of court decisions into synthetic overviews or treatises that could organize and explain various areas of the law. Then the school would train future lawyers the way scientists are trained, teaching them to do legal research amid actual cases in the library, stimulated by Socratic dialogue in the classroom, and coached in written research and oral argument outside class. In these ways, Langdell thought the legal academy would advance the profession's level of expertise while also contributing to progress in the law itself.

This approach broke apart the older forms of induction into the profession, thus establishing a new method of training in legal knowledge—a method separate from learning to practice. Over the long term, these two aims of induction into the profession (the academic and the more practical) would prove difficult to reunify. One noteworthy exception in law schools was the fortuitous conjunction of Langdell's approach with the needs of future law clerks and eventual judges, as well as aspiring legal scientists. For those seeking the traditional jobs of legal advocate or counselor, the linkages would be more tenuous.

Medical education, by contrast, somewhat awkwardly accommodated both training in formal knowledge and direct preparation for practice by placing them in sequence. The first two years of medical school were—and still are—entirely devoted to basic science, while the second two provided clinical instruction. This arrangement has long been dogged by skeptical questions about how closely and how well the two parts are related. In the law, however, the consequence of the university model was more often simply the deferment of practice experience until entry into the profession.

Within academic circles, legitimacy and respectability accrued to whatever could be assimilated to the model of formal, science-like discourse.

Over the course of the twentieth century, legal scholarship would move further away from the concerns of judges and practitioners and closer to those of other academic fields. In the process, the cultural resources available to any who wished to defend the earlier practitioners' traditions within the legal academy seemed correspondingly thinner and fewer. In its quest for academic respectability, legal education would come to emphasize legal knowledge and reasoning at the expense of attention to practice skills, while the relations of legal activity to morality and public responsibility received even less direct attention in the curriculum.

The triumph of formal knowledge and the stance of objectivity in the university resonated with similar trends in the twentieth-century economy and society. It extended to American law an ordering and rationalizing process that was already far advanced in Europe. The unexpected (and certainly unintended) consequence of these efforts at modernizing, however, has been a recurrent complaint of loss of orientation and meaning. This shadow side of modern institutions has shown up in the professions as accusations of professional self-absorption and irresponsible disconnection from the public. Whatever the merits of "value-free" knowledge, they do not transfer well to the idea of "value-free" professionals.

Law schools, like other professional schools, have recurrently found themselves sites of conflict about how knowledge and values are to be understood and related in the academic preparation of lawyers. It is not surprising that law schools, located at the junction between academic and practitioner interests, have tried at different moments to go in different directions. Thus during the 1960s and 1970s, when law schools were expanding, there was new concern for social purpose, manifested in developments such as clinical-legal education. Yet at the same time, internal academic norms emerged as more powerful than ever, so that faculty research became more intensive and more like scholarship in the arts-and-sciences disciplines.

Practice as Pivot: Reconnecting the Sundered Parts of Legal Education

Thanks in part to the development of legal scholarship, the law schools of the leading universities no longer fear being dishonored as mere "trade schools." They enjoy secure reputations as well-established members of the academic world, with prestige and international visibility. Since the coin of that realm is productivity in scholarship and research, it is not surprising that law schools have increasingly emphasized this dimension of their faculties' work and identity. At the same time, insistence that law schools should also attend to the preparation of their students for professional life in its broad dimensions has grown stronger. Forms of legal education oriented toward the demands of professional careers and the desirability of fostering professional competence beyond the purely intellectual continue to grow in the law schools. However, one of the less happy legacies of the inherited academic ideology has been a history of unfortunate misunderstandings and even conflict between defenders of theoretical legal learning and champions of a legal education that includes introduction to the practice of law.

In recent decades, however, new intellectual resources have made it possible to provide a theoretical, as well as a practical, alternative to the view of knowledge inherited from the positivist ethos of the research university. For professional education, moreover, this alternative viewpoint offers hope for healing old rifts between theory and practice, as well as new possibilities for reconnecting the dimensions of craft and meaning with formal knowledge. For this alternative conception of knowledge, the pivot is not limited to the detached position of the theoretical observer. Instead, it focuses attention on the stance of engaged practice, one shared by a community of practitioners. From this viewpoint, law is not simply science in the making, nor is it a set of general techniques for managing social relationships; law is a tradition of social practice that includes particular habits of mind, as well as a distinctive ethical engagement with the world. Learning the law thus loses a key dimension when it fails to provide grounding in an understanding of legal practice from the inside.

Developments in philosophy and in the learning sciences have made increasingly clear the reciprocal interpenetration of cognitive development and social interaction. This insight makes concentration on the teaching of practical judgment a compelling focus of research, as well as an immediate contribution to professional education. In contrast to the distanced stance of positivist theories of knowledge, the practical disciplines embody forms of knowing that blur distinctions among cognition, action, and intention. Skillful practice, whether of a surgeon, a judge, a teacher, a legal counselor, or a nurse, means involvement in situations that are necessarily indeterminate from the point of view of formal knowledge. Professional practice, that is, depends on judgment in order to yield an outcome that can further the profession's intended purposes. In law as in other fields, such judgment is reasoning not from a set of rules but by analogy to model cases and precedents so as to bring the particularities of each case into an illuminating relationship to the legal tradition's central principles and defining commitments.

All this has important implications for the education of lawyers. The mark of professional expertise is the ability to both act and think well in uncertain situations. The task of professional education is to facilitate novices' growth into similar capacities to act with competence, moving toward expertise. In order to do this, students need access to forms of social interaction that embody the basic understanding, skill, and meaning that, together, make up the professional activity. The contribution of the new epistemology of practice has been to direct the attention of researchers and educators toward grasping better the forms and spirit of expert practice, on the one hand, and, on the other, bringing novices into these practices while motivating their growth into becoming full participants in the profession. Starting from engagement rather than a claim of detached objectivity, this epistemology of practice aims to enlighten and enhance professional work through critical analysis. But the aim is neither to subsume nor to supplant the wisdom acquired through practice with an application of theory developed elsewhere.

As a tradition of research, the motivating question becomes how to grasp what makes possible a particular kind of skilled activity. By understanding professional practice as judgment in action, this approach aims to make practice more effective, comprehensible to students, and open to critical assessment. The focus of such attention naturally falls on teaching practices that enable learners to take part in the basic features of the professional practice itself. Such teaching presupposes a relationship between the academic institution and the settings of practice, such as relations with the clinic in the health professions. But it is also important to note that learning in these relationships between classroom and clinic has often gone both ways. New insights derived from the careful analysis of practice can be fed back into the stream of expert practice. One contribution of academic research to the field of practice derives from useful articulations of the insights derived from practical experience. These articulations then serve as theory to guide practice toward more reliable achievements of its ends.

Fortunately, professional education provides many examples of such pedagogy. Perhaps the most important and widespread is the case conference. In such settings, students observe, simulate, attempt, and then critically reflect on their work or performance. The case conference models the interaction of practitioners when, in consultation with colleagues or in solitary reflection, students analyze and assess instances of practice that require judgment. This kind of teaching practice is at the core of education in medicine and nursing, where it takes the form of the formal clinical conference, less formal teaching rounds, or highly informal feedback on students' clinical performance. It is also central to many fields of artistic production or performance, ranging from acting to architecture, where the ubiquitous critique session functions in much the same way. *Practicum* is a term sometimes used for this sort of pedagogy in fields such as teaching and social work. In legal education, the use of such pedagogy has been growing as well.

It is in these situations of intensive analysis of practice that the fundamental norms and expectations that make up professional expertise are taught. They are reinforced by the feedback that students receive as they attempt various approximations to expert practice. It is notable that in such teaching it is often difficult to neatly separate the dimensions of formal knowledge, know-how, and intention, except as an analytical exercise. Formal conceptual knowledge is brought to bear as a framework for thinking and as the source of principles underlying issues that case discussion confronts. Thus the teaching of case conferences in all their forms requires deciding, for particular purposes, how and how much conceptual learning and substantive knowledge is important for illuminating and guiding practice. The art of such teaching lies in knowing how and when an articulation of the particular meanings and issues in the situation at hand should be in dialogue with conceptual knowledge. In innovative practice, reframing the situation is guided by astute legal and moral perception in order to develop new precedents and new interpretations of the law. Such forms of professional teaching routinely connect what the positivist legacy in university education has sundered.

It would be a mistake, therefore, to take teaching centered on practice as hostile to generalization or theoretical formulation. Rather, careful analysis of intelligent practice reveals a more intricate relationship between theory and practice than in the positivist model—an understanding that is still poorly appreciated in the academy as a whole. In contrast to beginners, experts are able to perceive the features of the environment that are relevant to the profession's core practices and purposes. Learning situations such as the clinical case conference reveal the features of the environment in simplified forms so they can be understood by novice practitioners, who can begin to develop their own perception and judgment. In these situations, students often depend on conceptual knowledge to clarify the conditions of practice while they gradually build up their repertoires of experience. For example, novices can begin to learn the rudiments of litigation, or client counseling, or negotiation by attending to the core elements of the procedural and conceptual models exemplified in expert practice. The articulation and formulation of such core elements exemplifies the essential contribution of theoretical work to the domain of practice. Much more than "rules of thumb" or the lore passed on in practice situations, today's best teaching of practice encourages students to develop an analytically sophisticated approach to practice situations. Throughout this volume, we look at several examples of such pedagogies currently in use in law schools.

Considered in this perspective, the success of Langdell's own teaching innovations may have stemmed from his having invented a method that enabled students to analyze and research judicial decision making, thereby learning how to "think like a judge." On the one hand, Langdell's belief that law could be reduced to a science instilled confidence that legal principles were, in the end, mutually coherent. Much as did the scientific postulate of the uniformity of nature, this belief provided an imaginative background against which students could plot the actual vicissitudes of case law and judicial decision making over time. On the other hand, Langdell's method worked at an intermediate level of abstraction, between formal theory of the sort employed in the natural sciences and the kind of rules of thumb that might be passed on from judge to clerk while handling cases. At its best, law teaching in this mold makes accessible and intelligible to students the salient aspects of legal thinking in the judicial context.

A similar approach has shown considerable pedagogical promise when adapted for introducing students to those activities of legal professionals that involve both clients and cases, like counseling, solving legal problems, or litigating. Represented in case narratives and in conceptual form as procedures, the informal understanding that experts rely on in practice can be publicly represented and criticized for the purpose of raising the level of competence in the practice of law. The various aspects of practitioners' knowledge, like aspects of legal analysis, thus can be made visible and intelligible through the kind of theory that illuminates practice. With these conceptual tools, students can then be coached toward performing as professionals through increasingly complex and engaged contexts. This new look at practice can also make use of the systematic investigating and testing that are the strengths of the academy.

At the same time, the new epistemology reminds us, in ways that the old objectivism could not, that there is much more being taught and learned in any pedagogical situation than can be consciously abstracted in the form of procedures or techniques. Because it always involves social relationships with consequences, practice ultimately depends on serious engagement with the meaning of the activities—in other words, with their moral bearing. For professionals, the decisive dimension is responsibility for clients and for the values the public has entrusted to the profession. The pivot of practice makes it possible to accept this responsibility, not as an adjunct to legal knowledge but as one of its crucial constitutive parts.

Toward a More Integrated Model: A Historic Opportunity to Advance Legal Education

How then can we best combine the elements of legal professionalism— conceptual knowledge, skill, and moral discernment—into the capacity for judgment guided by a sense of professional responsibility? We are convinced that this is a propitious moment for uniting, in a single educational framework, the two sides of legal knowledge: (1) formal knowledge and (2) the experience of practice. We therefore attempt in this report to imagine a more capacious, yet more integrated, legal education. Our primary concern is both curricular (in particular, how to use the second two years of law school more effectively) and pedagogical (how to bring the teaching and learning of legal doctrine into more fruitful dialogue with the pedagogies of practice). Throughout, however, our emphasis is on fostering in the legal academy more focused attention to the actual and potential effects of the law school experience on the formation of future legal professionals.

A Framework for Legal Education: Putting the Pieces Together

In this report, we draw extensively from our investigation of existing patterns of legal education. But we are also attentive to the increasingly urgent need to bridge the gap between analytical and practical knowledge, as well as the demand for more robust professional integrity. These appeals and demands, from both within academic law and without, pose the new challenge to legal education. At the same time, they open to legal education a historic opportunity to advance both legal knowledge (theoretical and practical) and the capacities of the profession. We propose a framework that provides a structure for legal education that can be responsive to both the needs of our time and recent knowledge about how learning takes place. The framework we propose seeks to mediate between the claims for legal theory and the needs of practice, in order to do justice to the importance of both while responding to the demands of professional responsibility.

The two kinds of legal knowledge—the theoretical and the practical—are complementary. Each must have a respected place in legal education. Further, each sort of knowledge, with its own characteristic setting and ways of teaching, can be made to advance when it is understood in relation to its complement, so that neither remains what it would be if it continued to develop in isolation. This process of mutual development will progress best when it is directed by a focus on the professional formation of law students. Amid the useful varieties of mission and emphasis among American law schools, the formation of competent and committed professionals deserves and needs to be the common, unifying purpose. A focus on the formation of professionals would give renewed prominence to the ideals and commitments that have historically defined the legal profession in America.

In short, we propose an integration of student learning of theoretical and practical legal knowledge and professional identity. In order to produce integrative results in students' learning, however, communication and mutual learning must first occur among the faculty who teach in the several areas of the legal curriculum. The faculty responsible for curriculum and pedagogy in these areas must communicate with, learn from, and contribute to each other's purposes.

Legal education is complex, with its different emphases of legal analysis, training for practice, and development of professional identity. The integration we advocate will depend on, rather than override, the development of students' expertise within each of the different emphases. But integration can flourish only if law schools can consciously organize their emphases through ongoing mutual discussion and learning.

Legal Analysis

Recognizing the priority of analytical thinking in preparing lawyers, we place formal knowledge as the first element within the integrative framework we propose for legal education. However, this priority should not be misconstrued as sufficiency. Legal analysis—the categorizing and grasping of particular matters in terms of general principles and doctrines—is prior to legal practice, but not because practice is simply an application of general principles. Legal doctrine does not apply itself; rather, legal analysis is the prior condition for practice because it supplies the essential background assumptions and rules for engaging with the world through the medium of the law. The analysis, critique, and development of legal doctrine thus, in combination, constitute the first, essential element of legal education. However, this type of knowledge often comes most fully alive for students when the power of legal analysis is manifest in the experience of legal practice.

Practical Skill

The second element of our framework is, accordingly, the principle that effective legal preparation requires introduction to the perspective of practice. In contrast to legal analysis, which, as Langdell showed, can be taught in classroom settings to large numbers of students at once, the development of practical skill requires learning to understand and intervene in particular contexts. Practical skill is developed through modeling, habituation, experiment, and reflection. Thus teaching to develop practical skill, particularly when it involves work with clients, frequently requires settings and pedagogies different from those used in the teaching of legal analysis. Such teaching develops distinctive habits of mind, along with important skills of interaction. However, habits and skills should not be imagined as closed to rational analysis or essentially resistant to critique based on research and experiment. While honoring the learning passed on through the experience of various communities of practitioners, teaching practical legal knowledge should also draw insight from the social sciences and the humanistic disciplines. However, the significance and value of practical legal knowledge always depend on its relationship to the understanding of law that is the primary contribution of legal analysis.

Professional Identity

The third element of the framework—professional identity—joins the first two elements and is, we believe, the catalyst for an integrated legal education. The third element of our framework for legal education, which is sometimes described as professionalism, social responsibility, or ethics, draws to the foreground the purposes of the profession and the formation of the identity of lawyers guided by those purposes. We believe if legal education had as its focus forming legal professionals who are both competent and responsible to clients and the public, learning legal analysis and practical skills would be more fully significant to both the students and faculty. Much of law school's pedagogical activity presumes that issues of professionalism are somehow, somewhere, being handled. However, in a time when many raise questions about the legitimacy of the legal profession in both general and specific terms, professionalism needs to become more explicit and better diffused throughout legal preparation. Indeed, in this volume, we call attention to instances in which these concerns are well exemplified, and we urge ways in which movement in this direction can be strengthened.

Educating Lawyers: Part of the Legal Education Research Project

Educating Lawyers is one of a series of reports on professional education issued by The Carnegie Foundation for the Advancement of Teaching. Through its Preparation for the Professions Program, the foundation has been conducting comparative studies of education in five professional fields: law, engineering, the clergy, nursing, and medicine. The series began with an essay on the nature and value of the professions in American life: *Work and Integrity: The Crisis and Promise of Professionalism in America* (Sullivan, 2004). When completed, the series will include reports on the education of engineers, clergy, nurses, and physicians, as well as this review of legal education.

In conducting the research for this volume, the foundation assembled a research team drawn from its senior staff, assisted by research associates and assistants. Judith Wegner, a law professor and former dean at the University of North Carolina–Chapel Hill, directed the field work that underlies the study. She also contributed substantial analysis that, in significant respects, informed the study's present form. Psychologist Anne Colby and philosopher William Sullivan codirect the Preparation for the Professions Program and participated actively in all phases of the study. Lee S. Shulman, president of the Carnegie Foundation, was also an active participant and joined in the visits to law schools. Senior scholar Thomas Ehrlich, formerly dean of law at Stanford University and president of Indiana University, also took part, as did senior scholar and vice president of the foundation, Patricia Hutchings. Senior scholar Lloyd Bond, who studies psychological measurement and assessment design, joined the team in contributing to the report. Kelly Macatangay served as research coordinator, aided by several research assistants. Research scholar Matthew Rosin facilitated the research and writing of the report, supported by Sonia Gonzalez and Laura Ostenso.

The study began with a review of the literature on legal education, as well as consultation with the Association of American Law Schools, an association of 166 law schools. The research team also met with the Law School Admissions Council—the organization that oversees the development and administration of the Law School Admissions Test (LSAT). Over the space of two academic semesters, the team visited sixteen law schools in the United States and Canada. The schools, both public and private, were chosen to be geographically diverse, ranging from coast-to-coast and from

North to South. Several are among the more selective schools. Several are freestanding schools, whereas others are less selective institutions within large state university systems. One school is historically black; two (one in Canada, the other in the United States) are distinctive for their attention to Native American and First Nation peoples and their concerns. Several schools were chosen because they were judged as representing important innovations in legal education.

Typically, our visit to a law school involved a four-member team, which always included the study director and a senior scholar. During our visits, we observed and we listened carefully. We spoke with a variety of personnel, from academic deans and university presidents to admissions officers and placement directors. We visited classes of every type in use in the schools—from Socratic first-year classes to small upper-class seminars, from classes engaged in the simulation of practice to legal clinics where students worked with actual clients. We sought to understand how these different types of teaching, with their distinctive subject matters, differed from each other in approach and teaching style. We analyzed how students are assessed in law school by methods that vary across the kinds of courses offered. We especially inquired about the teaching of ethics and professional responsibility, clinical education, instruction in legal writing, and the provision of support for students in need of special academic assistance.

On campus, we interviewed, separately and in focus groups, hundreds of students. Most of all, we spoke with faculty, several hundred altogether, often after observing them at work teaching their classes. In all these conversations, our objective was to understand as well as possible what the experience of law school is like, both for today's faculty and administration and for today's students. We also asked about the goals and aspirations of students and teachers, about their successes and their difficulties and frustrations in negotiating the challenges of legal education. We inquired about faculty scholarship and how it was related to teaching, and we sought to understand how faculty life was different, depending on faculty background, the particularities of the school, and the nature of its student body. From all these conversations, we developed a richly detailed picture of how law school goes about its great transformative work, while we probed gaps and the unintended consequences of key aspects of the law school experience.

To broaden our perspective, we consulted widely with eminent scholars of both the law and legal education in the United States, Canada, and the United Kingdom. We presented the preliminary findings of the study in several forums, including a research meeting hosted by Rhodes House at Oxford University.

All these experiences modified and enriched our understanding of the achievements and the shortcomings of American legal education today. The result is this volume—not a comprehensive survey of law schools but an attempt to interpret what law schools do and do not do, with a sketch of some of the consequences for the legal profession, for higher education, and for American society. We conclude with a set of recommendations for the improvement of the preparation of lawyers, along with suggestions for how ongoing self-study and improvement might be made a part of the regular business of legal education.

The Plan of This Book

We have sought not only to learn *about* law school but to learn *from* law school. We believe that legal education has refined important lessons of value to other professional fields. The chief of these is the extraordinary power of the first-year experience as a way of beginning the formation of future professionals. We explore several aspects of this experience in the volume, successively focusing on the intellectual cognitive training, the preparation for practice, and formation of professional responsibility that law schools provide. To emphasize key findings and insights, we also make frequent comparison between practices in legal education and those in other fields of professional preparation.

Chapter One provides a summary statement of the angle of vision that informs this study, illustrated through examples of two programs that provide exceptional degrees of integration among the goals of legal preparation.

Chapter Two, through an in-depth look at the Socratic case-dialogue pedagogy, addresses the core teaching method of law school's first phase of instruction. This chapter emphasizes the strengths of this teaching practice, while it traces the implications of the Socratic classroom experience for the rest of law school and future practice.

Chapter Three examines how law schools provide an introduction to the practice of law, with special attention to "lawyering" courses, particularly legal writing instruction, simulated practice, and clinical-legal courses, as illustration of the complexities involved in law schools' efforts to teach key areas of legal practice.

Chapter Four examines the overall experience of law school as a context for professional formation, surveying a variety of current efforts to provide instruction in ethics in light of research on education for moral development.

Chapter Five analyzes the assessment procedures that form a very important complement to the classroom practice in both case dialogue and other forms of teaching. Using the latest findings of learning theory, we conclude the chapter with suggestions for making assessment a more effective formative device in legal education. Finally, we summarize the study's argument and findings, using the integrative framework described earlier; we highlight the importance of leadership and vision for advancing the aims of legal education.

Educating Lawyers: *A Link to the Past and a Vision for the Future*

This essay on legal education stands in a line of studies of professional education carried out by the Carnegie Foundation that reaches back to the landmark Flexner report on medical education of 1910. Historically, the Carnegie Foundation's identity and sense of mission have been closely bound up with that and other pioneering efforts to study professional education. Over its hundred-year history, the foundation has continued to exert considerable impact on the improvement of professional preparation. In addition to the Flexner study, which is still cited with regularity, the then-fledgling foundation undertook a series of "surveys of the professions," including engineering, architecture, and teaching. This early phase of investigation included several major studies of legal education, including Joseph Redlich's *The Common Law and the Case Method in American University Law Schools* (1914), Alfred Z. Reed's *Training for the Public Profession of the Law* (1921), and two subsequent studies by Reed during the 1920s.

In the middle of the post–World War II boom years in higher education, the foundation, at that time sharing offices (and a president) with the Carnegie Corporation of New York, organized the Carnegie Commission on Higher Education in 1967 and, later, the Carnegie Council on Policy Studies in Higher Education in 1973, both led by Clark Kerr. These bodies commissioned important studies of medical and legal education, including *New Directions in Legal Education* by Herbert Packer and Thomas Ehrlich (1972). In the 1980s and 1990s, under the leadership of Ernest Boyer, the again-independent foundation sponsored a series of new studies, including the highly influential *Scholarship Reconsidered* of 1990. More recently, for example, the 1996 report on architecture education—

Building Community: A New Future for Architecture Education and Practice by Ernest Boyer and Lee D. Mitgang (1996)—continues to influence policy and practice in that field at the levels of campuses and affiliated professional societies.

This volume, under the presidency of Lee Shulman, is intended primarily to foster appreciation for what legal education does at its best. We want to encourage more informed scholarship and imaginative dialogue about teaching and learning for the law at all organizational levels: in individual law schools, in the academic associations, in the profession itself. We also believe our findings will be of interest within the academy beyond the professional schools, as well as among that public concerned with higher education and the promotion of professional excellence.

Our second hope is that this volume will stimulate an interest in and support for better teaching and more effective programs of legal education wherever possible. Critics of the legal profession, both from within and without, have pointed to a great profession suffering from varying degrees of confusion and demoralization. A reawakening of professional élan must include, in an important way, revitalizing legal preparation. It is hard to imagine that taking place without the enthusiastic participation of the nation's law schools. We wish, therefore, to encourage legal educators to build on their justifiable pride in accomplishment a stronger commitment to the public mission and purpose of the vocation and the institution they have chosen to serve. Moreover, we hope to throw into relief the importance of teaching.

Teaching makes visible the invisible processes of thinking. By representing in a public way the content and movement of thought, teaching makes it possible for students to enter the ways of thought represented by the teacher. This public representation in gesture, action, word, symbol, and diagram that theorists call scaffolds for learning, enables students and teachers to collaborate in developing knowledge and skill. Effective teaching permits students and teachers to approach alignment of understanding. From this springs the possibility of cooperative activity, such as the exploration of ideas or the solving of problems together. When this activity becomes self-conscious, the learner can practice independently, spurring improvement and growth. Pedagogy is thus at the heart of the wonder of human culture—our species' capacity to collectively represent our world in ways that permit the sharing and transmitting of understanding, as well as the criticism and improvement of our understanding over time.

NOTES

1. Critiques of the limitations of the case-dialogue method on these grounds go back to the early twentieth century. See, for example, Redlich (1914), the first study of legal education by The Carnegie Foundation for the Advancement of Teaching.

I

LAW SCHOOL IN THE PREPARATION OF PROFESSIONALS

PROFESSIONS OPERATE WITHIN AN EXPLICIT CONTRACT with society as a whole. In exchange for privileges such as monopoly on the ability to practice in specific fields, professions agree to provide certain important social services. In exchange for the privilege of setting standards for admission and authorizing practice, professions are legally obliged to discipline their own ranks for the public welfare. The basis of these contracts is a set of common goals shared by the public and for which different professions take responsibility. For example, medicine, nursing, and public health are chartered for the maintenance and improvement of society's health, just as education exists to promote the goal of an educated citizenry, law to regulate social transactions and secure justice, and engineering to develop technologies for the improvement of life. These are public values, and the core of professional privilege is based on the professions' willingness to commit to them.

On this basis, professions have been given significant grants of public trust. Lawyers, for example, are allowed—even required by law—to hold in confidence their communications with their clients to a degree far beyond what is legally allowable in ordinary social relationships. Professions are guardians of practices vital to society's well-being, in which all citizens have a stake. This responsibility and orientation toward the public good set off professionals as members of a distinct type of occupation, one directly pledged to ideals of service to their clients and the public as a whole. A significant mark of professional privilege and social responsibility is the authority that professions wield to require of their members training in specialized institutions and to assess the fitness of candidates for admission to practice.

In our research on the professions, we have seen how this social contract shapes—and makes distinctive—professional training. Across the otherwise disparate-seeming educational experiences of seminary, medical school, nursing school, engineering school, and law school, we identified a common goal: professional education aims to initiate novice practitioners to think, to perform, and to conduct themselves (that is, to act morally and ethically) like professionals. We observed that toward this goal of knowledge, skills, and attitude, education to prepare professionals involves six tasks:

1. Developing in students the fundamental knowledge and skill, especially an academic knowledge base and research
2. Providing students with the capacity to engage in complex practice
3. Enabling students to learn to make judgments under conditions of uncertainty
4. Teaching students how to learn from experience
5. Introducing students to the disciplines of creating and participating in a responsible and effective professional community
6. Forming students able and willing to join an enterprise of public service

To be sure, the different fields emphasize some characteristics of a professional more than others. Professional education rarely gives equal attention to thinking, performing, and conducting oneself as a professional. (In legal education, as we shall see, the primary emphasis on learning to think like a lawyer is so heavy that schoolwide concern for learning to perform like one is *not* the norm.) And, of course, professions do not always embody all these core features well. However, it is impossible to organize or teach a curriculum to prepare future practitioners without at least tacitly commenting on what each of these six core tasks contributes to the profession's knowledge, skill, and attitudes.

Because, in essence, these tasks of professional education represent commonplaces of professional work (a normative model in which each feature is essential), we believe that the more effective the preparation for the profession is to be, the more consciously the educational program must address all these purposes.[1] As we have considered, over the course of our studies of professional education, the educational tasks that the nature of professional work imposes on professional schools, we have found useful two key concepts: (1) the idea of signature pedagogies and (2) the notion of apprenticeship. As we explore legal education in this volume, drawing insights from contemporary understanding of learning, we use these two key concepts to illuminate what we believe are the major challenges—and great promise—of today's legal education.

Signature Pedagogies

The typical practices of teaching and learning by which professional schools induct new members into the field can enlighten us about the personalities, dispositions, and cultures of the fields they serve and partly embody. Moreover, to the extent that they serve as primary means of instruction and socialization for neophytes in a field, they are worthy of our analyses and interpretations, better to understand both their virtues and flaws. We call these key educational practices "signature pedagogies."[2]

Some of these pedagogies are clearly visible to everyone. In the law, the quasi-Socratic dialogues so vividly portrayed by Professor Kingsfield and his students in *The Paper Chase* are the obvious candidate for a "signature"—readily identifiable and uniquely individual to the field. In medicine, the practice of bedside teaching is the clear candidate. There the formative teaching practice takes place not in a classroom but a hospital ward, in the context of daily clinical rounds, in which a senior physician or resident leads a group of novices from bedside to bedside, engaging them with questions and discussion about the diagnosis and management of the illness embodied in the patient.

Professional education is preparation for accomplished and responsible practice in the service of others. It is preparation for "good work."[3] Thus the pedagogies of the professions must attempt to bridge and resolve tensions between the competing imperatives to which future professionals must respond. The students must learn abundant amounts of theory and vast bodies of knowledge, but the "bottom line" of their efforts will not be what they know but what they can do. They must come to understand thoroughly so they can act competently, and they must act competently in order to serve responsibly. Thus the most distinctive of the signature pedagogies—the case dialogue in law, the varieties of design and performance studio in engineering and architecture, bedside teaching and clinical rounds in medicine and nursing, the interpretation of texts and instruction in preaching in seminaries—are pedagogical attempts to build bridges between thought and action, between relative certainty and rampant unpredictability. These are pedagogies invented to prepare the mind for practice.

The concept of signature pedagogy is an analogue to an idea common in modern linguistics—that there is a distinction between the observable linguistic performance of speakers of a language and the deep structure of grammatical and syntactical knowledge that these speakers are presumed to have in order to be able to speak with competence. A signature pedagogy is a kind of language of a particular profession. It can be imagined to have four dimensions: (1) its observable, behavioral features—the surface structure; (2) the underlying intentions, rationale, or theory that the behavior models—the deep structure; (3) the values and dispositions that the behavior implicitly models—the tacit structure; and (4) its complement, the absent pedagogy that is not, or is only weakly engaged—the shadow structure.

Law's signature case-dialogue method plays out across all four of these dimensions quite clearly. The surface structure is a set of dialogues entirely focused by and through the instructor. In these dialogues about legal texts, students are expected to engage in intense verbal duels and competitions with the teacher as they struggle to discern facts and principles of interpretation within a case. By contrast, the deep structure of the pedagogy is that "thinking like a lawyer" is about processes of analytic reasoning and the grasp of legal "doctrine" and principles rather than learning a system of statutory or "black letter" law. This is modeled through the relentless confrontation of interpretations in the inherently competitive character of the classroom.

We find that in the case dialogue, the third dimension—the tacit structure—is consistent with the surface and deep structures. As we discuss in detail later in this volume, students are often disappointed or disillusioned to discover that legal understanding can diverge significantly from what they understand as moral norms or standards of fairness. So the tacit teaching of the pedagogy is that legal encounters are of a different order than everyday moral behavior. This is an important part of the hidden curriculum of case-dialogue teaching.

Finally, there is in legal education a weakly developed complementary pedagogy. With some important exceptions, the underdeveloped area of legal pedagogy is clinical training, which typically is not a required part of the curriculum and is taught by instructors who are themselves not regular members of the faculty. Compared with the centrality of supervised practice, with mentoring and feedback, in the education of physicians and nurses or the importance of supervised practice in the preparation of teachers or social workers, the relative marginality of clinical training in law schools is striking.

The Impact of the Learning Sciences: Apprenticeship Reappraised

Research about human learning has recently brought back into prominence a term long connected to the preparation of professionals: *apprenticeship*. The most momentous change in professional training over the
past century has been the movement of professional education into the
academy. This has entailed a shift away from apprenticeship, with its intimate pedagogy of modeling and coaching, toward reliance on the methods of academic instruction, with its emphasis on classroom teaching and
learning. The central role of academic methods and patterns of thought
in professional training is today taken for granted. But the transition from
on-the-job training by practitioners to instruction carried out far from the
sites of professional practice and by full-time educators has transformed
professional life. It has reduced the arbitrary and often haphazard nature
of old-time apprenticeships. It has opened the induction of neophytes to
a measure of quality control, as well as the likelihood that the knowledge
imparted will be well tested and reasonably current. But it has also
bequeathed a legacy of crossed purposes and even distrust between practitioners and academics, as well as between the academy and the public,
which still besets the preparation of professionals.

Precise psychological analysis of experts performing, from scientists to
musicians to chess players, has revealed that high-performing individuals
share a set of cognitive skills that can be documented and compared. In
this research, two features of expert performance stand out.

First, compared to novices, experts possess not only knowledge but
highly structured knowledge. That is, they understand concepts basic to
their domains, and they have mastered well-rehearsed procedures, or
"schemas," for thinking and acting. These schemas enable experts to bring
their knowledge to bear on situations with remarkable speed and accuracy.

Second, expert knowledge is conditioned, or related to contexts. Experts
can perceive aspects of situations in ways that are relevant to deploying
their knowledge in ways beginners cannot. This finding has long been part
of the lore regarding lawyers, doctors, nurses, and teachers. But it has now
been documented for the law and other fields.[4] These two traits characterize measures of expertise regardless of domain, although the content of
the knowledge and specific features of experts' skilled perception and ability to act are highly specific to particular domains of activity.[5] In the language of the learning theorists, these features of expertise are what underlie
the ability of experts to solve problems in their domains.

Learning, then, entails embarking on an effort to gradually grow into the complex abilities of an expert. This is where the idea of apprenticeship enters. Research suggests that learning happens best when an expert is able to model performance in such a way that the learner can imitate the performance while the expert provides feedback to guide the learner in making the activity his or her own. This describes an expert-apprentice relationship in its simplest form. Expertise, however, is always shared among members of a community who have mastered certain practices. When such communities organize ways of transmitting this expertise to new members, they create apprenticeships. A great contribution of modern cognitive psychology has been to place apprenticeship, so understood, once again at the heart of education.

Learning theorists talk about rendering the informal, interpersonal kind of knowledge transmission typical of apprenticeship into more publicly available patterns of activity. They call this a *creating* within the more formal contexts of classroom learning of a "cognitive apprenticeship"—an educational experience focused on teaching beginners and journeymen the more advanced knowledge of the domain. The emphasis is not on acquiring information, as such; rather, it is on learning the concepts and procedures that enable the expert to use knowledge to solve problems. This requires learning the "subject matter" of law, medicine, engineering, and so on, but in a way that is already structured for performance, according to the explicit norms of the professional community. In many professional fields, though less so in law, these insights into learning have given rise to the widespread use of simulation as a form of teaching and learning. Particularly in medicine, carefully developed simulation practices have improved student learning and performance over traditional apprenticeship techniques.[6]

Much of the learning in apprenticeship is by observation and imitation because much of what experts know is tacit. It can be passed on by example, but often it cannot be fully articulated. By carefully observing expert performance, however, learning theorists argue, it is possible to render important aspects of expert practice explicit. As in the case of the simulation techniques employed in clinical domains, these articulations of good performance can then become objects of imitation and practice for learners. By making explicit important features of good performance through various conceptual models and representations, teachers can guide the learner in mastering complex knowledge by small steps. These devices of representation serve as scaffolds (in the language of learning theorists) to support efforts at improved performance. Feedback from more accomplished performers directs the learner's attention, supporting improved attempts at reaching a goal.

Academic expertise is not the same, even in professional schools, as actual on-the-job performance. In a similar way, "thinking like a student"— a skill that all students entering professional programs have mastered—is not the same thing as "thinking like an apprentice" to the domain. In order to become expert in a profession, making good grades with minimal effort has to give way to a complete involvement with learning new ways of thinking, performing, and understanding oneself. Today's renewed interest in apprenticeship can direct the attention of educators toward providing for their students clear notions of what professional expertise entails, along with carefully worked-out approaches to acquiring it.

The Three Apprenticeships of Professional Education

As understood in contemporary learning theory, the metaphor of apprenticeship sheds useful light on the practices of professional education. In these recent Carnegie Foundation studies and reports on professional education, we use the metaphor but extend it to the whole range of imperatives confronting professional education. So we speak of three apprenticeships. The signature pedagogies of each professional field all have to confront a common task: preparing students for the complex demands of professional work—to think, to perform, and to conduct themselves like professionals. The common problem of professional education is how to teach the complex ensemble of analytic thinking, skillful practice, and wise judgment on which each profession rests.

Drawing on contemporary learning theory, one can consider law, medical, divinity, or engineering schools as sites to which students come to be inducted into all three of the dimensions of professional work: its way of thinking, performing, and behaving. For the sake of their future practice, students must gain a basic mastery of specialized knowledge, begin acquiring competence at manipulating this knowledge under the constrained and uncertain conditions of practice, and identify themselves with the best standards and in a manner consistent with the purposes of the profession. Yet within the professional school, each of these aspects of the whole ensemble tends to be the province of different personnel, who often understand their function differently and may be guided by different, even conflicting goals.

The great problem for professional education is to square this circle by bringing the disparate pieces of the student's educational experience into coherent alignment. These pieces fall roughly into three large segments, or apprenticeships, each based in different facets of professional expertise as the particular school teaches these and guided by a variety of distinct pedagogical intentions.

The first apprenticeship, which we call intellectual or cognitive, focuses the student on the knowledge and way of thinking of the profession. Of the three, it is most at home in the university context because it embodies that institution's great investment in quality of analytical reasoning, argument, and research. In professional schools, the intellectual training is focused on the academic knowledge base of the domain, including the habits of mind that the faculty judge most important to the profession.

The students' second apprenticeship is to the forms of expert practice shared by competent practitioners. Students encounter this practice-based kind of learning through quite different pedagogies from they way they learn the theory. They are often taught by faculty members other than those from whom they learned about the first, conceptual apprenticeship. In this second apprenticeship, students learn by taking part in simulated practice situations, as in case studies, or in actual clinical experience with real clients.

The third apprenticeship, which we call the apprenticeship of identity and purpose, introduces students to the purposes and attitudes that are guided by the values for which the professional community is responsible. Its lessons are also ideally taught through dramatic pedagogies of simulation and participation. But because it opens the student to the critical public dimension of the professional life, it also shares aspects of liberal education in attempting to provide a wide, ethically sensitive perspective on the technical knowledge and skill that the practice of law requires. The essential goal, however, is to teach the skills and inclinations, along with the ethical standards, social roles, and responsibilities that mark the professional.

Through learning about these different aspects of professional knowledge and beginning to practice them, the novice is introduced to the meaning of an integrated practice of all dimensions of the profession, grounded in the profession's fundamental purposes. If professional education is to introduce students to the full range of professional demands, it has to initiate learners into all three apprenticeships. But it is the ethical-social apprenticeship through which the student's professional self can be most broadly explored and developed.

The three apprenticeships reflect competing emphases within all professional education—a conflict of values that has deep roots in the history and organization of professional training in the university. In the chapters that follow, as we describe how law school is experienced by aspirants to the profession, we use these three apprenticeships as metaphors or analytical lenses through which to see more clearly how the business of professional training is conducted in today's law schools. Although law schools have long been an object of study and criticism, approaching legal education as a threefold apprenticeship reveals, in the current organization of legal education, ambiguities that have not been examined before. As we shall see, today's legal education is sometimes able to marshal the three kinds of apprenticeship in support of the larger goal of training competent and committed practitioners. As we also note, however, in other ways the current system undermines that aim by failing to do justice to the full range of apprenticeship necessary to orient students to the full dimensions of the legal profession.

In their passage through law school, students apprentice to a variety of teachers, but they also apprentice to the aggregate educative effects of attending a particular professional school and program. That is, they are formed, in part, by the formal curriculum but also by the informal or "hidden" curriculum of unexamined practices and interaction among faculty and students and of student life itself. As is typical of organized apprenticeship, much of this informal socialization is tacit and operates below the level of clear awareness. However, abundant studies have confirmed socialization's great importance for the process of learning what it is to be a professional. Looking at law school from the perspective of the three apprenticeships reveals that the relation between the academic life and the demands of practice is seldom as straightforward and logical in reality as it is imagined to be by many of the faculty and administration. This will turn out to be especially true in the crucial apprenticeship of professional purpose and identity.

The Crisis of Professionalism: Recovering the Formative Dimension

Many in our time regard with a skeptical squint the authority, even the legitimacy, of the professions. Crisis, scandal, weakening of public confidence, popular outrage—all have become familiar associations of the fortunes of medicine, law, accounting, the clergy, teaching, and the academy. Many, including some in government and positions of influence, question the point and value of the peculiar features of the professions, especially their guild-like structures of esoteric knowledge and their corporate monopoly over practice within an occupational domain, including the recruitment, training, and licensing of personnel.

Law has certainly not been exempt from this questioning. Deborah Rhode (2000) of the Stanford University Law School has provided an overview of how these trends have been played out in the law, both in declining public trust in the profession and the erosion of morale among attorneys. It is good that amid these signs of internal disarray, the American Bar Association has several times during the past decade called for major efforts to both strengthen the profession's sense of public purpose and to address these issues in a serious way in legal education. We will take up these issues in more detail in later chapters. For now, it is enough to emphasize that we believe that these problems have given a new urgency to the question of how best to educate future professionals.

The question is clearly a matter of wide importance to American society, as well as to the members of the professions themselves. Any revitalization of professional mission must take into account what goes on in the professional schools—one area in which professions have significant leverage. It is also the source of their future—in a literal sense. The starting point of this concern has to be the social contract between the profession and society, as embodied in the terms of licensing and the code of ethics by which the profession declares its intent to regulate its own life in order to maintain the trust and cooperation of the public. But codes and contracts, as every lawyer knows, rely, in the end, on the good faith of the parties. As the old adage has it, *leges sine moribus vanae*: effective laws need the support of everyday practice and belief.

For professional education, the question is how to provide a powerful experience of the best sense of what it means to take up a profession. The answer, we believe, lies in understanding the whole of student experience as a formative process—a time of apprenticeship, during which the novice starts on the road toward assuming the identity of a competent and dedicated professional. To be a professional in the full sense is to understand oneself as claimed by a craft and a purpose in whose service to use that craft. Yet precisely because that purpose is a public one, directed toward others, professionals can also be conscious of the limits and specificity of their domain. With this awareness, professionals can appreciate other ways of living and contributing to the larger life of their times. They can be citizens as well as experts.

Professional education is, then, inherently ethical education in the deep and broad sense. The distillation of the abilities and values that define a way of life is the original meaning of the term *ethics*. It comes from the Greek *ethos*, meaning "custom," which is the same meaning of the Latin *mos, mores*, which is the root of "morals." Both words refer to the daily habits and behaviors through which the spirit of a particular community is expressed and lived out. In this broad sense, professional education is "ethical" through and through. Even to disparage any ethical intent is to declare one: the purely instrumental view of education as the acquisition of a set of tools by means of which to enhance one's competitive advantage in life. Ethics in a professional curriculum ought to provide a context in which students and faculty alike can grasp and discuss, as well as practice, the core commitments that define the profession. It can also be a place where the alternative, instrumental view just described can be squarely reckoned with. For lawyers, just as for other professionals, the practices they learn give them extraordinary powers. But the meaning of the practices—and therefore the object to which the powers are directed— is never morally neutral. Ethics rightly includes not just understanding and practicing a chosen identity and behavior but, very importantly, a grasp of the social contexts and cultural expectations that shape practice and careers in the law.

The centrality of professional and moral identity is obvious but is easily taken for granted. A surgeon wielding a scalpel and a lawyer equipped with potent arguments are positive figures, not simply through what they can do but because of who they have become. It is because of their sense of who they are and how they understand themselves in the world that these professionals' skills become positive assets for everyone rather than threats to well-being. Professions are communities committed to maintaining those positive moral identities. They are also obligated to disenfranchise any of their members who seriously betray this purpose. However, because identity is a comprehensive and integrative achievement, it is difficult to address in a specialized way, as one might address the study of calculus or Chinese language. The moral development of professionals requires a holistic approach to the educational experience that can grasp its formative effects as a whole.

The obstacles to improving this situation are quite real. There is evidence that law school typically blares a set of salient, if unintentional, messages that undercut the likely success of efforts to make students more attentive to ethical matters. The competitive atmosphere of most law schools generates a widespread perception that students have entered a high-stakes, zero-sum game. The competitive classroom climate is reinforced by the peculiarities of assessment in first-year courses. The ubiquitous practice of grading on the curve ensures that, no matter how talented or hard-working the students are, only a predetermined number will receive A's. Such a context is unlikely to suggest solidarity with one's fellow students or much straying from a single-minded focus on competitive achievement. What these instances point to is the way in which the hidden curriculum shapes, or misshapes, professional education. The only remedy for this problem is greater awareness on the part of faculty and academic leaders. The issues of meaning and identity, so central to the time of life in which most students are in law school, provide a lens for examining and a potential handle for grasping this otherwise elusive, if often decisive, matter of the moral climate of the institution.

Given these realities, effective pedagogy to address the students' formative development must be a highly self-conscious, reflexive one. The pedagogy of the small-scale seminars used to teach lawyering and ethics seems well suited to enabling students to look at and analyze their law school experience, with an emphasis on connecting their current experience to their transformation into lawyers. For this effort, a great deal of knowledge, even theoretical knowledge, is essential, including the history of American legal education, legal practice, and professions more broadly. Like landmark cases, biographies of notable figures in the law are valuable as concrete manifestations of the principles under discussion. Contact with practicing lawyers is another important aid to this process.

These educational emphases—self-reflexivity, the development of understanding of how the past has shaped the present and how one's own situation is related to the larger social world, as well as entertaining and probing possible models of identity—are all important elements of a formative pedagogy for tomorrow's professionals. They are also central themes of liberal education. Writing as a working journalist who had lately become dean of Columbia's School of Journalism, Nicholas Lemann (2004) made a case that the professional school and liberal education do indeed have important links. "Professionals," Lemann argues, "have goals and ideals and purposes having to do with the history, the techniques, and the social role of their field, which rise above the daily demands of work . . . Professionals have to deal with complexity in their work, [they] do work that has a public purpose." Lemann concludes that there is a big difference between "job training and professional education," that "liberal education and professions make for a good fit . . . because they have crucially in common a transcendent quality, a commitment to a broad and not necessarily utilitarian perspective" (p. 15).

If this is so—and we strongly agree that it is—recovering the formative dimension of professional education for the law lies in forging more connections with the arts and sciences in the larger academic context. The point is to engage the larger academy around the perennial themes of liberal education, particularly focused on the formation of a life of the mind for practice. But placing common focus on formation almost certainly will require a searching examination of the importance of experience with all three of the apprenticeships—cognitive, practical, and formative. Much of the humanizing and inspiring aspects of the law have always resided in actual contact with clients and their needs. It is difficult to imagine a stronger emphasis on formation that does not also require schools to place more relative weight on preparation for practice, including exploration of the ethical demands of the profession.

The Opportunity for Legal Education

In most of this report, we focus on the practices of teaching and learning that are at the core of legal education. However, it is worth emphasizing that many of the features of today's legal education stem not from the desires of law faculty or educational imperatives but from powerful external forces. Many external factors constrain legal education. Most law schools, aside from the most illustrious, must worry about how well they are "teaching to the test," as schools are indirectly measured by the percentage of their graduates who pass the state bar examination. All schools also think a good deal, whatever they may say for public consumption, about how they are ranked by the annual *U.S. News & World Report* survey of law schools. Deans and faculty alike complain, and rightly so, about some of the criteria by which this influential survey assesses their institutions, but very few can simply proceed without trying to improve their rankings within the bounds of institutional integrity. Or consider the pressure exerted on many schools, especially those aspiring to institutional prestige—something needed to attract the most competitive student body and most productive faculty—by the hiring practices of leading law firms. If prospective students believe that they are less likely to be hired by such firms because they typically recruit fewer new hires from a particular school, few of the institution's intrinsic, educational virtues are likely to offset this disincentive to many desirable applicants.

Above all, perhaps, schools face the demand that they recover their costs from tuition. How much of their costs they must recover is, of course, related to the size of their endowments—another factor that is tied to their success in achieving prestigious standing. But the consistent effect is to keep tuitions very high indeed. The prospect of graduating with massive educational loans has long acted as a damper on the idealism of students as they consider their career choices.

These and other constraints weigh heavily on law schools, pushing all schools toward a single model. Efforts for change, reform, and innovation become struggles against these constraints. Thus the climate of legal education is always subject to the pressure of unending inter-institutional competition, which drains energy and attention from the imaginative work of considering, creating, trying, and evaluating alternative possibilities.

In spite of these often daunting challenges, the range of variation and efforts at innovation apparent among law schools is striking. Differences in student bodies (especially the students' educational backgrounds and preparation), variations in consciously chosen missions, and various schools' efforts to respond to educational opportunities and needs as they see them—all these have contributed to making legal education a dynamic part of higher education. The vitality of legal education is manifest in the attention given to large questions about how legal education should adapt to changing conditions, improve performance, and respond to new potentials. From our perspective, many of the ongoing questions in legal education, such as how much uniformity is needed versus how much variation to promote or how broad a preparation for practice law schools should provide, concern relations among what we have called legal education's cognitive, practical, and formative apprenticeships. In our study, we were especially interested, for reasons that will become clearer in later chapters, in efforts to improve integration among the three apprenticeships—programs that strive to resolve the conflicts among theory and practice, technique and ethical engagement.

We encountered a number of examples of such efforts. In New York City, which many regard as a kind of microcosm of the United States, we found two of the longest-running integrative efforts. The City University of New York and New York University are very different institutions. But they are alike in that they have benefited from institutional leadership that has fostered intense faculty conversation and experimentation around integrating their students' educational experience. They are both imperfect examples, yet they provide "proofs by existence" of the feasibility of more intentional, more integrated educational strategies and programs in law schools.

Lawyering to Advance the Cause of Justice: The City University of New York

Consider the first-year experience at the City University of New York (CUNY). Although part of the CUNY system, the law school operates out of a former municipal building just south of Flushing, in the borough of Queens. A microcosm within the New York microcosm, Flushing is today a thronged meeting place of new Americans, not far from the site on which the 1939 World's Fair envisioned a very different "World of Tomorrow." At CUNY, all first-year students take a two-semester series of courses called a "lawyering seminar." The number of students in each course is never greater than twenty. Several prestigious law schools provide one small-section experience for students in their first year. What is distinctive about the CUNY seminars is that they are part of the school's requirement over a three-year curriculum of lawyering whose aim is to integrate the students' learning of the skills of practice and the ethical demands of professional identity with the more typical courses in civil and criminal procedure, contracts, torts, and so forth. Each lawyering seminar is linked to a "doctrinal" or substantive course, and both are taught by the same instructor.

For example, in the lawyering seminar linked to a substantive course on family law—Law and Family Relations—the professor, John Farago, leads students through the development of a simulated case of child educational neglect under adjudication in family court. To give beginning students the experience of thinking and working in context, Farago assigns them to act as lawyers representing the various parties to the case, organizing the course around the task of developing strategies and writing briefs on behalf of their clients. He begins class by posing questions about the legal issue in dispute, asking students to formulate written answers on the points of law. Students work in pairs, questioning and coaching each other before presenting their formulations to the rest of the students. Farago next extends the questioning, posing hypothetical problems based on the argument the students are making.

He then changes tack, and the rhythm of the class changes as well. The students watch a short film that dramatizes a courtroom argument about the issue at hand. Farago then addresses the students directly, asking them to compare their work with what they have watched, noting similarities and variances. The class concludes with each student returning to the points at issue, writing a very short, revised version of his or her original approach to the problem. Farago then uses this short written piece as the basis for an assignment that students will bring to the next class.

What is the pedagogical purpose behind this meticulous effort at fostering students' development of legal thinking, writing, and argument? CUNY law school, Farago notes, is committed to the proposition "that students learn law best by linking it to practice." Behind that commitment lies the understanding that, as he puts it, "What I have and the students do not yet have is the professional culture, what an oral or written argument must look or sound like, how this legal culture has evolved through defining cases." So the primary objective of law teaching for him is to make the forms of legal reasoning visible to students in ways they can imitate and gradually make their own. That includes grasping the narrative and rhetorical forms of legal argument, as well as the social and communicative contexts within which lawyers must do their thinking. As another professor put it, the effort is to teach "writing in context, interviewing, counseling, negotiation in context, learning from doing." With a background in theater and film, as well as the law, Farago is well positioned to provide a variety of ways for students to enter the legal imagination. But he notes that this kind of teaching and learning is premised on intense faculty involvement with students, meeting weekly or at least bimonthly for feedback and coaching, especially for helping students master strategizing and legal writing.

To carry out these ambitious goals, the CUNY law school has organized its building into a warren of small, simulated law offices for each "student associate." In addition to traditional classrooms and seminar rooms, the offices adjoin to a number of library-conference rooms for the performance of a variety of simulations: students are coached in interviewing, counseling, and negotiating sessions. In the first year, students concentrate on simulation exercises, including writing and speaking, built around legal issues that arise from their doctrinal courses.

What is perhaps most remarkable about this approach is that while their counterparts at the other schools around New York are typically in class with up to seventy or eighty of their fellow first-year students, CUNY students spend much of their first year in seminar settings that are focused on linking legal theory to practice and in which contact between students and faculty is close and frequent. Asked how CUNY, hardly a well-endowed, affluent institution, can afford to provide such an introduction to legal study when their more affluent competitor institutions obviously seek the economy of scale afforded by large first-year classes, CUNY administrators answered, "We cannot afford not to do it."

In part, they "cannot afford not to" because CUNY was founded in 1983 with a vision shaped by Charles Halpern, the first dean, to provide local students of limited means with access to a legal career, but particularly to serve the goals of social justice through the legal representation of the underrepresented, such as racial and cultural minorities and, increasingly, immigrant groups. The often weak academic preparation of such students places special burdens on faculty. At the same time, it seems to have been the stimulus to much of the creativity in teaching that is evident in the lawyering curriculum.

Where many law schools emphasize aspects of legal training of value for careers in business and corporation law, at CUNY the lawyering curriculum focuses on public interest law, family law, civil rights, mediation, immigration, health law, and elder law. This emphasis is continued through the second year of the curriculum and reaches its culmination in the third year of lawyering. Then students experience real-world lawyering in either a supervised field placement or through the school's on-site legal clinic, Main Street Legal Services, Inc. There students handle actual cases under the tutelage of faculty.

Faculty who teach in the clinical program at CUNY combine considerable practical experience with theoretical expertise in various areas of legal practice and teaching. Clinical courses are team-taught, often by a full-time faculty member and an adjunct professor who spends most of his or her time in practice. The faculty emphasize that clinics "teach a lot of law" simply because, in the words of one, "students learn to practice best by linking their activities to substantive law." The crucial factor for learning in this context is really the depth of student involvement with the issues of practice. For this reason, the elder law clinic insists that students parallel their actual work with clients by directed research in the area, involvement in legislative advocacy, and active dialogue with practitioners in order to expand their conception of the lawyer's role, as well as to see the larger nonlegal, social context that bears importantly on their clinic work.

Professor Susan Bryant, a former academic dean who was one of the formative figures in developing the clinical program, gives the example of how trying to obtain justice for clients from different cultural backgrounds not only enhances students' practical skills but also enriches their understanding of the deep structure of American legal thinking. A Spanish-speaking client—a recent immigrant—brought her brother to an important case conference. The student handling the case was at first dismayed. Why was the brother there? Did he expect to be involved in the interview? Would his presence compromise confidentiality? How to explain this to the client? What this student was up against was the difference between the individualistic assumptions of American law embodied in the confidentiality concerns and the more collectivist ethos typical of many cultures in which immigrants have been formed. In order to fulfill her fiduciary responsibility to her client, the student had to find ways to negotiate this conflict without, she hoped, either losing her client's trust or devaluing her client's dignity. In coaching this student, Bryant urged her to draw on not just her formal legal knowledge but her ability to "imagine alternatives, to work in parallel cultural universes and so always to ask questions—and to think expansively!"

This imperative to use ingenuity in pursuing justice through the law is what ties together the CUNY experience. Even during their orientation period, beginning students visit real courtrooms. They are asked to watch and listen carefully and then to describe, to faculty and each other, what they have seen. They are asked point-blank whether they could discern justice being done. The aim of their three-year experience is that, by the time they graduate, students are well on their way to being able to advance the cause of justice by serving their clients as competent professionals.

Lawyering on Washington Square: Integrating Theory and Practice at New York University

The elegant neo-Georgian main building of New York University's (NYU's) law school looks onto Washington Square in lower Manhattan. In style and setting it could hardly be more different from the utilitarian Flushing campus of the law school of CUNY. However, NYU announces in its catalogue that it is "the only top tier law school committed to giving sophisticated, in-depth attention, from the first year of legal study, to interactive, fact-sensitive and interpretive work that is fundamental to excellence in practice." It is the lawyering program, the catalogue continues, that "makes good on that commitment" by complementing NYU's "superior doctrinal classes, giving every first-year student closely structured, collaborative experiences of law in use." The concern that "collaborative experiences of law in use" be made integral to the learning of legal reasoning for the sake of "excellence" in practice resonates clearly with the focus of CUNY's curriculum on lawyering in order to train effective professionals.

The catalogue's reference to the school as a "top tier" institution is a subtle boast of NYU's recent ascent to the highest peaks of eminence within American legal education. "Top tier" designates a distinguished, well-published faculty that includes leaders of the field. It also means a highly selective admissions process. Unlike CUNY, the law school of NYU admits only students who are very high performers on the LSAT and high achievers in their undergraduate schooling. NYU students are drawn from across the nation and beyond. They come from all sorts of majors and backgrounds, but a large number have attended prestigious private colleges and universities where they majored in the liberal arts. So they are familiar with the ways of elite higher education and are typically much closer to faculty attitudes and culture than are most CUNY students, many of whom are the first in their family to graduate from college. The faculty uniformly note that NYU students are poised, highly articulate, ambitious, and competitive.

NYU impresses on entering students that its curriculum deliberately links theory to practice. Students take required courses in the usual first-year doctrinal subjects, but they also must do work in the area of lawyering, an involvement that often culminates in the third year with a variety of experiences in clinical legal education. Doctrinal and lawyering courses are mandatory for all students. Work in the clinic is widely available and promoted but is not required. A major aim of the lawyering program is to move students with demonstrated academic talents and interests in the direction of what one professor called "an enthusiasm for legal practice, a love of lawyering."

Within this broad purpose, the first-year lawyering program is intended to equip students with the tools and the vocabulary that will enable them to learn from their legal experience both in and beyond their three years at law school. Professor Peggy Cooper Davis, the director of the program, explains that the first-year lawyering program, which is typically taught by special faculty employed on the basis of three-year contracts, "consists of a series of exercises in which students are (1) given concepts and vocabularies for thinking about an aspect of practice, (2) given a related lawyering problem and guided through the process of working collaboratively to plan and execute a response, and (3) engaged in intensive collaborative critique of their planning and execution." The ultimate goal is to lay the groundwork for "a lifetime of professional self-reflection and improvement." In order to do this, Davis contends, "it is important that students see expertise in a sense broader than the competent manipulation of a body of rules, which is what some students take away from their doctrinal courses. They need to understand expertise within interdisciplinary, ethical perspectives that have to do with the role of law and lawyers in society."

The course is graded pass-fail. This means that lawyering runs the risk of being treated as less than serious by highly competitive, ambitious students. At a place like NYU, this is a particular problem in the first year, when the stakes represented by final grades are highest. (In law schools, key future career possibilities of clerkships and legal teaching are available more readily to the students at the top of their class after their end-of-first-year examinations.) So, Davis argues, it is important to engage students as early and as fully as possible in the intrinsic rewards offered by the lawyering experience. One of these is confidence in writing: "When students arrive, legal writing often seems intimidating to them, but by the time they are developing full briefs, their confidence has risen . . . they can see the benefits of the course."

Simulation of legal tasks in context—what NYU faculty like to call working in role—is the core pedagogical practice in lawyering courses. The announced aim is to provide every student the opportunity to think critically about practice as they develop legal arguments, develop facts, interview and counsel clients, negotiate a transaction or a dispute, mediate a claim, and plead a motion before a simulated court. Furthermore, students are judged on their adherence to the program's "Code of Lawyering Standards and Responsibilities," which is modeled on the American Bar Association Code of Ethics. The program's own code stipulates the expectations that faculty hold for student performance, but it also specifies the norms to which students are to hold each other. Because so much of the work is done in small groups, the code takes on reality as students often see each other's work and ask and answer questions about it.

The hope is that with so much feedback, including videotapes of simulated student interviews, as well as lots of writing, the lawyering program eases some of the peer-generated competitive pressure that typically develops during the first year. Does this work? Davis argues that "by working together, students begin to focus more on the prospect of client and public service and less on competition. They also come to see how important collaborative planning and preparation really are for lawyers." All the while, this is anything but divorced from the students' doctrinal study of contracts, torts, civil procedure, and so forth. As an instructor in the program pointed out, in order to have students engage the simulated cases used in the courses, "we [faculty] must also teach a lot of substantive law, just so students can do the assignments." And, as Davis repeatedly insists, a student's capacity to understand and interpret doctrine is inevitably deepened as the student attempts to use it in the service of a client or a cause.

In contrast to the faculty, students approach their first-year experience from a variety of points of view, often shaped by their academic lives before coming to law school. Where the case-dialogue classes work to enforce homogeneity of viewpoint and reasoning, molding diverse beginners into a corps of legal apprentices, the lawyering seminars seem to allow students to sort it all out, working to relate these new parts of their identity to their developing professional biographies as lawyers. This seemed to be the case for a group of students who met with us as they approached the end of their first year. In that meeting, the students offered a range of different perspectives on what they had learned and its significance to them.

Prior to law school, several of the group had been in Ph.D. programs— one in history and another in the sciences. Other students had tried high school teaching or social services. None had come directly from college. All agreed that their case-dialogue classes had taught them a useful way to "approach problems." It had also provided common ground by giving all students "a shared experience." Some found this exhilarating: "Legal reasoning is framed objectively," said one. Another commented that "the emphasis is on formally structured arguments. That's refreshing compared to the mushiness of many of my undergraduate seminars. It's great to be in a class where your personal experience doesn't get emphasis!" To which another student countered, "But that, too, is a box. The creative process is extremely limited. I'm eager to place legal reasoning into an interdisciplinary context."

When asked how the lawyering seminars had worked for them, however, these otherwise contentious students showed surprising unanimity. As one student put it, they "provide time to try to find out how to use this kind of reasoning that you're learning in the [case-dialogue] doctrinal classes." They also provided "a good deal of feedback," said another, "so, you could really get into a groove with writing assignments. . . . I found I had an affinity with legal composition and arguing." Still another student focused on the way the simulations supplemented the more formal processes of the substantive courses: "It's easy to get lost in cases, which can seem like just one following another. [In the seminar] I found myself discovering new skills and I enjoyed that—applying the ideas and seeing them in different ways. Everything really started to come together."

As at CUNY, many students at NYU see the high point of learning to practice law in the clinical legal experiences available to students in their later years in law school. Although NYU does not require clinical experience, it does offer an exceptionally large number of clinical courses and has tried to link clinical experiences with doctrinal courses—an effort to ensure that students hear, as one of the clinical faculty put it, "echoes across the street." The clinical program is indeed housed "across the street," tucked away it seems, behind the main academic building that faces Washington Square.

The clinical program, however, is not simply an add-on. The core of the clinical program is full-time faculty. Furthermore, it has developed a sophisticated, cross-disciplinary theory of its learning practices under the rubric of "problem solving." Promoted by a series of former deans, the program has also benefited from the groundbreaking work of a professor, Anthony Amsterdam. One of the distinctive features of this program is its team-taught, small-group seminars, where faculty and students are, in the words of another professor, Robert Mandelbaum, "always working with new material and in the process learning from experience." The high morale of the clinical faculty is perhaps indicated by Mandelbaum's judgment that teaching clinics there "keeps you young." One of the school's vice deans, Steven Gillers, described the value of the clinical experience as enabling students to grasp a basic truth: "much of becoming a lawyer is really a long-term process of developing performance skill." In experiencing work with real clients, sometimes in collaboration with professionals from outside the law, students report a new realization. As lawyers, they may often find that they are "someone's only link" to survival in an often-threatening or baffling legal system.

The lawyering and clinical curriculum at NYU has served as a kind of laboratory for the testing of theories about how best to train legal professionals who are at once scholarly, competent, and ethically committed. In 1991, the school began a faculty research colloquium led by Davis, along with Amsterdam, who had already been working to develop more theoretically grounded approaches in the clinical area, and Jerome Bruner, a noted cognitive psychologist who had recently come to NYU on a joint appointment in psychology and the law school. (The innovation of joint appointments with the School of Arts and Sciences was the device invented by the law dean, John Sexton, to breach the isolation of the law school. Subsequently, Sexton, in effect, reversed the direction of cross-fertilization by going on to the presidency of the university.) The colloquium brings together theorists and practitioners of all the areas of legal education. It was catalyzed by years of interchange with faculty colleagues, lawyers in full-time practice, and the feedback of students. Taken together, these efforts have produced a curriculum and set of teaching practices that, as an ensemble, is remarkably self-conscious about its aims and means. Its gradually developing scope has resulted in a plan for integrating the education of lawyers during their three years in law school.

At the center of the pedagogical process in NYU's lawyering curriculum is Amsterdam and Bruner's insistence that the narrative structure of legal reasoning provides a natural deep structure capable of uniting theory and practice. Simulation of legal activity "in role" is very important here. It is through the experience of actually making and criticizing legal arguments, in light of precedent and exemplary cases but also under the constraints of uncertain outcomes, that beginners can grasp the fundamentals of legal reasoning. That reasoning, argue Amsterdam and Bruner, always begins from some particular event that disrupts the expectations members of a community have of each other. Legal proceedings are therefore always narratives—stories—about the nature of the problem at hand, usually offered from competing, adversarial perspectives. The aim of legal activity, whether adjudication, negotiation, or mediation, is always to either bring matters back into accord with previous expectations or to adjust those expectations so as to create a new equilibrium in practice.

Seen this way, the deep structure of all legal argument follows a standard plot: there is a beginning—an earlier stable state. This state is disrupted, leading to the story's middle phase: a problem caused by a disruption that has to be precisely defined. Legal thinking, that is, the law's "artificial reasoning" about categorizing facts, finding plausible precedents in previous legal actions, and wielding proper procedures to attain goals in an adversarial context, is concentrated in this phase. Crucially, however, there is an end: an authoritative holding or account of how the balance is to be restored and why that conclusion is the right one. Despite the formidable esoteric language and technical precision used in legal proceedings, this narrative structure is not peculiar to the law. It is rooted in our shared culture as a society. Therefore, law is more than a trade or esoteric specialty. It is concerned with very widespread understandings and values, without which complex social life would simply be impossible.

Amsterdam and Bruner (2000, p. 140) write:

> [Practicing the law is therefore about ingenuity in] maintaining continuity in value judgments across time and changing conditions . . . it is centrally concerned [not with all value judgments] but with those that are seen as affecting the stability of a community. . . . Such value judgments must evolve through a process of repeated applications in which they are simultaneously reaffirmed and tested, made to fit anew through mutation and thereby preserved.

The point of legal education, in this vision, is to induct students into an understanding of how this complex system of society's self-regulation works—or should work—to uphold and extend socially vital ends and values, and to put students on the path toward developing expertise as practitioners of the legal art.

Why Study Law Schools? Defining the Challenge of Professional Education

From this brief encounter, it is obvious that the CUNY and NYU law schools are very different sites for preparing professionals. Yet across their obvious differences—in location within the New York metropolis, their relative positions within the national system of law schools, their student bodies, and the emphases of their faculty—each presents the compelling spectacle of a struggle to invent and sustain a well-defined educational mission in the face of strong contrary forces. Enlivened by these missions, the schools have been able to form communities of learning in which the form of curriculum and pedagogy follows, or anticipates, their students' future professional functions.

At CUNY, the effort has been to devise means to equip students from groups underrepresented in the law to work effectively in a great cause: social justice and wider inclusion in U.S. society. NYU's law school has moved out of its relative isolation toward greater involvement with the rest of the university, seeking to employ the expertise of the academy to discover and teach insights into law and its potential for bettering life in modern society. Both missions have led their communities to concern with improving the teaching and learning of law. The ways their faculty have engaged their missions differ. At CUNY, individuals find their direction by contributing to a powerfully collective educational enterprise. NYU's larger mission provides a context within which individual scholars can craft distinct niches as part of a larger ensemble. But both schools show the power of intentionally designed institutional pedagogy: for students, it is in both cases the school as a whole that educates, making teaching and learning more a shared concern than is typically the case in many other law schools.

Lawyers fill a bewildering variety of roles in American society. Early in the twentieth century, the great jurist Karl Llewellyn tried to analyze the field by gathering all "law jobs," as he called them, under three great functions of counselor, judge, or advocate (Llewellyn, 1940). But what unites them? The very diversity among law jobs has long been a matter of heated dispute within the profession. Today's law jobs remain in form much as Llewellyn described them. Today, as then, most young lawyers begin their careers in private practice; the majority begin in firms, though a small percentage strike out solo. Today, however, 16 percent enter government service, with two-thirds employed by state and local government and the remainder in federal employ. Nearly 10 percent of law graduates go to work directly for businesses, and 2 percent either do not practice law in any form or proceed directly to law teaching. As we will note later, these gross statistics conceal great diversity in the kinds of work done and, especially, the differing kinds of satisfaction and dissatisfaction experienced by new lawyers across this range of work setting (Dinovitzer and others, 2004).

Even before Llewellyn, Reed's 1921 study of legal education unwittingly created a firestorm in the American Bar Association. Reed was an educator rather than an attorney; he was commissioned by The Carnegie Foundation for the Advancement of Teaching to improve legal education the way its Flexner report had influenced medical training a decade earlier. Reed argued for acceptance of America's de facto division into two kinds of legal profession. One, to which entrance was through the major university law schools, was a world of big firms that dealt with large corporate clients, government, and the wealthy. The other, much larger bar of solo practitioners and small partnerships served most people's day-to-day legal needs. These practitioners were often children of immigrants and studied in ad hoc institutions such as the YMCA night law schools.

In the context of the anti-immigrant sentiment widespread in the early 1920s, Reed's proposal for accepting this diversity of mission, and its implicit effect of enhancing the upward mobility of immigrants through entry into the nation's most prestigious profession, was vigorously overruled by the leading figures of academic law and the practicing bar. Led by former secretary of state Elihu Root, the American Bar Association endorsed the view that the nation needed but one standard of legal expertise and training and that it should be defined by the leading law schools of the great Eastern universities whose graduates dominated the legal world. Root and his colleagues were not above making the claim that non-Anglo Saxons should not be trusted to handle the precious legacy of English law.[7] That conflict has never entirely faded away, however. We will encounter its echoes throughout this study.[8] We may depend on the fact that Root would have vigorously protested a school such as CUNY, perhaps regarding it as a latter-day return of the repressed.

Today, despite—or perhaps because of—the great diversity of careers for which legal education prepares its graduates, law schools exemplify in a particularly vivid way the challenge that defines all forms of professional education. This is how to draw on the genius of academic life, with its urge toward intellectual elaboration, without drifting away from the specific profession's defining focus. In the case of law schools, this focus is provided by engagement with the complexities of the law and its functions in the society in which lawyers must practice. The challenge is to align the practices of teaching and learning within the professional school so that they introduce students to the full range of the domain of professional practice while also forming habits of mind and character that support the students' lifelong growth into mature knowledge and skill.

Notes

1. For fuller explication of these six commonplaces, see Shulman (2004).

2. Shulman provides a fuller treatment of this notion in "Searching for Signature Pedagogies: Teaching and Learning in the Professions," in Shulman (2005).

3. The importance of the idea of professional activity as "good work" in the contemporary moral landscape has been powerfully illuminated in the study by Gardner, Csikszentmihalyi, and Damon (2001).

4. For example, see the work on clinical expertise in nursing practice by Benner, Tanner, and Chesla (1996). Blasi (1995) has provided an account for law.

5. These features of the research literature are laid out in a widely influential summary of the new learning theory (Bransford, Brown, and Cocking, 1999), published by the National Research Council.

6. See Groopman (2005) and also Velmahos and others (2004).

7. See the discussion of this argument in Lagemann (1999), pp. 75–84.

8. An updated picture of today's profession, including the diversity of the practicing bar, is provided by two studies sponsored by the American Bar Foundation. These were studies of legal practice in the Chicago metropolitan area conducted about ten years apart, but they are suggestive for the nation as a whole. See Heinz and Laumann (1994), and Heinz, Nelson, Sandefur, and Laumann (2005).

2

A COMMON PORTAL

THE CASE DIALOGUE AS SIGNATURE PEDAGOGY

ON OUR VISITS TO LAW SCHOOLS, we were repeatedly told by both students and faculty that the first-year experience typically results in a remarkable transformation: a diverse class of beginners somehow jumps from puzzlement to familiarity, if not ease, with the peculiar intricacies of legal discourse. The legal-case method, in all its variations, has dominated the first year of most legal education through much of the past century. Its purpose was described to us in straightforward terms: the case-dialogue method, pioneered by Langdell and his Harvard Law School colleagues from the 1870s, is designed to prepare students to "think like a lawyer."

To American legal education, the significance of being able to think like a lawyer lies not only in its potential to encompass significant educational imperatives but also in the powerful pedagogy with which the phrase is inextricably linked. However, when we asked how students learn this expert form of thinking, the answers were delivered with the broadest of strokes: "by observing faculty in action," by "reading cases," "by repetition," or "by osmosis, so that one day the light just dawned." In this chapter, we attempt to unlock the secrets of the learning process in the case-dialogue method and place it within the overall process of preparing legal professionals.

As a first step in examining the case-dialogue method as a process of teaching and learning, we address two questions: What does the case-dialogue method accomplish? How is it done? We then examine the method in relation to current theories of learning and, using examples drawn from our observations, apply these theories to illuminate the learning processes involved in case-dialogue instruction. After comparing case-dialogue teaching to other forms of instruction, drawing on recent research on both law schools and other professional schools, we consider the effects of the case dialogue, not just on students' thinking processes but on their formation as legal professionals.

The Pedagogical Prototype

If you ask most lawyers to cast their minds back to the first encounter with images of law school and legal education, they can usually provide a vivid image that seems indelibly etched in memory. The dramatic form of most students' first encounter with legal thinking has been presented with riveting effect in John Osborn's *The Paper Chase*. This is a work of fiction, and the portrayal of Professor Kingsfield does not provide an exemplary or even typical picture of today's law teachers. Still, the book's depiction of teacher-student interaction in the classroom provides clear and accurate insight into the logical structure and pedagogical drama of teaching law through the case-dialogue method. The interchange between Professor Kingsfield and Mr. Hart can help us begin our analysis of law school's signature pedagogy (Osborn, 2004). The course depicted in the novel is Contract Law, which remains a first-year required course for most law students. The particular case that becomes the focus of the dialogue that follows, *Hawkins* v. *McGee,* is still widely used to introduce students to contract law.

> "Mr. Hart, will you stand?"
>
> After some difficulty, Hart found, to his amazement, that he was on his feet.
>
> "Now, Mr. Hart, will you give us the case?" Hart has his book open to the case: he had been informed by the student next to him that a notice on the bulletin board listed *Hawkins* v. *McGee* as part of the first day's assignment in Contracts. But Hart had not known about the bulletin board. Like most of the students, he had assumed that the first lecture would be an introduction.
>
> His voice floated across the classroom. "I . . . I haven't read the case. I only found out about it just now."
>
> Kingsfield walked to the edge of the platform. "Mr. Hart, I will myself give you the facts of the case. *Hawkins* versus *McGee* is a case in contract law, the subject of our study. A boy burned his hand by touching an electric wire. A doctor who wanted to experiment in skin grafting asked to operate on the hand, guaranteeing that he would restore the hand 'one hundred percent.' Unfortunately, the operation failed to produce a healthy hand. Instead, it produced a hairy hand. A hand not only burned but covered with dense matted hair."

"Now, Mr. Hart, what sort of damages do you think the doctor should pay?"

Hart reached into his memory for any recollections of doctors . . . Hart tried to remember the summation he had just heard, tried to think about it in a logical sequence . . . .

Hart said nothing.

"As you remember, Mr. Hart, this is a case involving a doctor who promised to restore an injured hand."

That brought it back . . . .

"There was a promise to fix the hand back the way it was before," Hart said.

Kingsfield interrupted: "And what in fact was the result of the operation?"

"The hand was much worse than when it was just burned. . . ."

"So the man got less than he was promised, even less than he had when the operation started?"

Kingsfield wasn't looking at Hart now. He had his hands folded across his chest. He faced out, catching as many of the class's glances as he could.

"Now, Mr. Hart," Kingsfield said," how should the court measure the damages?"

"The difference between what he was promised, a new hand, and what he got, a worse hand?" Hart asked.

Kingsfield stared off to the right, picked a name from the seating chart.

"Mr. Pruit, perhaps you can tell the class if we should give the boy the difference between what he was promised and what he got, as Mr. Hart suggests, or the difference between what he got, and what he had?" (Obsorn, 1971, pp. 7–9)

Ask most lawyers to recall their first encounter with law school and legal education, and they usually describe a vivid image that seems indelibly etched in memory. Many of these memories are not much different from Obsorn's fictional portrait. The lawyers recall the encounter (though they tell it in largely undecipherable legal language) in a large classroom full of strangers, with a towering teacher who asks challenging questions, goading students to take uncertain steps into the maze suddenly before them.

When we observed a first-year class in core common-law subjects like property, torts, or contracts in a typical law school, we immediately noticed that the room was not designed like most university lecture halls. The rooms often accommodate seventy to eighty students (perhaps 120 in older class-rooms), with seats arranged in a semi-circle so that the students can see not only the instructor but many of the other students. The instructor, however,

is clearly the focal point, positioned at the center of the long side of the rec-
tangle, rather than at the short side, as in most undergraduate lecture halls.
The instructor faces the students and, rather than lecturing, asks questions
of one student at a time, waiting for answers and then following up with
the same student, asking more questions, one after the other.

Even if the classroom layout is familiar to students who had small
classes as undergraduates, the form of teaching they encounter is almost
always experienced as something dramatically new. As the class proceeds,
the instructor will turn to another student and focus on her for a while.
Again and again, the instructor asks a student to read aloud the precise
wording of a contract or a legal ruling given in the large book of legal
cases that forms the text for the course. When, inevitably, the student
becomes confused, the instructor repeatedly asks the student to look carefully at the language. It is relatively rare, however, for students to address
one another directly. The instructor may use the board or PowerPoint, but
this varies considerably, according to the instructor's pedagogical aims
and style. For most of the hour, the professor of law is facing the students,
interacting with them one by one through exchange of question and
answer, using the board or other visual displays to support the verbal
exchanges. Students can respond easily by raising their hands if the
instructor solicits additional proposals or responses. Again and again in
our observations, at the end of the hour we would be struck by the single-minded focus on the close reading of texts, analytical reasoning, and
a discourse of rapid exchanges and responses—a focus that the first-year
students are typically encountering for the first time.

Legal Education's Signature Pedagogy

As we discuss in Chapter One, a signature pedagogy is a key educational
practice by which a given field creates a common frame through which it
can induct new members. For example, bedside teaching during hospital
rounds, in which instructors pose questions to medical students regarding the patient at hand, is the instantly recognizable signature of clinical
medical training. For their part, law schools use case-dialogue teaching
almost exclusively in the first phase of doctrinal instruction. It is the vehicle through which the profession ensures all entering legal students,
whichever school they attend, a common experience important to their
professional formation. With its focus on teaching students how to think
like a lawyer, the case-dialogue method constitutes the legal academy's
standardized form of the cognitive apprenticeship.

Like all professional schools, law schools function as institutionalized
sites for apprenticing new professionals. The way the case-dialogue

approach presents the law is thus, by and large, the way novice lawyers come to understand the law as both a subject and a field of endeavor. As we shall see, with its heavy predominance in the first year, this pedagogy emphasizes a view of the legal profession as constituted not so much by a kind of knowledge as by a particular way thinking, a distinctive stance toward the world. It is, moreover, distinctive to North American legal education and quite sharply different from the method used in the United Kingdom, continental Europe, and, indeed, most of the world: a more typical academic presentation of material through classroom lecture.

Learning to Think like a Lawyer: The Purpose of the Case-Dialogue Method

As we explained in Chapter One, every signature pedagogy has four dimensions: (1) its surface, behavioral features—the surface structure; (2) the underlying intentions, rationale, or theory that the behavior models—the deep structure; (3) the values and dispositions that the behavior implicitly models—the tacit structure; and (4) its complement, the absent pedagogy that is not engaged—the shadow structure.

We can understand the purposes of the case-dialogue method through these four dimensions of pedagogy. First, the surface structure of the teaching practice is the teacher-initiated question-and-answer session. However, the pedagogy's underlying intention and rationale—its relation to the goal of teaching students to think like lawyers—is less obvious. Understanding the deep structure of the case-dialogue method requires serious engagement with both the teaching practice and its content. It is also a key step toward understanding the values and dispositions the classroom behavior implicitly models (the tacit structure) and what the method leaves out (the shadow structure).

What, really, is the subject matter in the case-dialogue classroom? Is it knowledge of the particular case under discussion in relation to some larger legal theory or principle? Is it the ways of reasoning that the instructor relentlessly employs through exchanges with students? Is it the excitement of the tournament, evident in so many of the exchanges? Or is it all of these at once—and, if so, what gives coherence to these apparently disparate purposes?

Elizabeth Mertz, a lawyer and anthropologist who is now a senior research fellow at the American Bar Foundation and a professor at the University of Wisconsin–Madison Law School, takes us further toward understanding what is at stake in the repeated classroom drama of the case-dialogue method. Mertz recently carried out a detailed study, funded by the American Bar Foundation and the Spencer Foundation, of the classroom activities of eight first-year contracts classes, taught by men and women of various races, in eight different law schools, chosen to represent the different types of law schools. Mertz, in a forthcoming work, found considerable variety at the level of surface structure. For example, the amount of class time given to lecturing, as opposed to faculty-student dialogue, varied enormously: from 95 percent of time spent on lecture to only 21 percent of time given to lecture. However, she concluded that while there is no single "Socratic method," there are more similarities than differences represented across her eight courses (Mertz, forthcoming, chapter five). The deep structure of the pedagogy—its underlying intention and rationale— was also highly congruent across the range of individual classes. Mertz also found that beyond the structure of the teaching practice, the courses were pervaded by the ethos of living in what she described as an "acontextual context" that emphasizes the formal, procedural aspects of legal reasoning as the central focus, making other aspects of cases peripheral or ancillary. (chapter five). This ethos is not always present in case-dialogue teaching, and we will see examples in which broader understandings of the law are deliberately taught in first-year courses, but in much of legal education, it remains an important aspect of the cognitive apprenticeship.

Drawing on her extensive research, Mertz has reported on the use in actual classes of the same case that Osborn's had his fictional Professor Kingsfield use. Mertz's retelling begins to clarify what the underlying purposes of the case dialogue might be. In the process, her analysis also begins to bring into relief the meaning of legal thinking, as opposed to other kinds of thinking. As Mertz presents it, in this particular class, the instructor begins the first day on *Hawkins* v. *McGee* with a significantly different kind of question from the fictional Kingsfield's more dramatic line of interrogation.

Whereas Osborn's Kingsfield seemed to be leading the class toward questions about what a fair settlement of the case would be, Mertz's instructor points the students toward legal procedure. Mertz's instructor asks students to think about what the lower court decided in the case: "What became of that?" So, from the very start, the students' attention is shifted from the obvious narrative of hapless patient and the failed surgery to what Mertz's students find "the oddest aspects" of the assigned case. The point only gradually becomes clear, as the instructor either takes up the individual students' proffered "facts" of the case or lets them fade into silence. Slowly, the class comes to realize that "the facts" that count toward figuring out what "really happened," are much less obvious than they first imagined, but they are also satisfyingly simple. The relevant facts, it turns out, are all framed by the technical language of legal procedure. Mertz asks the reader to imagine a newcomer's attempt to follow the story that emerges in this particular classroom interchange. "There was a jury trial" summarizes one of Mertz's students, and "Hawkins won and got lots of money; the doctor wanted to pay less money and filed a motion; the trial judge reduced the amount of money Hawkins could get; and Hawkins is appealing that decision by the trial judge [to the appellate court]" (Mertz, forthcoming, chapter one).

In learning to pay attention to some aspects of the cases they read, while discarding others, students are, in effect, learning a new definition of what constitutes a fact. In the law, they gradually are being led to see, facts are only those details that contribute to someone's staking a legal claim on the basis of precedent. As Mertz's student's response suggests, students tend to think of legally relevant facts as they are presented in the appellate opinions that they typically read for class discussion. These opinions, however, are highly redacted accounts of legal proceedings that render fact-patterns in condensed formulas. As a first encounter with legal facts, this can give the misleading impression that facts are typically easy to "discover," rather than resulting from complex processes of interpretation that are shaped by pressures of litigation. It is important, therefore, that instructors also give students experience with fuller accounts of cases in which students can grasp the different meaning of "facts" from opposing points of view.

Mertz's fine-grained analysis shows that it takes at least a whole semester for most students to sufficiently internalize the basic shift in understanding necessary to a recognizably legal point of view. The case-dialogue method never spells this out for students. Rather, as Mertz shows, instructors inculcate this approach less directly. They do this by modeling and by indirect praise or blame, as instructors either take up students' answers and use them to develop points or consign them to oblivion by criticizing, burlesquing, or simply ignoring them. Through these processes, students are being taught not only how to think but also, from a legal point of view, what is worth thinking about.

Mertz's analysis reveals how the surface structure of the pedagogy—question and answer—relates to its deep structure, the teaching of legal reasoning. Gradually, case by case, students discover that reading with understanding means being able to talk about human conflicts in a distinctively legal voice. The question-and-answer format models this translation process by continually translating ordinary human conflicts into the distinctive "frame" defined by legal points of reference and the requirements of legal doctrine. For example, ordinary persons, such as the hapless Hawkins, become redefined, according to their position in legal argument and procedure, as the "plaintiff" or "defendant." As "parties" to legal conflicts, these "legal personae" (from the Latin *persona,* for "mask" in Roman legal doctrine) are understood to be defined by their positions in the proceedings.

Hawkins and Dr. McGee are both thereby cast in the role of "strate-gizers," in Mertz's phrase, who are constructing their rival versions of the story to win the judge's consent. Of course, in reality it was lawyers who were doing this translating and constructing of argument, but that is the not-so-tacit point of the class. The ability to think like a lawyer emerges as the ability to translate messy situations into the clarity and precision of legal procedure and doctrine and then to take strategic action through legal argument in order to advance a client's cause before a court or in negotiation.

Becoming a Lawyer: Living in the "Legal Landscape"

Recognizing the link—continuous translation of human conflicts into legal language—between the surface structure and the deep structure of case-dialogue teaching now makes evident the tacit structure of this peda-gogy, the important third dimension of a signature pedagogy: the dispositions and attitudes that it models. The habits of legal thinking are inculcated by having students repeatedly practice these acts of translation. The instructor models this practice and coaches students through it until the response becomes increasingly automatic—an act taken for granted. In the process, law students are also learning to distance themselves from other, perhaps more concrete, aspects of the persons and situations described in the cases. This distancing is crucial for assuming the profes-sional role, much as medical students must learn to distance themselves from their natural reactions to wounding, suffering, and death. Law stu-dents, that is, are learning to live conceptually in what Mertz calls a "legal landscape," a conceptual space that is defined purely in terms of legal argument (Mertz, forthcoming, chapter six). Thus, "People and problems are located in abstract individuals" who are seen as working in an oddly "acontextual context" of "two contracting parties interacting with each other—even speaking in the first-person singular—against the backdrop of legal rights, jurisdictions, and doctrines" (chapter six).

In their exploration of legal thinking that we encountered in the previ-ous chapter, Amsterdam and Bruner stress the central role of learning to classify and categorize in legal education. They point out, moreover, that all categories are for some purpose and serve particular functions (Ams-terdam and Bruner, 2000). In the case of law's signature pedagogy, the relentless stress is on learning the boundaries that keep extraneous detail out of the legal landscape. This enables students to practice a disposition to think in a specific way, to value and aim at both precision and generality in the application of categories to persons and situations. This is an important distinguishing feature of legal thought and of the guild of legal professionals. The tacit structure of the case-dialogue method models attitudes that strongly reinforce the deep structure.

Legal pedagogy initiates students into a language and landscape in which identities and motives are "configured around points of legal argumentation," so that persons come to be inevitably presented as abstract, "individual strategizers," whatever their actual social and psychological situation (Mertz, forthcoming, chapter six). So, whereas Hawkins was thinking about some kind of expectation for his damaged hand, his attorney was concerned about what might be actionable: the kind of damages for which he could find precedents to support his argument. As Mertz emphasizes, this provides an impersonal filter to screen out bias against types and groups of people, permitting socially stigmatized victims to be heard (chapter six).

At the same time, however, this translation can obscure underlying issues of fairness by ensuring that they do not appear as such in the legal context. Summing up the findings of an ethnographic study of a top-ten law school, Carrie Yang Costello formulates the "norm" in this way:

> The ideology which was considered professional to espouse was to define fairness in formal and procedural terms, and to express concern that faith in the legal system not be undermined by ignoring precedents in the shortsighted drive to achieve a particular outcome. (Costello, 2005, p. 64)

Legal scholars such as John T. Noonan have referred to such features of legal reasoning as "masks of the law," punning on the Latin origin of the term "person" (Noonan, 1976, pp. 19–28).

THE CASE BOOK. The legal texts that form the basis for the case-dialogue method are found in a unique invention of legal pedagogy—the case book. These are compilations of decisions handed down by courts of appeals at the federal and state levels, most but not all organized around topics in the common law such as contracts. Appellate cases lack the situational immediacy of transcripts of jury trials, so that first-year law students are always working from highly edited and abstracted versions of events. These are accounts whose narrative structure is driven by the demands of legal process. Like the classroom organization, the choice of appellate cases as the raw material for the teaching of legal reasoning also dates back to Langdell at Harvard in the 1870s. Indeed, Langdell's employer and Harvard's president, Charles Eliot, explicitly analogized the law library as the pedagogical equivalent of the patients in the medical school's teaching hospital.

CASE SELECTION. For Langdell, the criterion for selecting cases was their historic contribution to building up legal principles. Langdell's enthusiastic protégé and successor, James Barr Ames, further developed the case book, switching from Langdell's chronological organization to an emphasis on "striking facts and vivid opinions" so as to more effectively instill a sense of legal process in the student's mind (Stevens, 1983, pp. 51–57). Since then, case books have included additional materials, such as notes, questions, and other devices intended to aid student learning. Somewhat as language teachers use analysis of important literary texts to support learning of the language, the organization of the case books complements the classroom pedagogy's efforts to immerse students in the landscape of legal process from the start.

The Missing Component: The Shadow Pedagogy

What, in legal education's signature pedagogy, is the fourth dimension— the missing complement or shadow? In our study, we found a number of students who expressed significant unease about certain features of their newly acquired powers of thinking and speaking. They discovered that they were now able to frame arguments convincingly from opposing strategic positions while shifting quickly among points of view. In the competitive case-dialogue classroom, of course, this is the skill that typically receives the most public approbation from instructors. Demonstration of this capacity also appears to place a student high in prestige among her peers. Indeed, so powerful is the method and the ethos of competition that an instructor must make a deliberate effort to ensure that the bigger question of "Who is right, and why?" is not neglected or overshadowed by competitive zeal. The unease of our student respondents is, in one sense, testimony to the very power of the case-dialogue method. It is also an important statement about the imbalance that can occur when so much of legal education is based on this single pedagogy.

In our study, we found two missing complements to the case-dialogue method. The first and more significant of the two is something that is the natural concomitant of most lawyers' activity: experience with clients. It is noteworthy that throughout legal education, the focus remains on cases rather than clients. The analogy in medical training would be the tension between focusing teaching on disease processes, on the one hand, or on patient care, on the other. The skill of thinking like a lawyer is first learned without the benefit of actual clients, and the typical form in which the case books present cases may even suggest something misleading about the roles lawyers play, more often casting them as distanced planners or observers than as interacting participants in legal actions.

The Best Practices for Legal Education project, headed by Roy Stuckey, argues that the case-dialogue method is overused in law schools. In addition to criticizing the use of case-dialogue teaching as a "tool for humiliating or embarrassing students" (Stuckey and others, 2006, p. 209), the authors go on to quote Peggy Cooper Davis and Elizabeth Ehrenfest Steinglass, who suggest that case-dialogue teaching needs to be supplemented by assignments in which students are led to "analyze cases in role . . . [b]y looking at cases from the perspectives of the parties, of their lawyers" (Davis and Steinglass, 1997, p. 275), as well as the appellate court. By such practices, "students are more likely to grasp the significance—and learn the techniques—of interpretive, interactive, narrative, and problem-solving work" (p. 275). Significantly, this recommendation draws on the pedagogies already used in lawyering programs in many schools. The new idea is to consciously connect these with existing uses of case-dialogue teaching. The intention is to introduce students in their first year to a richer kind of legal reasoning—one that moves back and forth between the distanced, "acontextual context" that Mertz observed in contracts classes, on the one hand, and, on the other, perspectives opened up by implementing what the Best Practices project calls "context-based education" (Stuckey and others, 2006, pp. 109–122).

The second "shadow" that emerged from our conversations with students (and, occasionally, with faculty) is the worry that the profession itself lacks ethical substance. This is not primarily a matter of scandals or notorious failures. It seems deeply implicated in the signature pedagogy, perhaps in the tension between the process and substantive dimensions of the law itself. However, the problem seems especially salient in the kind of student reaction to the case-dialogue pedagogy that Mertz identified. In order to gain facility in legal reasoning, case-dialogue teaching often forces students to separate their sense of justice and fairness from their understanding of the requirements of legal procedure and doctrine. Matters concerning the "equities" of a situation may be aired in class discussion, but almost always as second thoughts about "policy." Or the theme of justice may arise negatively, much as the theme of "bias" might, when an instructor asks why a court reached a decision that seems clearly to violate precedent or accepted doctrine. In either case, the tacit message can be that for legal professionals, matters of justice are secondary to formal correctness.

A number of commentators have argued that these disjunctions have become more acute.[1] We believe that if this is so, law schools need to attend more intentionally to how well the various elements of legal education—the cognitive, the practical, and the formative apprenticeships, as we have styled them—fit together in their students' experience. As we argue in greater detail later, simply adding more requirements to the student's curriculum fails to get at this problem, because it is precisely how to integrate the acquisition of conceptual knowledge and competence with ethical intention that is in question.

Engaging these two complements, or shadows, of the signature pedagogy would mean forging strong connections between the cognitive, or academic, experience embodied in the case-dialogue method and so predominant in a student's first year, with practice and formation of professional identity and purpose. When seen as parts of a connected whole, the practical courses in lawyering and clinical-legal education make an essential contribution to responsible professional training. These courses are built around simulations of practice or law clinics involving actual clients. But they can do more than expand the legal apprentice's repertoire of knowledge and skill. Critically, they are the law school's primary means of teaching students how to connect the abstract thinking formed by legal categories and procedures with fuller human contexts.

In Chapter One, we pointed to examples, at CUNY and NYU's law schools, of programs that have been making efforts to address the imbalance and disconnection between the cognitive, practical, and formative apprenticeships in legal education. These programs are notable for a further, important reason. Recognizing the limitations of exclusive reliance on the case-dialogue method to teach law, these programs resisted the common tendency in higher education to respond by simply adding a special course to "fix" the problem. (Mandated courses on such topics as "professional responsibility" are typical attempts.) Although such an additive strategy for righting a perceived imbalance is certainly preferable to doing nothing, it nonetheless misses an important aspect of professional preparation that the apprenticeship metaphor illuminates.

From the student perspective, learning the law is an ensemble experience, its achievement a holistic effect. From the point of view of student learning, the apprenticeships of cognition, performance, and identity are not freestanding. Each contributes to a whole and takes part of its character from the relationship it has with the others. Because case-dialogue teaching is seldom explicitly connected with clinical teaching, few law schools achieve the full impact that an integrated ensemble could provide. As we will discuss more fully, we believe legal education requires not simply more additions but a truly integrative approach in order to provide students with a broad-based yet coherent beginning for their legal careers. It is the systematic effort to do this in their curriculum that makes programs like that at CUNY's law school so noteworthy.

Practical courses in lawyering and work in legal clinics are thus the logical complement to the forced decontextualization that students experience in the standard first-year curriculum. When these courses are done well, they counter the potentially alienating effects of an exclusive emphasis on legal reasoning that can result in the pure legal technician, so injurious to the profession's public legitimacy. In our discussion of the teaching of professional responsibility (in Chapter Four), we suggest that the case-dialogue method is, in fact, able to encompass distinctions between moral and legal issues, but neither the typical course nor the case book used ventures to raise the question. These are issues that will occupy us again in this and following chapters. For now, however, it will be valuable to look more closely at the cognitive activities actually involved in case-dialogue teaching.

Instructional Tactics and the Dynamics of Dialogue

The challenge of any pedagogy is to make the invisible visible, both in the mind of the teacher and the mind of the learner. When what is to be learned are the highly complex, uncertain, and contextually specific forms of thought characteristic of the professions, the challenge for both teacher and student becomes ever more daunting. Because new learning must always be grafted onto existing understanding, the pedagogy must somehow make the connections between what the learner knows and believes and the kinds of thinking needed for professional success. It must also slow down the process of "exposing" students to knowledge or "covering material" in order to engage, that is, to build new habits of mind and rearrange old ones.

When what is to be learned goes beyond observable tasks and behavior, the challenge becomes even more serious. When the setting for learning is quite different from the settings of application and use, the challenge is greater yet, for learners must first master new skills and understanding in one setting and then figure out how to bring them into use in an entirely different one. All these challenges are present in case-dialogue teaching.

The subject matter, as we have seen, is unfamiliar to most first-year students, the method of thinking often even more so. Few of today's law students will ever practice as appeals court judges or as advocates before appellate courts, yet that is the setting the classroom most resembles, and the textbooks and mode of discourse are both drawn from that judicial prototype. How their ability to think like a lawyer will be used in practice remains, for most students, only a vaguely imagined future.

In the absence of exposure to other legal roles, socialization to law school provided through the case-dialogue method may result in a confusing and even distorted socialization to the profession and its requirements. By contrast, in today's education of Jewish and Christian clergy (another profession centrally concerned with the interpretation of texts), seminary students must learn to read familiar texts in new ways, strongly influenced by form-critical theories of interpretation developed in the academy. Yet the seminary students must also someday make these texts meaningful for their congregants. Some of the most innovative developments in seminary teaching have involved connecting students' learning of textual interpretation to imagining and practicing aspects of their future professional lives, for example, by learning to preach on the same text they have analyzed formally (Foster, Dahill, Golemon, and Tolentino, 2005).

The Case Dialogue as Cognitive Apprenticeship

In considering the nature of case-dialogue teaching as a cognitive apprenticeship, the place to start is the classroom dialogue itself. The dialogue of professor and students that plays such a central role in legal education's signature pedagogy contains its own dynamic of question and answer, comment and response. It is also modulated by the professor's selection of various student respondents, given that much, if not most, student participation in case-dialogue classrooms results from being called on by the instructor; for that reason, the patterns of speech and silence and the sorts of voices that are included or excluded from the room are also guided by the professor. This dialogue and its underlying dynamic have subtleties that are rarely explored. It is not the same kind of teaching that is found in either academic lectures or discussion groups. The dialogue is part of an ongoing conversation between master and artisan or journeyman who seeks to learn. In a sense, the dialogue of the legal case-dialogue method is embedded in the context of an apprenticeship system, though it is different from that of law office study in early legal education and other traditional systems used to educate professionals, craftsmen, midwives, and others, from time out of mind.

Modern studies of learning have yielded new theories of cognitive apprenticeship with associated insights that shed helpful light on the classroom dynamics associated with formal instruction in law and other fields. The cognitive apprenticeship theories of John Seely Brown, Allan Collins, Susan Newman, Paul Duguid, and others argue that faculty-student interaction associated with effective learning involves a sort of "apprenticeship" through which intellectual development occurs (Collins, Brown, and Newman, 1989; Brown, Collins, and Duguid, 1989). Although the process of development parallels that of traditional craft apprenticeships, it is less obvious because the complex cognitive patterns of teacher-experts are generally not explicit and are thus difficult for their student-novices to observe. Likewise, it proves difficult for teachers to discern errors and misunderstandings that may be occurring in the students' minds. These difficulties are especially pronounced in large classroom settings such as those in which the case-dialogue method is often employed.

Theorists of the cognitive apprenticeship have created useful rubrics for articulating and observing the subtle dynamics of the teacher-student dialogue in situations such as first-year law courses (Collins, Brown, and Newman, 1989). Expert teachers may employ a variety of methods or strategies as they initiate or advance dialogue. Indeed, in the case-dialogue classes we visited, we observed four basic methods identified by cognitive theorists:

1. Modeling, by making cognition visible
2. Coaching, by providing guidance and feedback
3. Scaffolding, by providing support for students who have not yet reached the point of mastery
4. Fading, by encouraging students when they are ready to proceed on their own

In addition to offering these basic methods, cognitive apprenticeship theory offers helpful rubrics for observing and describing students' responses to the teaching methods implicit in classroom dialogue. Important strategies, which we will also see in use in the examples to follow, include students' "articulation" of their ideas as a way for the instructor to see students' level of knowledge, including misunderstandings that need to be corrected if further learning is to occur. Another valuable insight is that students learn best when they can "reflect on" their knowledge and performance in relation to models supplied by the teacher. Perhaps most important is the reminder that the aim of learning for the professions is hardly ever confined to understanding concepts in a single setting. The point of much teaching in law schools is to foster students' ability to transfer their learning so that they can apply what they have learned in one context to another, different one. Making this aim conscious, so that the instructor actively tests students' progress in such transfer, is another well-attested contributor to better learning.

For example, reflecting on the dialogue of the fictional Professor Kingsfield and Mr. Hart, previously invisible pedagogical moves become quite plain. We can now name the teaching techniques and the corresponding expectations of students.

So when Hart is unable to "give us the case," Kingsfield models for him by providing the facts of the case: "*Hawkins* versus *McGee* is a case in contract law . . . a boy burned his hand . . . A doctor wanted to experiment . . ."

Kingsfield then uses coaching: "As you remember, Mr. Hart, this is a case involving a doctor who promised to restore an injured hand."

He also provides some scaffolding when he prompts Hart: "And what in fact was the result of the operation?" enabling Hart to finally make a response. In this passage, it is noteworthy, however, that Kingsfield does not encourage or allow students to go on their own. In this class, he never fades from the center of the pedagogical action. But this is not some quirk of the personality Osborn created for him. Kingsfield does not fade because, as novices, his students will need explicit scaffolds for months to come before they can analyze cases on their own with real facility.

Using the cognitive apprenticeship template, the student's side of the interchanges also becomes more apparent and understandable. Hart's task is articulating his understanding by "giving us the case" and responding to Kingsfield's follow-up questions. Hart's embarrassing silence was an unsuccessful effort to introduce reflection, as when we are told that "Hart tried to remember the summation he had just heard."

Finally, Kingsfield demands of another student further exploration of key concepts in the case: "Mr. Pruit, perhaps you can tell the class if we should give the boy the difference between what he was promised and what he got, as Mr. Hart suggests, or the difference between what he got and what he had." Like the common pedagogical practice of putting "hypotheticals" to students, the purpose of exploration is to induce the student to apply the concept under discussion to other patterns of facts, thereby revealing the student's grasp of the underlying legal notion. This tactic is at the basis of most forms of critical analysis.

In a sense, the dialogue of the case-dialogue method is an offshoot of the apprentice system, with a master artisan guiding a roomful of novices through the early stages of learning a craft. As in a craftsman's studio, the apprentices watch the master artisan's actions and attempt to emulate them. But in this cognitive apprenticeship, the fundamental skills are related to memory, knowledge, comprehension, and interpretation and are impossible to observe. Only through question and answer can instructors make their thought processes explicit, observable, and available for imitation by students. Similarly, instructors can detect students' mastery and lack of mastery, their misunderstandings, misinterpretations, and faulty reasoning only by asking them to articulate their understanding of key concepts and then helping them correct errors in their articulations.

Intellectual Tasks and Instructional Tactics at Work in the Classroom

What follows are several snapshots of law schools' cognitive apprenticeship in action. These snapshots are characteristic of the teaching practices we observed through classroom visits and related interviews at a cross-section of sixteen North American law schools during the 1999–2000 academic year. The classes visited included those in six common first-year courses (Contracts, Torts, Property, Criminal Law, Civil Procedure, and Constitutional Law), taught by a wide range of faculty (untenured, tenured, and chaired professors), with students having varied backgrounds and professional goals.

As we have already noted, case-dialogue teaching inculcates several, often largely tacit, meta-lessons well beyond the particular case under discussion on any given day, about how to gather knowledge and bolster comprehension. The first of these skills is the ability to read a case as a legal professional would; this skill is taught largely by modeling, supported by scaffolding questions that direct the attention of the class to certain features of the case. In Mertz's *Hawkins* v. *McGee* session, for example, the key scaffolding device was the instructor's direction to look at "what happened to" the lower court's decision in the appellate court's holding, which the class had before it in the case book. In our experience, instructors typically employed these scaffolding questions over and over with each case; this prompted students to articulate their developing ability to analyze material in legal categories. Through these practices, instructors encourage students to construct a particular form of knowledge—a legal understanding of events that filters out some aspects of the narratives under analysis while selecting and extracting the legally relevant "fact pattern" for attention.

A TYPICAL CLASS: FITTING RULES TO FACTS AND BEYOND. A second, pervasive meta-lesson teaches the peculiar nature of legal language, at once ambiguous and precise. Take a situation from a contracts class we observed. The topic that day was the complex doctrine of what constitutes an "offer" in transactions of buying and selling. Notice how the instructor directs the students' attention, first to the relevant facts and then to the language of the case itself.

INSTRUCTOR: What does this [holding] mean?

STUDENT: [Gives a somewhat rambling disquisition]

INSTRUCTOR: So, then what happens?

STUDENT: [Describes the result in her own words]

INSTRUCTOR: [Pressing the student to assemble the facts in narrative order] So then what happens? And her defense was? And the result was?

STUDENT: [Virtually reading from the text, manages to provide the basic facts of the case]

INSTRUCTOR: [Pauses to prompt reflection] Did the court look at all the facts? Does everybody get that?

INSTRUCTOR: [Moving to a second student, asks the student to state the next case, asking questions similar to those asked of the first student in regard to the first case]

INSTRUCTOR: [Prompting with a question] And what was the decision?

SECOND STUDENT: [Continuing the informal style of the dialogue thus far, starts to paraphrase the decision]

INSTRUCTOR: [Bringing the student up short] What's *their* language?

SECOND STUDENT: [Now quotes from the case book, giving the exact language of the decision]

Here the instructor scaffolds the first student, soliciting the student's articulation of the fact pattern. The instructor then continues to lead the student to describe the relation of these facts to the court's decision by encouraging the student to tell the story as a legal argument—one that moved through stages of claim and counterclaim toward authoritative resolution by the court. The tone is informal, with attention directed toward extracting the plot line of the drama of legal argument moving toward resolution. When moving to the second case, the instructor continues in the same mode, reinforcing the line of questioning used in the first. But then the instructor abruptly changes tack, interrupting the informal flow of the narrative by a sudden demand for precision in statement: "What was *their* language?"

What was the purpose of this pedagogical move? One obvious purpose is for dramatic effect: stopping the flow makes everyone sit up, and the palpable embarrassment of the student doing the articulation is quickly communicated through the class. The message is unmistakable: when dealing with court decisions, precise quotation is important; do not paraphrase! However, there seems to be a deeper point involved, having to do with the ambiguity that inheres in much legal language and the resulting need for clarity about definitions and rules to cut through the ambiguity to the key legal point.

The class continues:

INSTRUCTOR: [Going back to the case narrative, picks a critical point and asks the class] Was there an offer at that point? Why?

THIRD STUDENT: [Raising hand and, recognized, makes a fumbling response]

INSTRUCTOR: [Coaching] Yeah, that's [basically] right. [Pauses, then continues] Suppose one party says: "We accept the offer provided that the flagstones in the patio stay in place." What is that? [The instructor throws out a number of similar examples, or hypotheticals, to prompt reflection. They take the form of "You offer me . . . I accept if you . . ." He then asks, "Do we have a deal?" And calls on another student.]

FOURTH STUDENT: Yes.

INSTRUCTOR: How about in the Y case?

FOURTH STUDENT: [Asks to be excused because unprepared]

FIFTH STUDENT: Yes, there's a deal there also. [Articulates a rationale]

INSTRUCTOR: [Accepts the student's articulation, in effect coaching again, by affirming the students' ability to explain complex ideas in their own right] This is a very important point in contract law. It has to do with whether a particular term is enforceable. This is what is called a "firm offer." There are two things: an offer (one thing) and a promise to hold the offer open for a given time (another thing). Everything you've said is right, but I just want to take it a little step further.

In the end, the instructor draws a lesson from the fast-moving question-and-articulation process. The instructor had been using hypothetical changes in fact pattern analogous to the actual appellate court case that the students had read and presumably analyzed. The point of this sudden shift to didactic statement is to clarify the students' gradually developing understanding of the criteria for determining whether a contract's provisions are or are not legally enforceable.

The lesson here is a statement of legal doctrine: the definition of a "firm offer." At the same time, the case-dialogue method has enabled the instructor to teach, model, and dramatically emphasize the key meta-lessons about legal reasoning that we noted along the way: how to read legal material and how to engage with the complexity of legal language. This class was typical of those we observed, in that the exclusive focus of attention was learning how to classify events according to legal rules and to apply those rules to various sets of pre-organized "facts." Students were challenged, scaffolded, coached, and, finally, instructed about how to make the "legal landscape" their own. The clear focus of classroom activity was on the tacit purpose of legal education's signature pedagogy: students and instructor were united in a sustained effort to understand the human world through legal categories.

FLEXIBILITY: ADJUSTING CASE DIALOGUE TO LEVELS OF STUDENT-PREPARATION. We found nearly all the law faculty with whom we spoke to be proponents of the case-dialogue method as the best means for inducting novices into the craft of legal reasoning. A feature that faculty particularly appreciate is its adaptability not only to the different areas of legal doctrine, such as contracts, property, and so forth, but also to students with different levels of preparation and pre-existing skills in reading and debating complex written argument. What this might mean became clearer to us in a class in criminal law at a school with a highly diverse population, including many students who are first-generation college graduates and many who are working their way through school. For a substantial number, English is a second, not a first, language. Many are single parents, have extensive work experience, or have faced more than their share of other challenges in life.

Notwithstanding these challenges, the questions this instructor asked about the day's principal cases are very similar to the ones posed in the contracts class noted earlier. However, this instructor very forcefully focused on reading, especially on reading statutory text. He said in a later interview that he tries almost daily to take his class through relevant provisions of the state criminal statutes and the Model Penal Code. In doing so, he makes an important, substantive point about legal knowledge: it is not confined to collected case reports. Indeed, the culture of learning here seems quite different from that of the first example. As the instructor walks up and down the aisle, he asks students to point to where they are in the text. The image is that of a determined class learning a new language—its vocabulary and its literature at the same time. Students are being introduced to the basic features of legal interpretation. As the instructor told us, statutory interpretation does not come easily to most law students. Yet its challenge is put to especially effective use here. Highly structured work with brief but dense statutory material seems especially useful for a kind of vocabulary drill, perhaps more so than diffuse case narratives that other law courses and instructors more routinely use.

INSTRUCTOR: Today's topic is "complicity." We'll begin with a famous nineteenth-century case involving a Cherokee defendant sentenced to death for a murder committed by his partner while the defendant watched. Who can give us the facts? What was the holding? And the reasoning?

STUDENTS: [Raise hands to volunteer; several are recognized and they, in sequence, articulate their understanding of the fact pattern, the holding, and the court's reasoning; language is informal but shows students have made the basic structure of case analysis their own.]

INSTRUCTOR: Okay, pull out your copies of the Penal Code. What's the relevant provision? Where is it? [Walks up and down the aisle, checking to see where books are open and tracking student reading of the specific text]

INSTRUCTOR: Let's read it, Mr. X.

STUDENT: [Begins reading the text]

INSTRUCTOR: Okay, stop there! Anybody. . . . What's that word mean, "Abetting?"

STUDENTS: [Raise hands; several are called on; in sequence, they each articulate their understanding of the term.]

More than obvious issues are being addressed through this method, the instructor explained in a subsequent interview. Many students in this setting have not been strongly socialized into academic life, and, he has found, they share a misconception that looking things up is not morally acceptable: one should know them by heart. He says that systematically working with statutes allows him to bring to the surface such questions and to emphasize to his students that lawyers who fail to look up statutory answers are putting their clients at risk.

Later in the class, the instructor turns to the students and asks a general question:

INSTRUCTOR: Did you see the story in today's newspaper about Colonel Z, whose wife was involved in smuggling drugs?

STUDENTS: [No response]

INSTRUCTOR: You should have read that. You have to read that! You should have asked . . . [He then discusses details of the charges against the colonel that involve claims of complicity. He goes on to ask further questions about criminal responsibility relating to complicity in drug sales that could occur in a poor neighborhood (using hypothetical questions to prompt exploration) and to raise issues of culpability when one spouse engages in criminal conduct known to the other.]

So while this class incorporated a narrowly focused lesson on reading statutes, it also clearly engaged a broader world. The instructor explicitly tapped into students' knowledge and capacities for comprehension in distinctive ways—modeling, coaching, and scaffolding—by drawing on the world of context, as well as text. By drawing a lesson from a major national newspaper and emphasizing the need to read it regularly, the instructor conveyed to students that lessons about the law can be learned outside the confines of law school. Incorporating the story about the colonel and potential problems in poor neighborhoods made the lesson on complicity more relevant, memorable, and motivating.

While the instructor was explicitly coaching students on how to transfer their prior life-based learning into the context of learning the law, he was also reminding them that the tools they were developing in law school would have practical use later. This instructor was thereby beginning to link the apparently abstract doctrines of criminal law to the students' possible lives as lawyers. He was outlining a connection between the apprenticeship of knowledge and the apprenticeship of practice. Each effort like this one—an effort to interpret legal rules—adds a valuable layer of commentary, extending the students' understanding of what the law means. Moreover, by raising, through his examples, questions about race, poverty, and the law's role in the society, the instructor was also opening potential connections to the larger issues of ethics and the nature of legal work, the concerns of professional identity that typically do not receive much discussion in basic doctrinal courses.

INDETERMINACY AND THE APPLICATION OF RULES: EXPLORING LEGAL THINKING. As a contrast, consider an instance that illustrates the pedagogy's flexibility in another dimension. This time the setting is a first-year contracts course taught in a very selective, nationally recognized law school. Here the students' intellectual skills have been honed prior to entering law school, at least if undergraduate grade point averages and admissions test scores tell the truth. These students may have developed their capacities through a variety of high school and college experiences, ranging from English literature to philosophy, physics, or engineering, or from more informal experiences in families, libraries, or jobs. Students with demonstrated analytical abilities very likely have also developed well-internalized skills of managing their own cognition by monitoring and diagnosing their own understanding and learning strategies. In short, such students typically enter law school with pre-existing intellectual scaffolds that have often become habitual and unconscious. This intellectual infrastructure supports their further work in becoming expert legal analysts in significant ways.

Within a classroom where such students predominate, a teacher may perceive her task as quite different from that described by the instructor in the previous case. Here effective teaching might be thought to aim at motivating students to attend to their own learning. The surface structure of the pedagogy might then shift away from the typical emphasis on articulation in response to questions on the immediate case at hand and toward prompting students toward exploration of the implications of their understanding in domains related to, but somewhat different from, the areas under discussion. Effective teaching would also try to stimulate a dynamic learning cycle by bringing into the discussion students' reflection on what they are learning in relation to their previous knowledge. In such settings, certainly by the second semester, teaching might be expected to aim at moving students beyond the beginner's stage toward a more comprehensive and holistic grasp of legal thinking.

On this day in a contracts class, the topic is a set of cases involving what are called "illusory promises." The instructor had been absent from several classes due to illness, but the students seem eager and prepared. The instructor launched the class with a fast-paced set of questions, pausing on occasion to look at the ceiling as she struggled to remember students' names. When she succeeded, students laughed and clapped. The instructor led several students through a standard analysis of questions: "What are the facts? What was the holding? What was the court's reasoning?"

Finally, the instructor settled into an extended dialogue with a student sitting in the top row of seats, asking questions that caused her and her classmates to focus quite intently on key issues from both the buyer's and the seller's points of view. By deliberately shifting the viewpoint among parties to the dispute, the instructor was able to generate varied twists on a seemingly simple hypothetical fact pattern and turn what seems like reasonable assumptions inside out and upside down.

INSTRUCTOR: Why is that a problem for the client?

STUDENT: [Answers by placing the client within the case narrative]

INSTRUCTOR: What problem is that for the client?

STUDENT: [Replies by citing the proper legal definition of "illusory promise"]

INSTRUCTOR: But is that what the court is saying? I mean, consider that it may not be obvious here what the court is actually saying? Why would the law do that?

STUDENT: [Has to place the court's decision, repeating the precise formula, within her interpretation of the doctrine within which the decision could make sense]

INSTRUCTOR: Yes. Yes, very good. [Pausing to encourage reflection to let the class regroup, the instructor then turns to another student.]

By the end of the session, the instructor and the class have together constructed a complex understanding of key cases, pertinent statutes, and relevant reasoning to both make sense of the various holdings and to justify these in terms of an overarching concept of "illusory promise." This active process of constructing, rather then simply finding or being given, a concept in the law illustrates the signal strength of the case-dialogue method. As the students left the room, the student who had carried the weight of the day's discussion caught her breath—and beamed.

The instructor in this class has fully appreciated the possibilities that the case-dialogue method provides for training potential legal "stars," such as the student who left the class smiling and confident. While continuing to reinforce the importance of certain basic questions designed to guide the students quickly through the same standard steps of case analysis we have seen in the earlier examples (holding, reasoning, arguments), this instructor modeled a more fluid performance of legal reasoning by shifting key elements of the hypotheticals to spur wider, more experimental exploration on the students' part. She also tailored her questions to provide an exhilarating stretch for the student who was the center of the instructor's attention that day, neither demanding rote recitation nor presenting hurdles beyond the student's stride.

The visitor was left with the sense of having observed an artistic performance jointly produced by the instructor, the principal student speaker, and the class as a whole. Part of the impression stemmed from the fit between the instructor's teaching methods and the class with which she worked. It may, in fact, be such contexts in which the traditional, though nonabusive, Socratic method may work best—a context established by the high level of the pre-existing student skills and the versatility of the instructor.

INTERPRETATION AND POLICY: EXPANDING THE REPERTOIRE. In our study, we encountered a number of instructors of required first-year courses who had devised ways to encourage students to think about the significance of what they were learning about how the legal system operates. Some of these faculty led students toward reflection on their developing professional identities, providing opportunities to be let in on the game, as it were, of what lawyers think and do. Some introduced students into ways of reflecting on the contested issue of what the law does and should do as a central institution of democratic society. We single out these teaching practices because they seem to function well for the formation of competent and responsible lawyers. In the instances when we encountered such teaching, expanding the repertoire of typical case-dialogue teaching meant giving explicit attention to pedagogical scaffolding. The instructors provided explicit supports to enhance the students' ability to recognize what they were doing as they learned the basics of legal process. In the language of learning theory, this is called meta-cognition and is associated with enhanced learning.

Consider a first-year class in civil procedure in a leading law school. Though perhaps the quintessential "process" course, civil procedure in this instance was taught as a vehicle to enable students to reflect on the nature of legal reasoning, not simply as training in how to do it. The instructor presented the subject matter as an evolution in which judges had developed legal rules and concepts in order to resolve new kinds of disputes and problems. The course highlighted the role of creative analogy in this process, calling attention to how various judges draw new possibilities from concepts they borrowed from other areas of law in order to resolve the disputes at hand.

For example, in teaching the concept of jurisdiction, the instructor began by reminding the class that the case they were to analyze—an arcane nineteenth-century ruling by the Supreme Court—was an important step in an evolutionary narrative explaining how concepts of jurisdiction have been worked out.

INSTRUCTOR: Let's see where we are in our story. [Addresses a student] Will you state the case for today?

STUDENT: [Presents the case in informal language, noting that the case was essentially a dispute about jurisdiction]

INSTRUCTOR: [Probes students' understanding of the case by asking what was novel in the court's opinion, finally asking a summary question] Now, where did Justice Field derive his concept? He cites whom? [Calls on a student]

STUDENT: An [earlier] opinion by Justice Storey.

INSTRUCTOR: Correct. Now, what does the cite tell you about where Justice Storey got his notion?

STUDENT: He got it by drawing an analogy from the concept of sovereignty.

INSTRUCTOR: And where did he derive that?

STUDENT: It seems from the theory of international law.

INSTRUCTOR: Exactly! Have we seen other examples of this kind of borrowing by analogy?

STUDENTS: [Various students offer examples from earlier in the course.]

INSTRUCTOR: [Summarizing] So, what's interesting in this case is not the punch line but the various processes of reasoning that Justice Field used to justify a rule that would enable courts to settle such disputes.

The instructor then presented a scaffold in the form of a reflexive principle: "In the law, how you frame a question or approach will shape the possible answers." Continuing the reflexive theme, he posed a question for the whole class: "What does today's case show us about lawyers' epistemology, about how they think?" The result was a freewheeling discussion about the use of analogy in legal reasoning, drawing on cases read in the civil procedure course.

Following that discussion, the instructor turned to the blackboard to emphasize a distinction between two kinds of legal argument. As he stated the distinction, "category arguments—arguments from precedents, showing 'the ways things have always been done'—can end a case. It's always important to look for these. But 'principle arguments' are equally important. These provide the means to either justify or attack an application of category arguments. That's where inventive legal analogies, such Justice Field's and Justice Storey's, play a big role. You've got to understand the role of both kinds of arguments."

Here the instructor was drawing out the underlying principle of "lawyers' epistemology" that the case discussion had surfaced. He was leading the students to take a metacognitive stance toward what they had just learned. He then gave the core concept a memorable formulation by classifying arguments as two types. The instructor finally changed pace to conclude the class on a less dramatic note by posing questions for the students to use in preparing the cases to be discussed in the next class.

A second, quite different instance of expanding the case-dialogue repertoire comes from a weekly small-section class offered in another leading law school. Some schools offer their first-year students one required course that is taught in case-dialogue format twice a week but complemented with a third weekly meeting in a smaller, twenty-student seminar group. A course in torts organized this way used the weekly small-group session to link case-dialogue methods of teaching the subject with theoretical reflection on the basis of tort law. The pedagogy of the section meeting was more typical of upper-level legal courses taught in seminar format. For many of the first-year students taking the class, it seemed similar in style and format to some of their undergraduate liberal arts courses. The tone was casual but quite academic, with the instructor working methodically through an outline of a topic, engaging the students in intense, focused conversation about the assigned readings.

This instructor's approach was to assign students to read various, often opposing, legal theorists who offered arguments about the moral bases and policy implications of key topics in tort law. In effect, the section provided an ongoing jurisprudential commentary, with a set of arguments, about the topics being covered in the case law on the other class days. Students were reading and writing argumentative papers, taking up questions from the opposing viewpoints: Should tort law be conceived as a system for regulating the outcomes of disputes over fault in order to maximize economic efficiency? Or is it really a branch of applied legal philosophy and ethics, with important bearings on the moral quality of social relationships? The instructor alternately presented summaries of arguments and asked students to evaluate these, sometimes prompting debates among contrasting points of view. The aim, as the instructor saw it, was to prompt students into a kind of meta-cognition of the point of what they were learning in the case law. From the students' point of view, the small section provided more familiar pedagogical ground and also a (generally welcomed) chance to think about law in a way that is more critical of law and its workings than was provided in the case-dialogue meetings of the course. The class expanded both the pedagogical repertoire and the context in which legal reasoning was examined—and learned.

Toward a More Powerful Legal Education

The case-dialogue method is a potent form of learning-by-doing. As such, it necessarily shapes the minds and dispositions of those who apprentice through it. The strength of the method lies, in part, in how well it results in learning legal analysis, and in part in its significant flexibility in application. As our examples suggest, it is a highly malleable instructional practice. It encourages, at least for skillful teachers, the use of all the basic features of cognitive apprenticeship. It seems well suited to train students in the analytical thinking required for success in law school and legal practice. In legal education, analysis is often closely integrated with application to cases. The derivation of legal principles, such as we witnessed in our classroom examples, generally occurs through a process of continuously testing, using hypothetical fact patterns or contrasting examples to clarify the scope of rules and reasoning being distilled. This central role of analysis and application, then, is well served by the method.

From our observations, it also seems clear that the motivational power of the pedagogy is considerable, though here again it is perhaps most effective with classes that are primed for challenging analytical work. It is not only fear, however, as in law students' notorious dread of receiving a "cold call" from the instructor, that concentrates students' minds in class. In the best-taught classes we observed, it was the narrative nature of legal argument itself, especially its dramatic character, that motivated students. It frequently took the instructor's skill, however, to reconstitute the drama beneath the formal language of the opinions. As we saw in the previous chapter, legal argument is often triggered by conflicts—events that confuse or contradict a community's expectations. Legal proceedings, especially litigation, therefore, have an inescapable narrative dimension, with story and counter-story being constructed by the contending parties to the dispute.[2] We submit that this "conflictual" structure accounts for students' willing suspension of disbelief that the "actors" involved could really be, as the case books keep insisting, those odd, strategizing "personae"— the "plaintiffs" and "defendants" and "parties" who strive relentlessly to stake the better claim on the basis of precedent and principle. As we saw, when performed in back-and-forth argument by a professor and an advanced student, the fine points of legal arguments, especially when they serve as the turning points of these abstract dramas, can rivet students' attention. At such moments they generate the sort of collective effervescence that burns particular classroom events into the memory, gradually reshaping students into legal professionals.

Using the Signature Pedagogy with Possible Diminishing Returns

The findings of the Law School Survey of Student Engagement study, or LSSSE, released in 2005, are based on a national sample and represent the largest effort so far to document the actual learning activities of law students. Although the LSSSE does not directly evaluate the performance of either students or law schools, it provides useful information about how students allocate their time among various activities, as well as how they experience their legal education. The majority of students reported having learned between "quite a bit" or "very much" about thinking critically and analytically, developing legal research skills, and writing clearly and effectively, and that their classes emphasized the application of theories or concepts to practical problems (Center for Postsecondary Research, 2005). These data do not tell us what aspects of law school pedagogy produce these results, but they do corroborate the faculty's sense that valuable legal learning does take place for most students, though it is unclear precisely how much first-year case-dialogue classes contribute to this overall result.

Other data do suggest, however, that case-dialogue teaching is not seen by recent law graduates as particularly helpful in enabling them to move from school to professional practice. In *After the JD,* a study of a large national cohort of new lawyers, jointly sponsored by the National Association for Law Placement Foundation for Law Career and Research and Education and the American Bar Foundation, respondents were "not especially enthusiastic about the specific role of their law schools in the transition to practice" (Dinovitzer and others, 2004, p. 79). Specifically, when the survey asked recent graduates if they thought law school had prepared them well for their legal careers, "the median response is exactly in the middle (neither agree nor disagree), while respondents tended to agree, though not strongly, with the proposition that 'law school teaching is too theoretical and unconcerned with real-life practice'" (p. 79). The most useful experiences for making the transition to practice, according to respondents, were real work experiences, either in the summer or during the academic year, followed by legal writing and clinical courses. These were trailed by upper-year lectures and course concentrations, with the first-year curriculum receiving the lowest rating except for pro bono work and ethics courses (p. 81).

Taken together with the LSSSE data, the findings reported in *After the JD* provide indirect support for our belief—a central contention of this book—that legal education could be significantly improved. In our experience, and as the Best Practices project report suggests, today's trend is to supplement rather than replace the inherited reliance on this venerable case-dialogue teaching in the first phase of doctrinal instruction. This is being done either by including other techniques, such as close reading drills, or by the direct incorporation of legal writing into the class itself, or by changing the pedagogical form altogether, with smaller classes organized more like seminars in the arts and sciences, much like those we describe in Chapter One, at NYU and CUNY. Even though these developments are generally modest, instructors seem to worry that decreasing the prominence of the standard case-dialogue method would diminish students' motivation. With far too little systematic investigation (and, therefore, too little knowledge) to enable anyone at present to draw firm conclusions, it is difficult to know whether the faculty members' fears are unfounded.

A rather disturbing, though not particularly surprising, finding of the LSSSE is the drop-off in interest and effort in classroom learning as students move through law school. Third-year students, especially, reported a significant reduction in the amount of time and effort spent on their academic work, compared to their earlier years (Center for Postsecondary Research, 2005). This trend is consistent with anecdotal lore, long circulated in law schools, that many students, having at first been intimidated by the demands of case-dialogue classes, gradually become disengaged from their course work. As we have noted, the Best Practices project report suggests that case dialogue is overused as a pedagogy, resulting in unbalanced learning (Stuckey and others, 2006). It may also be that its overuse, or perhaps unvaried use, in the first year leads some students to disengage from the process—a disengagement that even later experiences with fuller approximations to practice and actual clients may not be able to reverse. As the Mertz study documents, the case dialogue inculcates a narrow and highly abstract range of vision. This, in turn, can have a corrosive effect on the development of the full range of understanding necessary for a competent and responsible legal professional. Some critics, such as Robert Stevens, have argued that the relentless emphasis on process tends to eclipse the importance of legal doctrine itself, leading to lawyers who are more technicians than professionals invested with a sense of loyalty and purpose (Stevens, 1983). Legal education may have a problem of diminishing returns—one that a better integration of the cognitive apprenticeship with the practical and professional could help to prevent. On the curricular level, this need for integration points toward a reconfigured third year (and probably some reconfiguration of the second year as well), marked by pedagogies of practice and professionalism that enable students to shift from the role of students to that of apprentice professionals.

The underlying problem was well articulated by Karl Llewellyn, who, besides being a great jurist, is one of legal education's legendary figures. In *The Bramble Bush,* a still widely read collection of essays that began as talks to first-year law students at Columbia, Llewellyn explained the problem of the first phase of legal education succinctly:

> The first year . . . aims to drill into you the more essential techniques of
> handling cases. It lays a foundation simultaneously for law school and

law practice. It aims, in the old phrase, to get you to "thinking like a lawyer." The hardest job of the first year is to lop off your common sense, to knock your ethics into temporary anesthesia. Your view of social policy, your sense of justice—to knock these out of you along with woozy thinking, along with ideas all fuzzed along their edges. You are to acquire ability to think precisely, to analyze coldly, to work within a body of materials that is given, to see, and see only, and manipulate the machinery of the law. (Llewellyn, 1996, p. 116)

We certainly discovered that the same process is very much at work in today's law schools. Faculty, like students, vary considerably as to how worrisome they find this "lopping" and "knocking," this temporary moral lobotomy. However, virtually everyone with whom we spoke was aware that this process was a major facet of the case-dialogue pedagogy of the first year. Warming to his theme, Llewellyn continues:

It is not easy thus to turn human beings into lawyers. Neither is it safe. For a mere legal machine is a social danger. Indeed, a mere legal machine is not even a good lawyer. It lacks insight and judgment. It lacks the power to draw into hunching that body of intangibles that lie in social experience. None the less, it is an almost impossible process to achieve the technique without sacrificing some humanity first. Hence, as rapidly as we may, we shall first cut under all the attributes of *homo,* though the *sapiens* we shall then duly endeavor to develop will, we hope, regain the *homo.* (Llewellyn, 1996, pp. 101)

Our experience in law schools gave rise to the question of how effectively today's legal education reconnects the "sapiens" with its underlying humanity. At the very least, this disconnection in the first year sets up a major problem of reintegration in the remaining two years. This disconnection has important implications for the way in which today's legal education forms future legal professionals and, perhaps, for the fate of the legal profession itself.

Legal Education in the Context of Professional Education

Let us try for some perspective. Is law school really egregious in the degree to which it disconnects knowledge from meaning and purpose? We already noted in passing that medical school demands of its students a seemingly unnatural distancing from the patients who host the "cases" of disease that are the actual subject matter under study. Does something analogous mark all professional education? If so, what do other fields do about this? Do they offer models for reconnecting the separated elements of the lawyer in formation? What might law schools do that they are not doing at present?

From the law students' point of view, entrance into the professional school is the beginning of apprenticeship. In centuries past, learning as an apprentice typically meant exposure to the full dimensions of professional life, not only the intricacies of esoteric knowledge and peculiar skills but also the values and outlook shared by physicians, lawyers, or ministers. By contrast, today's law students encounter this once-unifying experience as three differentiated, largely separate experiences. Students encounter a cognitive or intellectual apprenticeship, a practical apprenticeship of skill, and the apprenticeship of professional identity and purpose, often through different faculty with different relationships to the institution. For many students, neither practical skills nor reflection on professional responsibility figure significantly in their legal education.

The academic setting clearly tilts the balance toward the cognitive and intellectual. Inasmuch as professionals require facility in deploying abstract, analytical representations (symbolic analysis), school-like settings are very good environments for learning. At the same time, however, professionals must be able to integrate, or re-integrate, this kind of knowledge within ongoing practical contexts. But in this area, students learn mostly by living transmission, through pedagogies of modeling and coaching. For law schools, as for all professional schools, re-integration of the now-separated parts is the great challenge.

ENGINEERING. The problem is well illustrated in the setting of engineering schools. There the university's values are prominently displayed in the courses in engineering science or physical analysis. These courses make up the preponderance of all programs for entry into the field. In them, students are taught how the world works as understood by contemporary physical science. The distinctive strength of the engineering mind lies in its powers of analysis. Engineering students are trained to abstract from the welter of everyday situations neatly bounded problems, described with quantitative precision, which can then be solved by elegant mathematical means. However, like all the professions, engineering is finally about doing—exercising practical judgment under conditions of uncertainty. If the students are to become functioning professionals, the analytical clarity emphasized in the courses in engineering science must be tempered by experience with actual materials and conditions in the world.

Experience with actual materials and conditions in the world is the stuff of the apprenticeship of engineering practice. Students learn how to work the world. Such learning can, and does, take place in several curricular areas, but chiefly in laboratory courses, in which students learn that actual situations may not behave precisely as described in theory, or in design studios. In these settings, students begin to understand the fuller dimensions of solving problems in engineering—that economic, social, environmental, and esthetic considerations have a place, often confusingly juxtaposed to purely physical requirements.

Besides learning how the world works and how to work it, future engineers also confront the question of how to be in the world—how to live as professionals. Today this is often understood as the realm of "ethics," which is correct in the older, expansive sense of ethics as the investigation of how best to live. Compared to the courses in engineering science, labs, or even design courses, this area remains curiously unaddressed, or only haphazardly addressed, in many engineering curricula. The reason is often that the question of how to be in the world is beyond the competence of engineering to answer. This kind of reflection does not come easily to many engineers, despite a half-century of efforts to bring the humanities into the undergraduate engineering curriculum. Yet engineers must answer the question in practice, just as must everyone else. Furthermore, because of their peculiar knowledge and special skills, the attitudes and decisions of engineers often have effects on others and the larger environment.

In the past, the professional identity and conduct of engineers received virtually no attention in professional school. It was simply left to the on-the-job training that most beginning engineers received from the industrial corporations who employed them. Often the operative assumption was that the company, not the individual engineer, was the responsible party. The days when engineers were overwhelmingly employees of large, paternalistic corporations are rapidly coming to an end, however. Today, in the face of recent economic and technological changes that are placing more initiative and responsibility in the hands of engineers as inventors, managers, and entrepreneurs, perceptive analysts of the engineering world have begun to ask whether the old reliance on on-the-job training is enough to equip engineers to judge and decide as professionals.[3]

MEDICINE. Medicine is another profession that functions at the interface between the scientific and technological realm and the human and ethical world. Like engineering, its students must learn to abstract precisely measurable problems from the confusing range of organic breakdowns found in human ills. Hence, an array of basic sciences, such as biology and organic chemistry, are integral parts of learning to trace the physiological basis of pathology in the body. Like engineers, physicians-in-training must master the available technologies of treatment in order to "work the world" in a curative direction. The distinguishing feature of medical training, however, is that most of it is carried out in settings of actual patient care. The consequence is to provide medicine a real advantage, compared to engineering or law, for integrating its forms of apprenticeship. Current efforts to improve significantly the professionalism of physicians-in-training center on teaching better and more humane forms of patient care and on relations between doctor and patient.

A CONTINUUM OF INTEGRATION. If neither engineering nor medicine can provide direct models for how law might deal with its problem of integrating the cognitive, practical, and professional, they do provide some insight into law's particular problems and possibilities. One might imagine a continuum among types of professional education—one on which the poles are defined, at one end, by an exclusive emphasis on purely cognitive training in the classroom setting and, at the other, by an exclusive employment of forms of teaching tied directly to settings of practice. On such a continuum, law schools would clearly fall at one extreme; medical education, like nursing, would fall closer to the other pole, with engineering in between, though more on the classroom-cognitive side.

The strength of the classroom-cognitive end of the continuum lies in its ability to abstract concepts and principles from situations and to compress learning into controlled components that can be mastered more or less independently of any knowledge of the situations to which the concepts apply. In the modern university, furthermore, academic respectability goes with what Max Weber famously called value-free investigation (Weber, 1997). The signature pedagogy of law school, like engineering science, fits this end of our hypothetical continuum.

Once one poses the question of how this kind of intellectual training is to serve the end of preparing legal professionals for practice, however, the difficulty Llewellyn conjured up for his first-year classes looms large. It is difficult to imagine moving very far toward subsuming the skills or the habits of judgment needed by the competent and responsible legal professional into the case-dialogue pedagogy of legal analysis. The essential dynamic of academic procedures is the separation and specialization of analysis from the activities of professional practice. Professional activities typically blend and mix what the academic treatment of law works hard, for legitimate intellectual reasons, to keep separate: knowledge, know-how, and ethical judgment.

The essential dynamic of professional practice, especially in fields such as law, in which face-to-face relationships with clients are typical, proceeds in the opposite direction from the logic of academic specialization. Practice requires not the distanced stance of the observer and critic but an engagement with situations. The sort of thinking required to meet the challenges of practice blends and mixes functions, so that knowledge, skill, and judgment become literally interdependent: one cannot employ one without the others, while each influences the nature of the others in ways that vary from case to case. In counseling or advising a client, it is difficult to know what and how much legal knowledge to apply without also gaining a sure grasp of the complexities of the client's situation and outlook and coming to some determination about the appropriate professional response. For this reason, we believe laying a foundation for the development of practitioners requires that legal education expand along the continuum to include significant involvement in the experience of performing the tasks of practicing attorneys. Beginning students' legal education almost entirely at one end of the pedagogical continuum is simply not the best start for introducing students to the full scope and demands of the world of the law.

LEGAL EDUCATION'S UNIQUE SITUATION. Compared to medicine or engineering, the particular social position of the legal profession and the nature of law as a field of study together create a unique situation for legal education. First, legal professionals play a dual role in American society. Unlike physicians or engineers, legal professionals act as social regulators. The bar is not simply a guild or trade association. Those admitted to practice assume an official public role. This is most salient in the instance of judges, who decide authoritatively in civil disputes and criminal trials, and to a lesser extent, government lawyers at local, state, and national levels. But it is also part of the official designation of all licensed attorneys as officers of the court. This designation means that, in principle, lawyers have obligations to see to the proper functioning of the institutions of the law. Indeed, in numbers far disproportionate to the population, many of the nation's political leaders are lawyers. At the same time, lawyers are themselves social actors, functioning within rather than above the perpetual clash of interests we call civil society. This role is the more familiar one—the lawyer as zealous advocate for clients. The apparent conflict between these two roles is often muted in practice by the subordination of the social regulatory function to client advocacy, but it remains real and demands explicit attention in any law school curriculum (a theme we will return to in our discussion of social responsibility).

The tension between the advocacy and the regulative functions of lawyers is paralleled by another basic polarity within legal thinking itself. Modern legal systems yoke together two significantly different modes of thinking, two different social logics. This opposition can be formulated in several ways. Among the most influential has been the distinction between the everyday, practical or narrative mode and the formal or analytical.[4] In our observations, we have seen this contrast frequently in play in first-year classrooms. In the narrative mode of thought, things and events are given significance through being placed within a story, an ongoing context of meaningful interaction. The narrative is a mode of thinking that integrates experience through metaphor and analogy. It is employed in the arts and also in practical situations, including professional work. Meaning and value have their origins here.

In the analytical mode, by contrast, things and events are detached from the situations of everyday life and represented in more abstract and systematic ways. Historically, the evolution of autonomous legal systems has depended on the development of the technologies of writing and numeration as the media through which the intellectual skills of classification, argument, and proof can be represented and learned. These skills, in turn, have been essential to the development of science and technology, as well as the modern systems of administration. It is this cognitive style to which the modern common law, like other forms of Western law, has developed while retaining its necessary roots in narration, albeit of a highly technical kind.

On the one hand, then, law is a form of artificial reasoning, constrained by historical precedent but powerfully shaped by the demand for consistency in the application of formal rules and principles. In this aspect, the experience of learning the law resembles learning in the scientific and technical fields such as medicine and engineering. Legal education, too, needs to train students in the analytical mode of thought, with its reliance on formal procedures and general theories and ideas. Like engineering or medicine, facility in the law requires the ability to distance oneself from everyday contexts and meanings and to concentrate on abstract cognitive features of the environment, though in verbal rather than mathematical media.

On the other hand, law functions as a normative lattice in American society. Law provides a web of categories and rules that interpret and channel individual aspirations while regulating conflict. Its reliance on narrative, even if highly formalized, reveals this involvement in human contexts structured by cultural meaning and moral norms. Students cannot proceed very far in even their technical mastery of the law without encountering issues concerning matters of policy or the equities implied in particular rulings or general rules. Legal thinking naturally opens out onto the concerns of political philosophy, ethics, and religion, though as we noted earlier, the case dialogue's emphasis on formal and procedural issues tends to convey the view that a lawyer need not take matters of policy or "the equities" very seriously. Yet law regulates the world of human activity. In this way it is quite unlike the physical or biological systems underlying engineering or medicine, which can be adequately described in abstraction from intention and purpose. As we have seen, this cultural and ethical aspect of the law receives far less attention in the critical first year than its formal, analytical features. From the point of view of professional identity, the missing complements to legal analysis imply the need for a serious effort to re-integrate the severed components of the educational experience.

This internal tension between the analytical and narrative, formal and substantive, and technical and moral aspects of legal thought has given rise to the rich fields of jurisprudence and legal philosophy. It is noteworthy, then, that jurisprudence is rarely given an important place in the North American law school curriculum. For developing professionals, however, these two faces of legal thinking generate varying levels of existential strain. From the one side beckons the formal persona of the legal technician, while from the other calls the identity of the lawyer as moral agent. The former holds out the prestige of academic recognition, likely career success, and the apparent satisfactions of remaining too tough to fall into Llewellyn's "woozy thinking." The latter continues to make appeals to conscience and the ideals of the profession. However, by now it should be obvious that this is by no means an even contest for the hearts and minds of law students. The first-year experience as a whole, without conscious and systematic efforts at counterbalance, tips the scales, as Llewellyn put it, away from cultivating the humanity of the student and toward the student's re-engineering into a "legal machine."

The Formative Dimension of Legal Education

It is common in French, though not in English, to talk about education as "formation," as in *la formation medicale* or even *la formation humaine*. However, changing conditions of professional life have begun to give the term some educational currency. The preparation of the clergy has, for its own internal reasons, long been sensitive to the relation of character to professional legitimacy and competence. Recently, educators of future clergy have begun to look at how their educational experience as a whole contributes, or fails to contribute, to the formation of the sort of clergyperson they wish to cultivate.[5] Within legal education, too, recent and influential critical analyses of the unintended effects of law school on students, especially women and minorities, have opened up a new discourse about the formation of future lawyers.[6] As these studies document, all forms of education exert socializing pressures on the students—and faculty—who take part in them. This is the formative dimension of professional education.

Although obvious as a concept, outside clergy education, the formative aspect of professional education is still not a major topic in its own right. Certain features of contemporary educational thinking seem, on the surface at least, to discourage such reflection. From different points of view, in their writing about legal education Lani Guinier, Michelle Fine, and Jane Balin (1997) and Anthony Kronman (1993) have pointed out that recognizing the unequal effects of various kinds of habituation on different individuals or populations can be in conflict with our society's aspiration toward equality and freedom from bias (Guinier, Fine, and Balin, 1997; Kronman, 1993). Nevertheless, it seems beyond question that attention to the formative effects of pedagogical practice is a necessary step toward either assessing or improving legal education.

In actual professional practice, it is often not the particular knowledge or special skill of the lawyer or physician that is critical, important as these are. At moments when judgment is at a premium, when the practitioner is called on to intervene or react with integrity for the values of the profession, it is the quality of the individual's formation that is at issue. The holistic qualities count: the sense of intuitive engagement, of habitual disposition that enable the practitioner to perform reliably and artfully. Thinking about how to train these capacities inevitably calls up words such as *integration* and *focus* to describe deep engagement with the knowledge, skills, and defining loyalties of the profession.

Ultimately, the goal of formative education must be more than socialization seen as molding human clay from without. Rather, formative education must enable students to become self-reflective about and self-directing in their own development. Seen from a formative perspective, law school ought to provide the richest context possible for students to explore and make their own the profession's possibilities for a useful and fulfilling life. The school contributes to this process by opening apprenticeship to its students as effectively as its faculty is able. Concretely, this means enabling students to grasp what the law is, as well as how to think within it, just as it means giving students experience of practicing the varied roles lawyers play while coming to appreciate the engagements of self and the world that these entail. Preparation for the demands of practice is the topic of the next chapter.

Notes

1. For example, Glendon (1994), and Rhode (2000).

2. See Amsterdam and Bruner (2000) for their extensive discussion of the role of narrative in legal reasoning and judgment.

3. These issues receive more elaboration in the Carnegie Foundation study of engineering education; see Sheppard (forthcoming).

4. See Bruner (1986) for an extended discussion of these contrasting forms of cognition.

5. Formation is one of the themes of the Carnegie Foundation study of preparation for the clergy. See Foster, Dahill, Golemon, and Tolentino (2005). See also the discussion of formative education in Sullivan (2005) pp. 216—226.

6. For example, see Guinier, Fine, and Balin (1997). See also Mertz (forthcoming, chapters six and seven).

3

BRIDGES TO PRACTICE

FROM "THINKING LIKE A LAWYER"
TO "LAWYERING"

AS WE HAVE SEEN IN THE PREVIOUS CHAPTERS, the primary focus of future lawyers' education is legal analysis. Learning to think like a lawyer is, accordingly, the main occupation of students' first phase in law school. But developing lawyers must at some point learn another set of demanding skills, all the while negotiating the complex transition from the stance of student—the one we saw enacted in case-dialogue teaching—to that of apprentice practitioner. This movement toward practice is generally the secondary focus of legal education, the introduction to practice. When done well, the apprenticeship of practice can strengthen students' learning of legal reasoning, pushing them to more supple and inventive thinking. As reported in *After the JD*, new lawyers especially appreciate those aspects of their law school experience that they see as having helped ease their transition to practice (Dinovitzer and others, 2004). However, it remains controversial within legal education to argue that law schools should undertake responsibility for initiating and fostering this phase of legal preparation.

As we mention in the previous chapters, law schools now offer courses in a variety of areas, with the purpose of preparing students to practice, developing what are often called lawyering skills. These lawyering courses cover a wide range, from research and legal writing in the first year, through trial advocacy and practice negotiation to clinical experience with actual clients. Typically, these are elective courses, optional for the students. But whether they are optional or mandatory, they are most often taught by faculty other than those teaching the so-called substantive or doctrinal courses of the curriculum—a faculty that is not typically tenured and that has lower academic status. In many of the schools we visited, students commented that faculty view courses directly oriented to practice as of secondary intellectual value and importance. As other means to develop lawyering skills, students often work as summer associates in law firms or take other kinds of informal, apprentice-like positions, but these experiences are rarely graded or connected to course work.

However, there is evidence that this situation is changing. In recent years, the American Bar Association has advocated more use of supervised externships and now provides standards for linking such experiences to the formal curriculum (American Bar Association, 2005b). This is among the signs that education for practice is moving closer to the center of attention in the legal academy—a positive development and a trend to be encouraged. Making part of the standard legal curriculum students' preparation for the transition to practice is likely to make law school a better support for the legal profession as a whole by providing more breadth and balance in students' education. Educational experiences oriented toward preparation for practice can provide students with a much-needed bridge between the formal skills of legal analysis and the more fluid expertise needed in much professional work. In addition, we think that practice-oriented courses can provide important motivation for engaging with the moral dimensions of professional life—a motivation that is rarely accorded status or emphasis in the present curriculum.

Movement toward a more integrated curriculum would also make legal education more like preparation in a number of other professions. In medical education, for instance, most of the education consists in clinical teaching carried out in settings of actual practice rather than in classrooms. Nursing education also involves significant amounts of mandatory clinical training. Some amount of clinical training or internship is also a regular part of the education of teachers and members of the clergy. Engineering students must demonstrate their abilities to design functioning projects. At present, however, a law degree requires no experience beyond honing legal analysis in the classroom and taking tests. In most schools, this leaves direct preparation for practice entirely up to student initiative. Too often, the complex business of learning to practice is largely deferred until after entry into licensed professional status.

This situation is the result of the particular history of legal education in the United States and the way the field of legal education developed. Today, however, there are hopeful developments aplenty. In this chapter, we look at some current promising experiments in the preparation of students for legal practice. In doing so, we hope to call attention to the largely unrealized potential that these models offer for addressing many criticisms of today's law schools, those of the profession and the public alike. To make their potential clearer, we relate these pedagogical developments to discoveries in the learning sciences about how professional expertise is best developed. We note existing models in other professional fields, especially medicine, that suggest how law schools might better integrate the learning of legal reasoning with the grasp of practice. And we also consider the question of what could be done to move education for practice into the more central position it deserves to hold within the legal academy. Here we offer the emergence of negotiation within the area of clinical-legal education, to which we have already alluded, as a test, along with promising pedagogies in the important area of legal writing and communication.

Narrow Perspective: An Obstacle to Change

Underlying the imbalance between the cognitive and practical apprenticeships of legal education is clinical education's problematic legitimacy, which has made it difficult to bring institutional attention to the teaching of practice skills. In our study, we discovered that faculty attention to the overall purposes and effects of a school's educational efforts is surprisingly rare, partly due to the general tendency of faculty to focus on only their particular areas of the curriculum and partly due to the culture of legal education, which is shaped by the practices and attitudes of the elite schools; those practices and attitudes are reinforced through a self-replicating circle of faculty and graduates.

Most faculty are drawn from a very small number of leading academic institutions, from among lawyers who have taken predictable career paths. Students at the top schools who are identified after their first year as stars in analytical reasoning receive extensive apprentice-like training as law review editors during their second and third years; training comes from both faculty and more experienced peers. They then go on to yet more hands-on mentoring as law clerks for appellate judges before taking up such positions as appellate advocate, legal scholar and teacher, or judge. Drawing law school faculty from this pool has ensured great uniformity in career path and outlook, especially in matters of faculty promotion and curriculum, introducing little diversity of experience into faculty perspectives. The most prestigious law firms hire graduates of the leading standard-model schools. Because there is a tacit expectation that recent graduates from the elite schools will receive careful mentoring as part of these firms' staff development, the schools pay scant attention to preparing their students for practice.

The contest for distinction and influence is relentless and consuming, so it would not be surprising if many within this self-replicating circle were to lose sight of the rest of their fellow students—the majority of practitioners. It would require a change of outlook on the part of many law faculty to become interested in refashioning the curriculum to better serve the needs of the bar and the nation as whole. After all, it is the leading schools' most successful graduates—the judges, the professors, the partners at the blue-chip firms—who continue to dominate the profession and staff the law schools.

The attitudes and practices of the elite schools are replicated in other ways. The relative simplicity and low cost of the standard-model law school has also made it attractive to many less prestigious institutions eager to advance their standing. Especially during the postwar decades, general agreement about what a high-prestige law school should look like made a competitive rise in status a direct matter for any institution that could muster the resources. The ambitious school would recruit a highly credentialed faculty, preferably from the old, elite institutions, increase the library's holdings, induce prestigious figures to publish in the law review, and work hard to recruit well-prepared students, as measured by the LSAT. By the 1960s, for example, a number of law schools at state universities, many in the Midwest, had advanced their status in this way. After that, the competitive "gold standard" was set for the field of legal education.

The standard is so securely established that there are few leverage points from which to effect change in the model. In American law, academics have long enjoyed a strong position. Unlike the situation in other common-law countries, such as Britain, the American bar has never been able to directly control standards of either admission to practice or training, instead having to filter its control of standards for admission through often hostile state legislatures. There the suspicion of professional privilege long restrained the bar's power, allowing law schools, by the late nineteenth century, to establish an independent niche for themselves by selling the credential of a formal legal education as a competitive advantage in a field once made up mostly of former apprentices. The subsequent movement of legal education into the university, along with the rise of the standard model that has given legal education its basic uniformity, has also successfully entrenched the independent position of academic law. On the one hand, American law schools enjoy a substantially free hand in relation to standards and practices, which is good for academics. On the other hand, the strong position of academic law has made it difficult for the concerns of the practicing bar and the public to influence law school education, except around the edges.

The competitive dynamics internal to the existing system have long been strong enough to stymie well-reasoned and well-intended efforts at reform, while the prevailing view of legal knowledge continues to sharply separate analytical knowledge from practice. Still, law schools have collectively learned a good deal about how to provide the foundations for better legal practice. Despite a largely unresponsive field, some legal educators have already refined a number of promising ways of teaching for practice. Over the past decade, moreover, there has been significant progress in legitimating and advancing the concerns of advocates of a different epistemology of professional learning, one that more intimately connects theoretical understanding with practical competence.

Building Bridges to Practice: The Long March Toward the Center

Efforts to shift the present imbalance in law school curricula by emphasizing the teaching of negotiation, legal writing, and actual clinical experience, as well as the skills of legal analysis, have a long, distinguished history. In the Carnegie Foundation's 1921 report on legal education, Reed pointed out the dearth of training for practice in the leading law schools. Jerome Frank, a leader of the Legal Realist movement in jurisprudence between the World Wars, famously advocated a clinical "lawyer-school," rather than a "law school" (Frank, 1963, p. 230) that would focus on preparation for practice as an alternative to the exclusive emphasis on the case method invented by Langdell. A variety of experiments with different models of such curricula—models involving clinical teaching and close student-faculty interaction—marked the interwar years in a number of leading law schools.

Overcoming the Stigma of the Trade School

Prior to the 1950s, clinical legal education was impeded by law schools' efforts to distinguish themselves academically from the old apprenticeship models, which produced disagreement about the propriety of the clinical mission for academic law schools. This viewpoint was reflected in the standards for accreditation established by the American Bar Association and the Association of American Law Schools, which neglected the subject entirely. The 1950s, however, saw a renewed worry that legal education had neglected to provide students with sufficient grounding in practice. This concern did not close the traditional theory-versus-practice divide. It simply pushed law schools to add more practical skills education, with no attention to the relation of these practices with theory. It also led, briefly, to introductory courses, such as Harvard's course on the legal process, to provide students with some early sense of the nature of the profession they were striving to enter. The typical objection was that the profession itself should do a better job of acclimating students to their new lives upon completing law school—a charge that would appear again in later periods.[1]

The 1960s brought new emphases: social justice and professional responsibility. Curricula did not change much, but some law schools began to experiment with teaching the rules of professional responsibility within practice settings, though this approach lagged behind efforts to interject professional responsibility training into the traditional curriculum through the so-called pervasive approach, which will be discussed in the next chapter. During the late 1960s, in the wake of the civil rights and women's movements, the underlying motivation for interest in clinical education shifted yet again, this time toward an emphasis on community service, using legal clinics to provide pro bono access to legal services for low-income clients.

These currents were significantly strengthened by the infusion of Ford Foundation support to restructure legal education in order to give a prominent place to clinical training. A Council on Legal Education for Professional Responsibility spread the idea, while Harvard professor Gary Bellow sought to give it articulation and pedagogical sophistication. A perhaps unintended effect of the social-activist inspiration of this wave of clinical programs, however, was to keep the clinical courses (and often their faculties) isolated from the main doctrinal teaching of the law schools.

In 1972, the Carnegie Commission on Higher Education issued *New Directions in Legal Education*. There Packer and Ehrlich argue that clinical education—a high-cost endeavor—ought to be diagnosed and evaluated along three different axes: (1) the extent of student involvement in an experience, (2) the extent of supervision by a responsible person, and (3) the integration of experience into students' academic programs. These remain important criteria. The authors were supportive of clinical legal education, as well as other forms of education for practice, but they criticized some forms of clinical education, noting that the pressures of real life do not necessarily make for well-organized learning situations. They emphasized the need for educationally meaningful supervision and warned against the "intellectually low level" of much existing clinical teaching:

We doubt that clinical education is *the* solution that many of its proponents claim it to be or that it should be *the* dominant trend of legal education in the future. We are also concerned that an anti-intellectual tendency of clinical education will offer an allure to students and to some faculty members who seek "relevance" at any price. We do not see clinical education as *the* testing case for the legal education of the future. While we believe that clinical education has a useful role to play in legal education, its role is not unique. We prefer to think that the path of improvement lies in experimentation with many modest ideas, one of which is clinical education. (Packer and Ehrlich, 1972, p. 46)

Like Reed in the 1920s and Frank in the 1930s, Packer and Ehrlich recognized the growing diversity within the bar and the need to rethink legal education to prepare attorneys for a wide variety of careers, advocating more diverse curricula that would provide a more sensitive and penetrating interrelation between theory and practice.

Despite some initial interest at the American Association of Law Schools, however, these efforts failed to change the standard pattern of law school education. Today's standard model—the three-year curriculum, an emphasis on analytical training through the case-dialogue method, and work on a law review journal—took a long time to achieve dominance in preparation for legal practice. This model was promoted by the American Bar Association and the Association of American Law Schools as a way to raise standards, in order to protect the public and, not incidentally, to enhance the status of the profession. Still, for up to half of the twentieth century, legal education struggled to escape the "trade school" stigma. Law schools of the approved model, demanding an undergraduate degree as a prerequisite for admission, became the definitive portal into the profession only after the 1950s.

Recent Calls for Change

In recent decades, attempts by the organized bar to introduce more concern about preparing students to practice received a major boost with the American Bar Association's widely circulated MacCrate report of 1992.[2] The report recommended that law schools develop greater emphasis on instruction in skills, as well as the formation of values. These require, according to the report, opportunities for the performance of lawyering tasks with feedback, including ongoing reflective evaluations of student performance. The report did not attend to the fiscal implications of its recommendations, however. As Packer and Ehrlich had noted, because the teaching of practice is time-intensive and requires low student-to-faculty ratios, it is unavoidably more expensive than large classes. Nonetheless, efforts at increasing the presence and sophistication of lawyering courses have continued since the publication of the report.

Other sympathetic proponents of a more balanced legal education have noted that efforts to bring lawyering fully into the law school experience face a number of, as Tomain and Solimine call them, "strategic defects": clinicians operate from a devalued position institutionally; clinical legal education takes place within legal training that lasts just three short years, as opposed to the medical model of a longer training period; and no worthy pedagogical theory of legal practice on which skills training might be founded has been produced (Tomain and Solimine, 1990). (The inauguration of the *Clinical Law Review* in 1994 could be seen as one effort to respond to this continuing challenge.) These strategic defects are still in evidence fifteen years later, and skills training will continue to face an uphill battle unless it is linked with an accepted theory of lawyering that could provide a bridge between theory and practice and perhaps establish a rationale for more systematic continuing education beyond law school. The proposals first essayed by legal-realist icons such as Llewellyn and Frank still await their Langdell.

By contrast, the American Medical Association achieved tight control of standards by means of the 1910 Flexner report and so was able to create a uniform system well before the attempts of the American Bar Association and the Association of American Law Schools. Yet over the past three decades, medical schools have experimented extensively with curriculum and pedagogy. Toward the end of better integration of the teaching of science and clinical knowledge, they have employed a variety of means: new curricula, extensive use of simulation to train clinical skills, and problem-based learning, to name a few. Medical education has also benefited from the insights of empirical, historical, and conceptual studies that employ insights from the social sciences and the humanities. By contrast, in legal education the problem is not the absence of many models—there are some good ones—but the question of how to provide a wider and more integrated foundation for future practitioners. What has so often been missing is recognition of the importance of providing a broader form of legal education—one that includes strong interconnection among the elements of the curriculum and the full faculty.

Recently, however, the many independent efforts seem to have coalesced into a wider pattern. The 2006 *Best Practices for Legal Education*—the product of a team effort led by Roy Stuckey of the University of South Carolina Law School—has brought the movement to place the teaching of practice at the center of legal education a new visibility and maturity. Not simply a documentation of promising efforts, though it is that, this report draws extensively on the literature on educational effectiveness, including undergraduate learning, in order to propose for legal education adaptations of approaches found to be effective elsewhere. The key idea in the report is that the findings of the learning sciences have converged on what the authors call "context-based education" (Stuckey and others, 2006). The report's thesis: "Students cannot become effective legal problem-solvers unless they have opportunities to engage in problem-solving activities in hypothetical or real legal contexts" (p. 109). We concur with this thesis and in the next section examine some of the bases for such a claim in the findings of the contemporary sciences of learning.

The Apprenticeship of Practice: Enter the Learning Sciences

We intend the metaphor of apprenticeship as a reminder that, for practical purposes, the law school's demands and expectations define the legal profession for the student. With little or no direct exposure to the experience of practice, students have slight basis on which to distinguish between the demands of actual practice and the peculiar requirements of law school. The strengths of academic training lie in its efficiency in the systematic transmission of ideas and information, along with at least some guarantee that the knowledge communicated to students will be reputable and up-to-date. Its weaknesses lie in its relative abstraction from the actual application of knowledge to practice, along with its general avoidance of the embedded knowledge of practice itself.

A great challenge for all professional schools is how to provide grounding in this crucial aspect of apprenticeship, initiation into the wisdom of practice. The key, though largely unexplored, question is what the academic setting might provide that would not only avoid losing the benefits of apprenticeship but actually enhance the teaching of practice. As we have noted, the most elite levels of the academy do provide extensive direct mentorship for the small number of academic stars likely to go on to teach law, though the purpose of such mentoring is rarely described (or acknowledged) so explicitly. The problem is that little of this kind of close mentoring is typically available for the great majority of future lawyers.

Enter the learning sciences. The second half of the twentieth century has been called the time of the cognitive revolution—a broad, multidisciplinary movement of researchers in psychology, linguistics, philosophy, evolutionary and neural biology, and artificial intelligence that has produced important new knowledge about how human beings think and learn.[3] These developments provide new insights on the potential, as well as the limitations, of that venerable learning institution—the school. Schools seem to have been contemporaneous with the development of literacy and numeracy, as these skills emerged as the intellectual technologies that make organizing complex societies possible. In *Actual Minds, Possible Worlds,* psychologist Jerome Bruner, one of the leaders of cognitive science, argues that schools, like modern societies as a whole, depend on the yoking of two broadly different modes of thinking that do not fit easily together.

One mode of thinking is based on narrative; that is, things and events acquire significance by being placed within a story, an ongoing context of meaningful interaction. This mode of thinking integrates experience through metaphor and analogy. It is employed in the arts and in all practical situations, including professional work. Critically, this mode of thought is the source of meaning and value, even in contemporary society. Bruner sees narrative understanding as rooted in embodied skills. Mostly tacit, these forms of bodily perception are most noticeable when absent or widely different, as in encounters between persons formed by different cultures. Then the divergence of basic understanding at the tacit level can render more formal communication ineffective, even counterproductive, as efforts to transport institutions and ways of doing things between different parts of the globe attest.

Bruner calls the other mode of thinking, by contrast, "analytic" or "paradigmatic." Analytical thinking detaches things and events from the situations of everyday life and represents them in more abstract and systematic ways. Writing and numeration are the media through which the intellectual skills of classification, argument, and proof can be represented and learned. These intellectual skills have been essential to the development of science and technology, as well as the systems of law, administration, and communication that sustain modern civilization. Although learning through narrative seems universal in human cultures, it is particularly the analytical capacities that schools, at every level, exist to foster.

Modes of Thinking and the Role of Schools in Forming Professional Expertise

From this vantage point, schools can be seen as ambiguous sites for forming future professionals. Insofar as professionals require facility in deploying abstract, analytical representations—symbolic analysis—school-like settings are very good environments for learning. One of the key findings of cognitive research is how important conceptual models, or schemas,

are in human thinking. Establishing cause-and-effect, ranking and ordering, and finding logical relationships of inclusion and exclusion are all basic
cognitive devices that receive much attention and development at all levels of schooling. At the same time, professionals must be able to integrate
this kind of knowledge within ongoing practical contexts, which are organized by narrative modes of thinking and often convey meaning through
exemplary acts and cases.

Actual legal practice is heavily dependent on expertise in narrative
modes of reasoning. Indeed, in all legal reasoning, as Bruner points out,
the analytical and paradigmatic models depend on narrative and metaphor
for their sense (Bruner 2002; Amsterdam and Bruner, 2000). Hence both
judicial decisions and law teaching must invoke cases in order to give
intelligibility to abstract legal principles. It follows that the formation of
the habits of mind needed for legal practice also demand fluency in both
the engaged mode of narrative thinking characteristic of everyday practice and the detached mode of analytical thinking emphasized in case-dialogue teaching.

This twofold aspect of professional expertise is captured by Eliot Freidson when he describes medical education's aim as forming a "clinical"
habit of mind so that physicians could "work as consultants who must
intervene [with specialized, esoteric knowledge] in everyday, practical
affairs" (Freidson, 1996, p. 69). In order to treat the patient, the clinician
must be able to move back and forth between detached analysis of the
medical condition and empathic engagement with the distressed patient.
Medical education clearly demonstrates that this clinical habit of mind can,
like analytical thinking, be developed within a formal educational program.

Apprenticeship as the Heart of Education

Successful apprenticeship instills these habits of the practical mind as the
learner sees expert judgment in action and is then coached through similar
activities. To be effective preparation for the variety of legal careers, legal
education must provide a foundation in both kinds of learning. How to
blend the analytical and practical habits of mind that professional practice
demands is, we believe, the most complex and interesting pedagogical challenge in the preparation of legal practitioners. As we saw in Chapter One,
studies of expert cognition have reinforced the importance for learning of
access to the key features of a practice, which means coming to participate
in the ways of a community of practice. The insight that apprenticeship, so
understood, lies at the heart of all education has been the great contribution of modern cognitive psychology to understanding learning.

An Unexpected Possibility from Legal Practice

Traditional apprenticeship emphasizes the informal transmission of expert knowledge through face-to-face contact. As we have noted, law schools provide this kind of experience for the very few law students who find themselves on the track for the bench and legal scholarship. The experience of most law students, however, includes little of this highly particularistic kind of training or assessment of competence that will be central for their practice, as students typically have little close contact with faculty. However, one of the strengths of the insights from cognitive theories of learning is that they also open up an unexpected possibility. The very tools of thinking that display and develop analytical reasoning can also play an important role in enhancing and extending the model of apprenticeship.

Important features of good performance can be described using various conceptual models and representations. These conceptual models can then be employed to guide the learner in mastering complex knowledge by small steps. This new understanding of teaching and learning has only begun to be exploited for its potential to generate more effective ways to prepare future lawyers, especially in the second and third years of law school. As trial lawyers and school debaters have long known, arguments can be written down, then rehearsed, analyzed, criticized, and, in the process, improved. These devices of representation serve as scaffolds, in the language of learning theorists, to support efforts at improved performance. Feedback from more accomplished performers directs the learner's attention toward improved attempts to reach a goal.

The iterative process that cognitive researchers have discovered at work in the improvement of thinking and writing turns out to be at the center of core legal practices as well. It is, for example, the way in which judges generate legal opinions: judges, working with their clerks (former law students), draft appellate opinions through a series of meetings in which they compare, correct, and modify drafts, redrafting in response to each other's criticism until they reach a final product that reflects, as fully as possible, the judge's considered decision. These are the opinions that eventually find their way into the legal case books, through which students are taught to think like lawyers. This is a case where "theory" and "practice," in the sense of how the judges think and what they do in order to think, are inseparable in the execution.

Iteration is also the way that practicing attorneys produce many legal documents. For example, a partner at a metropolitan law firm and former law professor, Bryn Valler, has described spending his evenings at a conference on the teaching of legal writing "crashing out" an advice letter to a corporate client. His task was to synthesize in "a brief, punchy letter (intended for nonlawyers)" a complex, 150-page recent judicial decision. He developed his letter in e-mail communication with three of his partners, who reviewed his drafts and suggested changes. Valler described this work as a "process of organizing and re-organizing facts and ideas in a conceptual framework and with a concrete purpose." In such instances, well-established expert practices converge with findings from the learning sciences to highlight a model for training legal reasoning within contexts of practice (Valler, 2002).

Using Iteration

As these examples suggest, the iterative mode of improving skills can be applied to the teaching and learning of a wide variety of capacities, blending the intellectual and the practical. Features of expert performance, either of the analytical or narrative-practical sort, can thereby be made explicit for learners in the form of rules, procedures, protocols, and organizing metaphors for approaching situations or problems. Cued by these devices, students can then be coached through imitation and appropriation of various aspects of expert performance. As we shall see, a similar sequence is typical of pedagogy in clinical-legal courses. These findings call into question the long-assumed qualitative difference between the formal teaching of doctrine and the learning of the skills of practice. It is therefore important to re-examine the way in which law schools of the standard model have segregated the apprenticeship of conceptual learning from the apprenticeship of practice. Indeed, there exist empirical embodiments of such correlation: legal research and writing courses have long practiced ways of integrating the conceptual and the practical, and law schools such as those at NYU and CUNY have built successful curricular structures on similar practices.

Other professional fields provide some well-tested instances of pedagogies that teach complex practical reasoning and judgment, blending the cognitive and practical apprenticeships. For example, medical schools use various simulation devices, even professional actors, as "simulated patients," in order to train clinical skills. In such situations, performance can be rehearsed, criticized, and improved "off-line." This removal from the exigencies of actual practice permits the instructors to focus on particular aspects of the complex ensemble of skills they are trying to teach. The elements and sequence of skills can then be modeled and rehearsed in safety—without real-world consequences or immediate responsibility for the welfare of others. This kind of teaching makes it more likely that students will reach a basic level of competent practice from which expertise can be subsequently developed.[4] As we shall see, teachers of legal practice in several areas such as negotiation, writing, and clinical-legal education have begun to put these ideas to effective use. Such pedagogy is the heart of the Best Practices report's "context-based education" (Stuckey and others, 2006, pp. 109–122).

Understanding the Profession's Defining Practices

Whenever educators study expert performance in order to make its key features visible and available to novices for appropriation, they are opening access to the profession's defining practices. By giving learners opportunities to practice approximations to expert performance and giving these students feedback to help them improve their performance, educators are providing an apprentice-like experience of the mind. Understanding develops through the actual performance of modes of thinking. This process can be greatly enhanced by the skillful use of mental representations to provide the scaffolds through which feedback can become meaningful to the learner in the effort to achieve mastery of new concepts or abilities. All this has become widely disseminated through work such as Bransford, Brown, and Cocking's *How People Learn: Mind, Experience, and School* (1999).

A Theory for Practice: Cognitive Insights for the Practice of Law

The perspective of cognitive theory offers a different way to think about law schools: they are complex settings for apprenticeship—organizations for initiating the next generation of practitioners into the several dimensions of the expertise that defines the competent practitioner. Indeed, during the past decade, legal educators have begun to assimilate these insights from learning theory in order to make sense of the disparate forms in use to teach lawyering. However, further development of well-grounded principles of pedagogy and models of good teaching and learning are vital to the future of legal education. We might think of it as developing a theory for practice.

Developing theory for teaching practice has been a marked feature of much clinical-legal education. In the schools we visited, especially the highly ranked institutions with very well-prepared students, it was not uncommon to hear faculty voice deep skepticism about the intellectual value of practice-oriented courses. "Students will get better training when in a firm than from our skills courses," lamented one professor at an elite public institution, adding that, "our clinical program is not a good use of resources. . . . It is a side show in which the central faculty and students are not interested."

Not surprisingly, clinical faculty have felt themselves, at times, under a kind of special obligation to justify their pedagogical practices. We rarely found faculty teaching case-dialogue courses felt under similar pressure to demonstrate the educational effectiveness of their approach to teaching. (We will return to these themes in Chapter Five, when we consider how law schools assess what their students are learning through their legal education.)

As an example of efforts to develop useful pedagogical theory for clinical teaching, Gary Blasi has drawn on a number of strands from cognitive science and learning theory. In trying to explain "what lawyers know," Blasi makes use of the wide body of literature on the nature of expertise and how it is acquired. This is the same set of ideas and studies from which the notion of learning as cognitive apprenticeship derives. What is most relevant for courses in legal practice, notes Blasi, is recognizing that it is possible to go beyond using mere rules of thumb and informal, labor-intensive personal mentoring in teaching key aspects of legal practice (Blasi, 1995). Just as the case-dialogue method at its best can represent in a public way the processes of reasoning embedded in complex legal opinions, it is likewise possible to articulate the conceptual models involved in the important skills that define effective lawyering: in developing evidence, interviewing, counseling, drafting documents, conducting research, and negotiating.

In each of these areas, the expert first abstracts from a complex, often messy environment a set of factors that are most important. (This is just the skill the beginner does not have.) These are the aspects of the situation that the expert attends to and manipulates in order to render certain outcomes. Models and schemas that represent the objects of the expert's perception, together with the procedures by which the expert works on these objects, are the elements of what might be called "theories of practice." Once articulated, Blasi suggests, these general schemas can be probed and tested for their reliability, much like more formal scientific hypotheses (Blasi, 1995). In the realm of teaching expert practice, theories are really statements of technique in the classic sense of well-tested procedures for achieving specific outcomes in certain kinds of situations. Thus novices can begin to learn the rudiments of litigation practice, for example, by attending to the core elements of the procedural and conceptual models exemplified in expert practice. Teachers make this possible by allowing novices to work with and imitate multiple examples, using the conceptual models as scaffolds through which to understand feedback, in order to guide their assimilation of more skillful performance.

Teaching the Case

In earlier chapters we examine several promising lines of development of such theory for practice. Some of those who have developed and tested these innovations have made their ideas public. One of these is a team of faculty at UCLA's law school, who organized their framework for teaching legal counseling in a textbook, *Lawyers as Counselors: A Client-Centered Approach* (Binder, Bergman, Price, and Tremblay, 2004). The premise of their client-centered approach challenges the common assumption that because of professional expertise in understanding the law, the lawyer knows best. Instead, Binder and colleagues work from the premise that effective counseling depends on the lawyer's ability to recognize, solicit, and use not only his or her own legal knowledge but also the client's understanding of the extra-legal dimensions of the problem. This approach explicitly proposes that the client is likely to have important "local knowledge" that must be brought to bear in order to arrive at strategies for legal action that will genuinely resolve the client's problem. The textbook offers a set of practical guides and techniques to realize the implications of the starting assumptions by having the student develop a clear "theory of the case."

The task of developing such a theory of the case requires the student to take an active role, questioning yet supporting the client. In learning this often-unfamiliar role of counselor, the student is also learning a normative model of professionalism, a model that puts the lawyer in the role of cooperative problem solver with the client rather than the distanced expert who solves the client's problem. As a pedagogical approach, the Binder textbook incorporates many of those elements of actual legal situations that we found removed in the teaching of legal analysis by the case-dialogue method. In the case-dialogue method, as Mertz shows, the aim is to move students into operating within a legal landscape in which concrete clients disappear behind the conceptual masks of abstract legal actors (Mertz, forthcoming, chapter five). In the process that Binder and his colleagues developed, the student is given a set of scaffolds to support his or her engagement with the client's understanding of the situation.

THREE STEPS TO THE THEORY OF THE CASE. In order to develop the theory of the case, this pedagogy guides the student through three analytical steps. First, the apprentice lawyer must determine what the client's problem is a case *of*. This is legal categorization, as Amsterdam and Bruner describe it in *Minding the Law* (Amsterdam and Bruner, 2000). Is this fraud? Is this negligence? Categorizing will determine what body of legal doctrine applies.

Second, the student must parse this body of legal principles into the criteria that must be met for the client's problem to qualify as a legitimate case of that kind. However, the key step is the third one: the student must construct a narrative—a story that links the particulars of the client's case in a way that shows unequivocally that the client's problem should be remedied because it is a legitimate case of the legal doctrine identified in step one.

THE T-FUNNEL TECHNIQUE. An example of how Binder and his colleagues provide scaffolding to beginners is what they call the "T-funnel technique." The "funnel," they explain, "is a pattern of information-seeking that relies both on clients' paths of association and your legal judgment to produce persuasive and factually-rich stories . . . thorough information-gathering rests on a combination of open and closed questions" (Binder, Bergman, Price, and Tremblay, 2004, p. 167). Open questions solicit clients' own paths of association, while closed questions are designed to solicit evidence relevant to meeting the criteria of a specific legal doctrine. The scaffolds aid students in navigating the complexities and uncertainties of developing case theory.

The point to be made here is that the lawyer's own everyday experience of how people typically think and act is important for crafting a convincing legal argument. A good counselor, the student learns, is one who can enter the world of the client with a legal eye and join the client there in order to translate the client's problems into legal concepts, all the while anticipating opposing counsel's likely arguments. So in this pedagogy, legal analysis does not disappear. Rather, it serves as the sometimes tacit, sometimes explicit background of the lawyer's engagement with the client's problem. The sort of thinking learned in case-dialogue classes is relevant here—not least in the reflexive question about what arguments one's opponent might make—but the student has to use it in a new way, within a less definite, more complex context than is typically presented in case books.

Enriching Legal Knowledge and Professional Effectiveness

Theory for practice, then, is a kind of toolkit of well-founded procedures within clearly delineated areas of professional work. Developing this kind of theory is of more than practical value, however. It also expands knowledge of law as a profession and legal work as a form of expert knowledge.

Once represented in conceptual form, the rules of thumb and informal understanding embedded in expert practice can be publicly represented, criticized, advanced, and disseminated.

A similar model is scientific and technological progress through peer review and critique. As we shall see, there are important limitations to this model when applied to areas of judgment that carry human meaning, such as the law. There is simply much more being taught and learned in any pedagogical context than can be consciously abstracted in the form of rules or schemas. But the fact that some, and indeed key, aspects of practice can be rendered into teachable techniques removes, in principle, a chief objection to including an apprenticeship of practice in the legal curriculum: it refutes the charge of anti-intellectualism. At the same time, developing theory for practice demonstrates the value of social science for the enrichment of legal knowledge and professional effectiveness. The promise of an expanded theoretical repertoire, seen in this cognitive perspective, is an enrichment of legal science itself, with the intended result of both higher prestige and more effective teaching of key aspects of legal competence.

Connecting the Apprenticeships Through Legal Writing

In their visits, our research teams were impressed by how often students raised the topic of legal writing. One student's comment summed up many others. She noted, "It is the feedback you receive from the teachers, as opposed to just so much reading" in her doctrinal courses that made the writing course so important for her in learning the law. Writing assignments seemed more effective than expectations of being called on in class for "forcing you to read the case more than once" in order to be able to analyze it in writing, "to explain it to someone else." In a number of the legal writing programs we observed, students reported that they learned by "watching, following examples, being talked through what was being modeled in class." On the basis of this experience, students suggested that writing should be "more integrated into courses on doctrine" in order to speed up students' learning of legal reasoning.

The legal writing courses the students were describing provide a pedagogical experience that in many ways complements what is missing in the case-dialogue classes that make up most of the students' first year. Classes are typically small, with around twenty students, who meet both in class and frequently (sometimes weekly, but at least bimonthly) for feedback and coaching sessions with their instructor. Writing assignments are structured and paced to emphasize drafting and redrafting in response to the instructor's criticism and suggestions. Students often read each other's work and are encouraged to learn from each other.

Equally noteworthy, the syllabi for the best legal writing classes we encountered focused on learning tasks that are typical of legal work. The instructor led students through a sequence of writing projects that began with interviews, progressed to situations that simulated letters of counsel, then negotiation, and, finally, the construction of full-scale legal briefs—all critical skills of legal practice that receive little or no attention in the doctrinal courses of the first year. The emphasis was on learning legal doctrine by putting it to use in drafting legal documents. By learning to analyze facts and construct arguments in use, students were also being taught how to strategize as a lawyer would. They were beginning to cross the bridge from legal theory to professional practice.

For example, we observed writing being used at Hamline University Law School in St. Paul, Minnesota, to strengthen a program in Alternative Dispute Resolution (typically called ADR). The school sees its ADR program, which is concerned with techniques for settling disputes without litigation within the larger field of lawyering, as a distinctive area of strength and comparative advantage. ADR is also one of the manifestations of the problem-solving functions of legal work. Hamline's summer institutes on ADR were cross-registered with the university's management and public administration program, and the resulting certificate of completion was intentionally cross-professional. The first-year legal writing course introduced the writing of an ADR memo as one of the genres of legal composition that students were required to master. The aim, said faculty, was "to lead students to see Alternative Dispute Resolution as a part of the field of law . . . to help them get a philosophical road map" to "a problem-solving environment." Compared to typical legal research and writing, argued these faculty, the ADR memo "broadens the view of the case to *interests* rather than the simple 'legal relevance' of the facts," thereby "opening up other possibilities in the lawyer's practice besides standard litigation."

As we have noted, the question of the place of practice-centered subjects and courses, including clinical legal education as well as writing, has been a subject of intense debate in law schools for more than four decades. Among these "practice subjects," negotiation has perhaps come farthest in attaining academic respectability. Writing with Joanne Martin, Bryant Garth (then of the American Bar Foundation and currently dean of Southwestern Law School), has argued that this is because negotiation can claim a body of theory to bolster its claims to practical importance

(Garth and Martin, 1993). Although less fully developed, ADR teaching has been able to incorporate aspects of negotiation theory among its approaches. The interconnection that Hamline's summer ADR institute has made between such theory-based teaching of practice and the teaching of legal writing provides an illuminating example of how the teaching of writing can promote the learning of concepts, as well as practical skills.[5] We have already noted that the study reported in *After the JD* found that beginning lawyers saw their legal writing experiences as quite valuable in helping their transition into practice (Dinovitzer and others, 2004). The areas of ADR and negotiation also illustrate some of the potential in the area of lawyering for connecting the learning of legal reasoning and legal practice. We will look more closely at each of these examples in turn.

Legal Writing as Simulated Practice

Were Scott Turow, author of *One L,* the dramatic account of the first year of law school set at Harvard in the middle 1970s, to revisit law school today, he would find things both the same and, in some important ways, different. Nowhere would this be more apparent than in mandatory legal writing classes, especially their relation to doctrinal courses. Turow describes in heated detail his travails in the legal methods course that accompanied his first exposure to case-dialogue teaching as a "1L." This was an ungraded course regarded as an introductory supplement—a mere how-to class taught by teaching fellows rather than faculty. The practices he learned laboriously in Legal Methods received no attention in Turow's doctrinal courses. Turow found that most of his fellow students found the class to be an "unfair sacrifice of time that could have been put into the larger [graded] courses" (Turow, 1977, p. 128). He noted, however, that while the briefing and arguing that Legal Methods required provided a channel for the students' competitive bent, it also raised their already high levels of terror of potential failure.

In those days, a course in legal methods required students to pursue a fictionalized case through all its various stages, from interviewing clients through negotiation sessions, to preparing and arguing a legal brief and observing a mock trial performed by an actual judge and practicing lawyers. Although already an accomplished writer when he entered law school, Turow describes his frustrations when attempting to brief a case, finding legally significant facts within the mass of detail, organizing facts in relation to legal issues, and putting these into precise forms of reasoning in an attempt to frame a court's decision making. It was all trial and error, with little guidance provided by the teaching fellow and no feedback until a draft was returned—typically splattered with red ink.

Things were no better in the second semester, when Turow was preparing a brief to be argued, much as a practicing attorney might. He found that the problems of achieving fluency in the particulars of legal notation and verbal formulation were compounded by the difficulties of managing the interpersonal work of collaborating with the partners assigned to him for the case. Turow records his satisfaction at finally getting some control over the complexity of legal issues during the course of his research, writing, and arguing with his student partners.

Despite his struggles at the time, in looking back, Turow found these experiences to be among the more important of his first year. He was struck by the fact that he learned to reason legally within both the methods course and in the formal doctrinal classes. Yet the pedagogies of Legal Methods were largely divorced from the theoretical-analytical training in his doctrinal classes. Turow thought this reflected the valuing of certainty in legal education over the uncertainty and situational ambiguity of law revealed in the practice experience. Law school provided no formal place in which to come to grips with his momentous discovery that legal theory and the practice of law require very different habits of mind and modes of engagement.

HOW SIMULATED PRACTICE WORKS. Today's equivalent of first-year legal methods courses are in many schools informed by learning theory applied to composition research that did not exist in Turow's day. This new perspective sees the teaching of writing as a form of simulated practice. Students use simulated files of materials in order to develop full-blown legal memoranda that require students to relate a specific set of facts and procedures to a dispute at the trial level. This is far beyond the kinds of assignments Turow was given. There is more feedback and a good deal of scaffolding in the form of models and schemas. However, the clash between the quest for theoretical certitude and the need to engage with the indeterminacies of practice retains its considerable relevance to legal education. As we have seen in earlier chapters, the case-dialogue pedagogy of the cognitive apprenticeship in law school provides some learning by performing, but chiefly for the relatively few students called on in a given class. In the case-dialogue method, students are expected to learn, most of the time, by observing and noting the interactions between the instructor and other students. This is powerful pedagogy, but it has important limitations, and the transition to learning by engaging in professional practice can be difficult.

We encountered similar issues in medical education. For medical students, the first year of full-time clinical training, usually following two years of basic science taught in lecture classes, is a recognized point of difficult transition. To profit from clinical education, students must shift from learning by observation and discussion to learning by performance. Various experiments are under way in medical schools to make this transition easier and faster, such as starting the transition to practice at the very beginning of medical school, through simulations. These experiments are based on the recognition that learning professional knowledge and skill "in role" is a distinct pedagogical genre and needs the same care and attention as the didactic teaching that dominates the first two years of medical school.

USING COMPOSITION THEORY. In legal writing courses that are informed by composition theory, the pedagogy is, like that of clinical medicine, performative and learned in role. That is, students learn primarily by being led, coached, and given abundant feedback directed to improving their ability to practice legal reasoning in specific contexts. Many students with whom we spoke noted the ways in which their writing courses accelerated their progress in legal reasoning in their doctrinal courses, especially seminars beyond the first year; some wanted more such linkage. In these examples, legal writing is already coming to play an important role in helping students to cement basic patterns of legal thinking; it also serves as a bridge between the learning of legal thinking and the mastery of the skills demanded in order to practice law.

Studies in the theory of composition developed in two main stages. In the first burst of enthusiasm, cognitive researchers in the 1970s studied how individual writers bring together their stored knowledge with the rhetorical tasks at hand: organizing and shaping the knowledge to suit various purposes and conventions of discourse.[6] Further experimental work on differences among writers led to the distinction between "knowledge telling" and "knowledge transforming" writing processes. The former relies on existing knowledge structures and involves little or no solving of problems. The "knowledge transforming" writing, however, is necessary for the complex tasks of improving one's own performance in a given context. This kind of writing represents a highly sophisticated set of metacognitive practices through which students can learn to transfer the insights gained in one experience to other writing tasks (Bereiter and Scardamalia, 1987; see also Galbraith and Torrance, 1999; Flower, 1994). It is the kind of problem solving that legal professionals must master in order to function well in a variety of legal roles.

The Pedagogy of Legal Writing

Much of legal writing instruction today is concerned with developing better methods for promoting students' abilities to engage in knowledge-transforming performance. It is the kind of skill Turow struggled to acquire through the hard knocks of Harvard's moot court. The promise of the new pedagogical work is to make the insights available to more students more efficiently, with fewer hard knocks and assaults on self-confidence than in the old days. In a contemporary writing course influenced by composition research, students are not told to simply figure things out for themselves. In place of that kind of cold induction, a course is likely to begin with the instructor posing a task to students by giving some general prompts.

So imagine Turow's case-briefing assignment in today's context. (However, thanks to advances in learning theory, the assignment probably wouldn't be in the same position in the curriculum.) Rather than just being told to brief the case, students are asked first to provide concise narratives of the case, emphasizing what seem to be important "facts." To guide the process, the instructor introduces short prompts along these lines: How does A present the events; what issues emerge here? How does B present the events, issues? These prompts provide a scaffold for the students as they work up their narratives—a set of strategies that suggest lines of inquiry.

In class, students take turns presenting their versions to the group for comments. The instructor guides the analysis, providing feedback and modeling the use of the prompts in constructing a well-honed document. The class ends with the instructor and students discussing how to use the feedback to improve the drafts for the next session. These procedures help students learn to make their thinking visible in writing so that it can be worked over and improved under the instructor's guidance. An important part of the instructor's function is to call students' attention to the strategies they are employing as they strive to improve their performance.

This kind of instructor-led group process resembles the simulation pedagogies in use in other sorts of lawyering or practice classes, as well as the practice of clinical courses. Common features distinguish this pedagogy of learning in context. Among them is its surface structure, which consists of four typical steps: (1) the instructor defines the task; (2) the instructor provides the scaffold of prompts and rules for engaging the activity within a collaborative group context; (3) the students practice the activity and present their work to the group for feedback; and (4) the instructor coaches and models the activity in order to improve performance but also to call attention to strategies for improvement. This last step, which psychologists sometimes call metacognitive, turns the student's activity back on itself in order to produce awareness in the student of what is being learned—a "second order" or reflective awareness; then the process is reiterated, with gradually more difficult and complex tasks, toward the aim of improved competence in writing a brief, conducting an interview, carrying out a negotiating strategy, or developing an oral argument, depending on the aspect of practice being learned.

What about the deep structure of the pedagogy? How does it work? What ends does it realize? The pedagogies of legal writing instruction bring together content knowledge and practical skill in very close interaction. Writing makes language observable. Writing instruction—more accurately, the use of writing as a means of instruction—allows the communication process to be stopped for a while to enable students to observe and analyze the discourse being developed. As we saw in Chapter Two, this is similar to the deep structure of case-dialogue teaching. But in writing instruction, the focus is typically on the generation of a product for a specific rhetorical situation—a simulated or actual piece of legal work. Because of this, students are challenged to engage with the uncertainties of specific practical contexts and to search for solutions together, using the instructor (and one another) as coach and resource. The coaching is precisely intended to support this process of discovery and refinement within a complex context. In its fully developed form, the pedagogy makes this developmental process itself visible to the learners, so that they can become aware of the components of their growing abilities to write—and think—as legal professionals.

What of the tacit structure—the attitudes, values, and dispositions—modeled by the instructor regarding professional practice itself? As we have seen, the iterative, collaborative nature of the writing process simulates real legal production quite closely. When employed as a complement to learning legal reasoning in case-dialogue teaching, which is the most familiar role of legal writing courses, the tacit structure of the pedagogy reinforces important aspects of the doctrinal courses. It also goes beyond them into the complexities of uncertain rhetorical contexts. In more advanced courses, today's understanding of composition allows writing to become less a simple demonstration of content mastery and more a supple, pervasive device for developing reflective capacities to do legal research, critique and construct arguments, and draft legal instruments.

Through these activities, the new composition research suggests, students can grow into a more expansive and self-aware professional competence. They learn the importance of genre but locate it within a set of well-defined professional writing tasks. They are encouraged to become aware of their own performance and how to improve it. Recent literature on the teaching of rhetoric describes how the explicit teaching of strategies for inquiry can prompt students' development as scholars without determining the outcome of their inquiry. By providing strategies for inquiry, instructors can guide students' attention toward identifying and exploring a subject matter. By constructing a classroom context of collaborative work that presents legal expertise in its broad social significance, faculty can encourage students' engagement with a culture of public argument within which law finds one of its chief inspirations and to which legal scholarship can contribute (Lauer and others, 2000).

The teaching of legal writing can be used to open a window for students onto the full complexity of legal expertise. Composition is an area in which research in the learning sciences has had direct and significant impact on classroom practice, from elementary school through the undergraduate years. Like other forms of "theory for practice," contemporary composition theory has been developed from the careful study of expert practice for the purpose of improving the teaching of that expertise to learners. Composition studies' insights and practices have now entered even highly technical fields, such as engineering, which have previously given little attention to verbal and written reasoning and communication. Contemporary composition theory holds significant promise for legal education as well.

Another Case in Point: Teaching Negotiation

Among the long-standing goals of the clinical movement has been to develop a more cooperative, problem-solving model of lawyering that can enable students to anticipate a wider variety of future professional roles than litigation. These goals are strongly reaffirmed in the 2006 *Best Practices for Legal Education* as well. In this perspective, the emergence of negotiation as an area of the legal curriculum stands out. In the late 1970s, the American Bar Association issued a report on lawyer competency (American Bar Association, 1979). In its wake, the American Bar Association added to the requirements for law school accreditation that all students ought to receive rigorous training in legal writing, plus instruction in such professional skills as counseling, negotiation, advocacy, and drafting. Although many of the lower-ranked schools welcomed the idea, the president of the Association of American Law Schools, Albert M. Sacks, dean of Harvard Law School, noted, "One is tempted to treat the new proposal as a flyspeck to be ignored. . . . I hope it will be strongly resisted" (Stevens, 1983, pp. 257). It was.

Galvanized by admonitions from public sources, including chief justice Alan Berger, about the inadequacy of the adversary system to best settle all disputes, legal educators in the early 1980s launched a movement to develop the areas of mediation, negotiation, and alternative dispute resolution. Negotiation without a third party, already a common practice in some legal areas, can be thought of as standing at one end of a continuum of means for resolving disputes, with other forms of resolution that depend on a third party, such as mediation and arbitration, further along the line, at the end of which stands the full adversarial machinery of litigation before a court. Negotiation is a good example of a nonjuridical skill that is nonetheless important to the practice of law. How to teach it became an important question, as there was no strong case to be made that skill in negotiation resulted during the study of appellate decisions.

A 1984 issue of the *Journal of Legal Education* featured a collection of essays about these "alternative methods" of resolving legal disputes. Negotiation and ADR were treated as parts of one larger entity. It is interesting that the pedagogical practices associated with both negotiation and ADR were also treated alike in articles with titles such as Williams's "Using Simulation Exercises for Negotiation and Other Dispute Resolution Courses." By this time, Sacks was in on the discussion in a less confrontational stance, noting in a historical essay that the broad area of "alternative dispute resolution" was benefiting from renewed interest in the lawyer's role and the proper function of the law, on the one hand, and the new academic respectability of interdisciplinary approaches to law and legal practice coming from outside the law schools, on the other (Sacks, 1984).

Drawing on studies by the American Bar Foundation, Garth and Martin (1993) noted that by the 1990s, an increasing percentage of law school graduates indicated that law schools affirmed the potential value of negotiation. In contrast to the 1970s, a majority now believed that the subject, which had been a rallying cry for clinicians, could be taught effectively within the law school. By the late 1970s, innovative legal academics such as Gary Bellow and Bea Moulton of Harvard, influenced by practice experience in work with poor clients, began to develop textbooks on negotiation that drew on game theory and other intellectual devices for analyzing actual negotiation practice. By the 1990s, legal academics were emphasizing the importance of teaching the theory of negotiation. The theoretical literature on negotiation has grown and, in Garth and Martin's description, become a part of "legal science":

The MacCrate report, for example, emphasizes the importance of "skills, concepts, and processes" of negotiation—not simply practical training—and the use of full-time faculty in this area. Teachers now say that the subject is part of legal science; practitioners who teach what works in practice for them are no longer adequate. (Garth and Martin, 1993, p. 505)

With negotiation's entry into "legal science," the authors argue, law schools are pressured to hire negotiation faculty because firms can no longer compete for market position simply by hiring graduates who learned through clinical mentoring. Rather, access to state-of-the-art negotiation training is highly attractive in the marketplace for services.

Through these developments, Garth and Martin argue, law schools are responding to some of the canonical criticisms regarding their lack of attention to practical instruction. However, schools have responded best when new legal theory was developed by entrepreneurial professors. This new body of theory serves to legitimate the construction of new forms of recognized competence. Put another way, the mere recognition of a gap between law schools and legal practice is not sufficient to account for the success of negotiation. Rather, negotiation has raised its status through generating new legal theory. This development has been broadly linked to law firms' promotion of innovative legal services, which also expands the range of roles for lawyers. Perhaps most spectacularly, legal negotiation theory has been diffused into the wider culture of business and civil life through the widely read popular adaptation, *Getting to Yes* (Fisher, Ury, and Patton, 1992).

As to alternative dispute resolution, Garth and Martin also note:

ADR theory—or what is emerging, at least—is also becoming celebrated, including in the MacCrate report. Not as successful yet as negotiation, but a similar set of common purposes is developing between ADR scholars and firms: i.e., the new legal science of ADR has been taken up as a high-tech service of major law firms. (Garth and Martin, 1993, p. 506)

ADR, the authors argue, is therefore becoming better positioned to gain increased prominence. But it is noteworthy that Garth and Martin were, in 1993, portraying ADR as a separate issue from the success of negotiation, whereas the two were intermingled in the thinking of everyone writing in the *Journal of Legal Education* in 1984.

There is more than convenience at work here. As we have seen, the 1970s produced among legal scholars and law school faculty new interest in expanding the understanding of legal processes to include forms of civil regulation beyond formal adjudication. This carried with it an implied expansion of the lawyer's repertoire of skills, but it also potentially broadened the lawyer's roles and identity beyond the usual adversarial context. Over time, however, negotiation became increasingly identified with specifically professional functions that could be marketed by law firms. Mediation and other alternatives to adjudication, by contrast, were less easily confined to legal professionals and tended to shade off into quasi-legal, "lay" activities, as exemplified by the successful dissemination of some of these ideas in popular literature—a problem of blurred professional boundaries that continues to hobble the full acceptance of ADR as a professional specialty.

In addition, as Garth and Martin (1993) point out, "academia has trouble with skills that are merely learned by doing, especially when, as is often the case, practical teaching appears to be more expensive." Therefore, teachers of skills must find ways to "bring their efforts in practical areas within the recognized domain of legal science" (p. 504). That "science" consists in the three basic areas of knowing the law, finding the law (legal research), and arguing the law. For their part, faculty must find ways to "turn practice into legal theory in order to succeed in their academic careers" (p. 504). In short, the determining model for what becomes central to law schools has been the academy, not the profession. The American Bar Association itself has had to filter its recommendations through the career and reward structures of the legal academy, which have increasingly emphasized theory over practice, scholarship over teaching, cognitive over ethical engagement.

It is an important development that legal educators seem to have increasing appreciation for the usefulness of simulations, through which negotiation seems particularly successful in broadening law students' awareness of the multiple dimensions of legal actions. The trajectory has been what Carrie Menkel-Meadow called two decades ago, "strategies in search of a theory," a work in progress that the *Journal of Legal Education* featured in a 2004 issue(Menkel-Meadow, 1983). A fortunate outgrowth of this interest has been increased willingness to critically examine, in lawyering programs, the changing organization of the profession and its social responsibilities. The development of simulation pedagogies in negotiation and ADR provides an illuminating example of how a focus on pedagogies integral to the apprenticeship of practice can lead faculty and students toward concerns about professional identity, responsibility, and conduct.

Learning from the Wisdom of Practice

Those in law who have the "wisdom of practice" know how and when to draw on theoretical knowledge in order to respond to client needs, institutional context, and the demands of being a good lawyer in the situation. Law students' growth toward the wisdom of practice in the law can benefit significantly from effective pedagogies, that is, carefully constructed experiences in legal thinking and performance—the "active learning in context" promoted by the Best Practices project. Law schools, we believe, need to give the teaching of practice a valued place in the legal curriculum so that formation of the students' professional judgment is not abandoned to chance. The past several decades of progress in pedagogies for teaching lawyering, including well-organized clinical experiences with actual clients, hold the promise of rescuing this vital function of apprenticeship for practice from the vagaries of curricular accident and establishing it as a basic part of legal preparation.

The practice of law is, ultimately, a matter of engaged expertise. Like the experienced physician, the legal professional must move between the detached stance of theoretical reasoning and a highly contextual understanding of client, case, and situation. The habit of moving back and forth between these two different modes of cognition is learned primarily through experience, especially the intimate relationships of apprenticeship, but similarly expert teaching can greatly expedite students' progress.

What, exactly, is the goal of teaching that moves students toward the wisdom of practice? One part of expert practice consists of the fundamental techniques, as well as the patterns of reasoning, that make up the craft of law. The ability to grasp the legal significance of complex patterns of events is essential, but so are skills in interviewing, counseling, arguing, and drafting of a whole range of documents. Beyond these lie the intangible—but publicly evident—qualities of expert judgment: the ability to size up a situation well, discerning the salient features relevant not just to the law but to legal practice, and, most of all, knowing what general knowledge, principles, and commitments to call on in deciding on a course of action.

Research validates the widespread belief that developing professional judgment takes a long time, as well as much experience. It cannot typically be achieved within three years of law school, no matter how well crafted the students' experience. But those years in law school can give students a solid foundation and, as they begin their careers in the law, useful guidance on what they need to continue to develop—if the curriculum and teaching in law school are conceived and carried out with the intentional goal of promoting growth in expertise. Knowing the end is an essential step toward figuring out the best means for getting to it. If the final aim of legal education is to foster the development of legal expertise and sound professional judgment, then educators' awareness of the basic contours of the path from novice to expert, along with appropriate steps along this way, are very important.

Moving from Novice to Expert

As legal educators try to better understand how to help law students develop the wisdom of practice, educational theory can again be helpful, in part by clearing up widespread confusion due to the faulty assumption that thinking is like electronic computing. A persuasive body of thought argues that formal modes of thinking, such as information processing, are not only qualitatively different from skilled human performance but are, in fact, ultimately parasitic on it. This is the argument advanced by Hubert Dreyfus and Stuart Dreyfus—a philosopher and an engineer, respectively—who draw on both phenomenological philosophy and experience with artificial intelligence and systems engineering. Dreyfus and Dreyfus (with Athanasiou, 1986) advance a conception of how expertise is actually developed based on their experience in "knowledge engineering," meaning the invention of the most efficient means for enabling beginners to acquire complex skills ranging from chess playing to airplane piloting to clinical judgment in the health care fields. Their model has direct relevance to the education of practical judgment in law students.

The core of the Dreyfus model is an account of how expertise is actually developed in a variety of human activities. In all cases, they argue, the progression from novice to expert is the opposite of the common belief that learners simply move from concrete examples toward gradually more abstract conceptions. Instead, the Dreyfuses show that mature skill acquisition moves from a distanced manipulation of clearly delineated elements of a situation according to formal rules toward involved behavior based on an accumulation of concrete experience. Over time, the learner gradually develops the ability to see analogies, to recognize new situations as similar to whole remembered patterns, and, finally, as an expert to grasp what is important in a situation without proceeding through a long process of formal reasoning. Sometimes called expert intuition or judgment, such ability is the goal of professional training.

In learning lawyering skills, rules and procedures are essential scaffolds that enable beginners to gain a basic grasp on how to function in a variety of practice situations. Law students at this stage are what the Dreyfuses call novices. The prime learning task of the novice in the law is to achieve a basic acquaintance with the common techniques of the lawyer's craft. The novice should not be asked to exercise judgment or interpret a situation as whole. Instead, the novice must learn to recognize certain well-defined elements of the situation and apply precise and formal rules to these elements, regardless of what else is happening. Following the rules allows for a gradual accumulation of experience. But in order to progress, the student has to attend to features of the context, even to events that occur outside the rules.

With proper coaching and sufficient experience, the novice can progress toward competence. This development is triggered when the amount of accumulated situational information starts to overwhelm the carrying out of the rule-governed procedures. What saves the competent performer from situational overload is discovering a goal. (The novice is often too beset with remembering and following context-free rules to think about purpose at all, or, when imagining a goal, may attempt things that a competent performer knows from experience to be impractical.) The new capacity—what the competent person has that the novice does not—is the ability to judge that when a situation shows a certain pattern of elements, it is time to draw a particular conclusion, that one should act in a certain way to achieve the selected goal.

It is important that novices understand at the outset that they are embarking on a long and difficult path but that the reward is great. The end point is expertise—the ability to achieve goals dependably without either working through complex problem solving or devising explicit plans. Because this level of performance cannot be fully reduced to rules and context-free procedures, it often appears to the novice—or the layperson—as a kind of magical know-how. It is, in fact, the result of long training and practice, during which feedback and coaching are essential. The expert, such as the skilled surgeon, the great painter, the respected judge, or the successful negotiator, has made the tools and techniques his or her own, incorporating them into skilled performance, a smooth engagement with the world.

FROM EXPERT PRACTICE TO FORMAL KNOWLEDGE. Although it looks so to the outsider or novice, experts do not simply act intuitively. Expertise is judgment fully realized. This is not a cognitive either-or. Experts reflect and deliberate, especially when confronting difficult or strikingly novel cases and situations. In such reflection, experts may employ analytical techniques precisely to try out different analogies in a conscious process to suggest new or forgotten possibilities. In law school, novices are exposed to embodiments of juridical thinking in their case-dialogue classes. Developing competence in this kind of reasoning is a foundational skill for the profession. But there are other expert skills of the profession. As a foundation for developing legal judgment, it is also important that students encounter and gain insight into legal expertise in its various manifestations.

The expert's knowledge is well grounded in subtle, analogical reasoning achieved through a long apprenticeship to more expert practitioners. In this process of learning, formal models and rules play an essential role, as the Dreyfus model stresses, but the formal models are themselves based on practice. Put another way, in the teaching and learning of expertise, practice is often ahead of theory. Formal knowledge is not the source of expert practice. The reverse is true: expert practice is the source of formal knowledge about practice. Once enacted, skilled performance can be turned into a set of rules and procedures for pedagogical use, as in the cognitive apprenticeship. But the opposite is not possible: the progression from competence to expertise cannot be described as simply a step-by-step build-up of the lower functions. In the world of practice, holism is real and prior to analysis. Theory can—and must—learn from practice.

LEARNING FROM PRACTICE. An important confirmation and extension of the Dreyfus model of learning expertise is provided by the work of Patricia Benner and colleagues. Benner has shown the relevance of "learning from practice" in order to improve the understanding of expert practice—and to use that understanding to point a direction for improved professional training in the field of clinical nursing (Benner, Tanner, and Chesla, 1996). Benner and colleagues argue that the educator's key aim ought to be to develop a sufficiently broad viewpoint to be able to coach students on negotiating the gaps between formal theory and clinical practice. With such a perspective, it becomes possible to guide students toward progress from novice status toward competence and expertise.

Benner and colleagues' work emphasizes the use of analytical thinking to foster rather than replace the cultivation of analogical and practical reasoning. This may be true in all areas of expert practice, and there may indeed be unsuspected analogies between nursing and the practice of law. They note that there has always been a large part of the domain of nursing practice that has been historically "private and not formalized" (Benner, Tanner, and Chesla, 1996, p. 306). Much of the clinical expertise of nursing is, therefore, embodied in judgments within contexts that are often highly charged emotionally, as well as biologically complex. For example, nurses do essential health care work by coaching patients (and sometimes apprentice physicians) through illness and recovery. For this work, what Benner and colleagues call "skillful ethical deportment" is indispensable but is difficult to teach through the usual techniques, which focus on procedures and skills out of context. Ethical deportment depends on complex traditions of living that can only come alive through apprenticeship experiences with exemplars of judgment and skill. Thus the apprenticeship of practice takes on aspects of the critical apprenticeship of ethical engagement.

Fostering Judgment in Context

All this research points to the crucial role of practice experience in the development of expertise. Practice experiences need not be entirely "authentic," however. The value of simulation, for example, is increasingly recognized in legal education as in other fields of professional education. In a study of the use of simulation pedagogies in the teaching of practice in a variety of professional contexts, Pam Grossman and colleagues concluded that such teaching enables students to improve their performance of key components of practice through "targeted instruction." Grossman and others (2005) show that by identifying specific components of expert practice, such as taking a deposition, interviewing a client, or questioning a witness, skillful teachers can break down complex practices so that students can "see" and enact specific parts of the activity through various approximations of practice. Teaching professional practice, they discovered, typically involves an exaggeration and repetition of key activities that could not take place in real-time interaction with actual clients. As a result of this decomposition of practice for the sake of learning, students can be given detailed feedback on elements of their performance. As they develop some competence with each of the elements of the practice, these parts can then be put back together, with a considerable gain in the quality of the overall performance.

We saw this strategy at work in a number of lawyering courses in a variety of schools. In programs that deliberately integrate the learning of skills with learning doctrine (programs such as we describe in Chapter One, at CUNY and NYU), many of the basic skills, including interviewing clients, counseling clients, and negotiating transactions, are indeed "decomposed" into discrete elements that are then "exaggerated," slowed down, and rehearsed, with students receiving critique from faculty and peers. Writing is a device instructors frequently employ, and, indeed, the kinds of legal writing practices we discussed earlier exemplify "approximations of practice" that allow for careful correction and improvement of learners' skills. One of the interesting shifts from the doctrinal classroom that we observed in a number of lawyering courses was the instructors' involvement of students as peer coaches. In such classes, not only is the teacher less exclusively the focus of attention, but students are at least temporarily placed in less directly competitive relationships with each other, so that learning from and working with peers gets direct, positive reinforcement. Such an approach can also be seen as an approximation to practice.

Decades of pedagogical experimentation in clinical-legal teaching, the example of other professional schools, and contemporary learning theory all point toward the value of clinical education as a site for developing not only intellectual understanding and complex skills of practice but also the dispositions crucial for legal professionalism. In their modeling of and coaching for high levels of professionalism, clinics and some simulations exemplify the integration of ethical engagement along with knowledge and skill. In part because they recognize this rich potential, some schools have modified the standard first-year curriculum to make clinical courses more prominently available as first-year electives. Yale Law School, for example, has restricted the required first-year courses to the first semester. A significant proportion of the first-year class elects introductory clinical courses during the second semester and then continues to take part in clinical courses intermittently throughout their academic careers. The Yale arrangement offers students the possibility of real experience in all three apprenticeships—developing knowledge, skill, and professional identity—throughout their three years, enabling them to move back and forth among emphases on legal analysis, practice, and professionalism in different courses.

The Potential of Clinical-Legal Education

The potential of clinical-legal education for bringing together the multiple aspects of legal knowledge, skill, and purpose has long been noted. Clinical teaching resonates clearly against the well-documented importance of active learning in role. Its most striking feature, however, is perhaps the power of clinical experiences to engage and expand students' expertise and professional identity through supervised responsibility for clients.

Although we had little direct experience observing students in field placements or externships, it seems likely that many of the principles and practices developed in clinical-legal education apply to those contexts as well, though issues of supervision and coordination between the law school faculty and supervisory personnel are more salient than in the typical in-house clinic. These issues are discussed in the Best Practices report (Stuckey and others, 2006).

As we observed clinical instruction, one of its striking features was the pedagogical shift from reliance on the hypothetical questions typical of other phases of legal education (such as "What might you do?") to the more immediately involving and demanding: "What will you do?" or "What did you do?" Responsibility for clients and accountability for one's own actions are at the center of clinical experiences. Assuming responsibility for outcomes that affect clients with whom the student has established a relationship enables the learner to go beyond concepts, to actually become a professional in practice. Taught well, it is through this experience of lived responsibility that the student comes to grasp that legal work is meaningful in the ethical, as well as cognitive, sense. Or rather, the student comes to understand that the cognitive and the practical are two complementary dimensions of meaningful professional activity that gets its point and intensity from its moral meaning. Taking the role of the lawyer in real cases makes visible the ways in which the lawyer's decisions and actions contribute to the larger functioning of the legal order. At the same time, it reveals the value of that activity as part of the larger function of the law in securing justice and right relations for actual persons in society.

Clinics can be a key setting for integrating all the elements of legal education, as students draw on and develop their doctrinal reasoning, lawyering skills, and ethical engagement, extending to contextual issues such as the policy environment. A community lawyering course at the University of New Mexico provides a striking illustration. As in many clinical courses, students in Community Lawyering learn by being of service to individuals or organizations in need. Each student establishes a placement with an organization that serves low-income people. For some students, the clients are the low-income individuals served by that organization; for other students, the clients are the organizations themselves. Early in the course, students draft engagement letters for their placements, spelling out their expectations, describing what they are offering and are prepared to commit to the client. In choosing their placement sites, students are asked to think carefully about whom they want to serve. A therapeutic day-care center, for example, sees itself as serving families. Students who want to serve children need to consider what it means to serve families rather than children.

As they think about whom they will be serving, the professor, Antoinette Sedillo Lopez, asks students to approach their relationships with their clients more holistically than is usual in some kinds of legal practice. She asks students to think about what it means to serve survivors of domestic violence, keeping in mind the full range of their needs, not simply "doing domestic violence cases," or serving seniors by "doing wills."

During class meetings, Sedillo Lopez gives advice and guidance, leading brief discussions of issues raised by the various placements and tying practical issues that students are confronting to legal issues. The discussions frequently raise public-policy questions as well. In the context of one placement, for example, the group discusses problems with some pending legislation about domestic violence, which would make it a felony to allow a child to witness domestic violence. Sedillo Lopez encourages students who have studied the issue to consider weighing in on the pending legislation by contacting their legislators.

Thus clinical courses can go well beyond simply filling gaps in students' legal preparation. If one were to search for a single term to describe the ability they hone best, it is probably *legal judgment*. In a wide sense, of course, this is the end of all legal education. The particular power of clinical courses to advance this goal becomes clear when faculty reflect on the complexity of the educational task such courses address. Clinical courses are always taught seminar-style, with a very low faculty-student ratio. They are either preceded by a lawyering course that teaches, typically by simulation and coaching, a number of skills needed for actual practice, such as client interviewing and discovery, or they provide instruction in these capacities in their early phases. These skills provide the basis for one of the most challenging features of clinical instruction, often referred to as teaching the theory of the case, or case theory.

The Use of Case Theory

As we saw in the counseling-theory textbook developed by Binder and colleagues, *case theory* refers to the lawyer's task of understanding the client's legal needs and constructing a strategy to address those needs. Actual strategies always involve counseling the client and may demand negotiation, mediation, litigation, or some combination of all three. Case theory involves complex strategic issues; finding the proper doctrine and case law precedents for the client's problem requires analytical expertise. Moreover, constructing a strategy is also complicated by questions of the lawyer's responsibility to the client, issues of confidentiality, conflict of interest, and duties to the legal order. Thus all the dimensions of legal practice are, at least in principle, involved in developing a theory of the case. Furthermore, the client's material well-being or even survival is frequently at stake, so that case theory entails assuming professional responsibility as well.

Arriving at a theory of the case is the principal educational task of most clinical courses. In practice, this usually means, as one student put it, "legalizing the [client's] story," meaning by this that serving the client requires turning the client's narrative of difficulty into a viable strategy for obtaining a legal remedy. Discussing this idea, Binny Miller has argued that developing case theory means, in effect, bringing the very concrete, particular facets of the client's problem into illuminating and useful connection with some general principles of legal doctrine, of combining "narrative" with "analytic" thinking (Miller, 2002). Reflecting on her own growth in understanding as a clinical professor, Miller describes a process of cognitive development that is likely to be shared by many novices in legal thinking. Law school, Miller observes, mostly teaches legal reasoning as the "application of abstract rules to particular factual situations" (Miller, 2002, p. 301)—rules located in either statute or judicial opinion. In her early days, Miller says, she "misunderstood legal analysis as a hunt for the perfect case, or at least the better case. So I spent hours looking for more cases, when my time would have been better spent creating a legal theory with facts and law I already had in hand." In reality, she concludes, "creating a legal argument is like reading a map, in the old fashioned way . . . [y]ou need to notice what is around you, rather than going in a straight linear path from point A to point B" (p. 302).

Miller's use of the map-reading analogy to describe case theory, in contrast to finding the best "fit" between available cases and principles in legal analysis, resonates with the novice-to-expert learning trajectory developed by Hubert Dreyfus and Stuart Dreyfus and worked out in nursing education by Benner and colleagues. They describe "novices" as at first locked within a system of rules. Their chief cognitive activity is the subsuming of events and situations under those rules, attending mostly to the formal requirements—the logic of the system of rules. Only gradually, with experience and under the guidance of expert coaching, do learners begin to acquire the ability to attend to context, to "notice what is around you," in Miller's phrase (Miller, 2002, p. 302). It is by such expanded attention, which builds on the analytical rules already learned, that students develop the capacity to make judgments in practice.

This represents an important cognitive advance, as well as growth toward ethical engagement with the client in the situation. It should not be misconstrued as simply further application of principles to problems, as might be taught in a mathematics course. Philosopher Elizabeth Minnich has characterized practical judgment of this sort in terms that illuminate the aims of teaching case theory. Minnich notes that a person "who has good judgment" is one who "recognizes in a new situation what makes it familiar so that she can bring experience to bear; and yet she is also one who recognizes equally the claim of what is indeed new [in the situation]" (Minnich, 1991, p. 222). That is, practical judgment is not the subsuming of the "case" as simply an "instance" of a general rule. It is seeing the particular instance in light of the principle, so that the principle itself may take on a new or nuanced meaning that it might have in connection with a different situation. Awareness of narrative and context bring the principles alive while also giving conceptual nuance to their meaning. In this way, clinical experiences can qualify and expand students' comprehension of legal principles, potentially providing crucial insight for the students' progress toward mature legal judgment. This process is likely to be faster and more efficient if instructors in case-dialogue teaching share goals and strategies with those responsible for clinical teaching, and vice versa. This is an example of the synergistic advantages of an integrated approach to teaching and learning in professional education.

Teaching Case Theory: A Possible New Pivot for Legal Education

Developing competence in legal judgment is the goal of teaching case theory. Although clinical pedagogies engage students with specific clients in particular contexts, their intent goes beyond the particular subject matter studied or service offered.

It is worth emphasizing that the development of capacities for legal judgment that can be observed in successful clinical courses is deeply consonant with the larger purposes of legal education. Moreover, the iterative movement among the three apprenticeships that the best clinical instruction provides is isomorphic with the practice of law in virtually all its forms. That is, the threefold movement between law as doctrine and precedent (the focus of the case-dialogue classroom) to attention to performance skills (the aim of the apprenticeship of practice) and then to responsible engagement with solving clients' legal problems—a back-and-forth cycle of action and reflection—also characterizes most legal practice. The separation of these phases into distinct areas of the curriculum, or as separate apprenticeships, is always an artificial "decomposition" of practice. The pedagogical cycle is not completed unless these segregated domains are reconnected.

Seen in this perspective, case theory calls attention to the important role played by the problems of particular clients in specific situations in giving impetus to the legal process. In actual practice the parts are not attended to all at once or even sequentially in a once-and-for-all sense but iteratively, in a virtuous circle. Each of the elements should be present from the beginning. Each also demands special emphasis at different points in the students' development. The desired integration, like competent practice, requires constant mutual adjustment among the emphases of the three parts, so that conceptual analysis is not only taught in doctrinal classrooms, nor is practice only taught in lawyering courses, nor is professional purpose and identity taught only in courses identified as such.

These considerations point toward a basic question: Given what we now know about the kinds of learning that are foundational to professional competence, how might legal education be reshaped to better enable students to move toward that goal? In this process of rethinking, what should be the conceptual pivot? We affirm the argument of the Best Practices report that the best available knowledge points toward context-based education as the most effective setting in which to develop professional knowledge and skills (Stuckey and others, 2006). However, for a profession such as law, which is pledged to public service, a more encompassing center may be essential. That center is the development of responsibility, both for individual clients and for the law and its values. This is the subject of the pedagogies of the apprenticeship of professional identity, to which we turn in the next chapter.

NOTES

1. These developments are discussed in detail by Grossman (1974) and by Barry, Dubin, and Joy (2000). What is most striking is the similarity of issues and arguments over a period of three decades.

2. American Bar Association's 1992 report on legal education is commonly called the MacCrate report.

3. Gardner (1987) provides an overview of the first decades of this movement.

4. See Rose (1999) for an analysis of the effectiveness of this approach to teaching practice, as used in the training of physical therapists.

5. For an overview of the evidence, see Bransford, Brown, and Cocking (1999).

6. See, for example, the now-standard work of Hayes and Flower (1980).

4

PROFESSIONAL IDENTITY
AND PURPOSE

LAWYERS ARE UNIQUE AMONG PROFESSIONALS in that they are officially sanctioned participants in making the legal system work—officers of the court, as well as advocates for their clients. According to the American Bar Association's *Model Rules of Professional Conduct* (hereafter, Model Rules), "A lawyer, as a member of the legal profession, is a representative of clients, an officer of the legal system and a public citizen having special responsibility for the quality of justice" (American Bar Association, 2004, "Preamble"). Similarly, the 1996 report of the Professionalism Committee of the American Bar Association's Section of Legal Education and Admissions to the Bar places a concern for social contribution at the center of its definition of a professional lawyer:

> A professional lawyer is an expert in law pursuing a learned art in service to clients and in the spirit of public service; and engaging in these pursuits as part of a common calling to promote justice and public good. (American Bar Association, 1996, p. 6)

Essential characteristics of such a person include "ethical conduct" and "dedication to justice and the public good," as well as knowledge of the law, skill in applying it, "thoroughness of preparation," and "practical and prudential wisdom" (American Bar Association, 1996, pp. 6–7).

These official definitions suggest a demanding ideal of legal professionalism. They describe the lawyer as expert in legal thinking and practice, while committed to service of both clients and the welfare of the larger community that is organized by the legal order. Such expertise and commitment require an extraordinary degree of flexibility of mind and a highly integrated and focused character. In many professional settings, however, these lofty ideals of public spirit and service to clients can seem far removed from reality. The press of business demands, already experienced by many law students in summer clerkships in law firms, frequently focuses thoughts elsewhere than on the public purposes of the profession. Students rarely leave law school without having heard a variety of views about the "real" nature of their chosen profession—views that are often conflicting and based on varying degrees of experience, hearsay, and warranted evidence. Law schools face a formidable task in providing some coherence and guidance to their students in developing their identities as legal professionals.

The models of the lawyer that legal education transmits to students can, in fact, fall short of the articulations of the Model Rules. The focus of law school on the juridical-process-as-conflict resonates with the dominant images of the lawyer in popular circulation. In the popular understanding, vigorous advocacy for clients overshadows the other demands of legal professionalism. However atypical the tense courtroom drama may be in the careers of most lawyers, the important dimensions of the lawyer as counselor and court officer are simply less visible unless they are regularly analyzed, modeled, and practiced, as well as ceremonially invoked. As Mary Ann Glendon of Harvard Law School has noted, "peacemaking, problem-solving lawyers are the legal profession's equivalent of doctors who practice preventive medicine. Their efforts are generally overshadowed by the heroics of surgeons and litigators" (Glendon, 1994, p. 107). This is so, even though such careers may well provide the best opportunity for students to contribute to the well-being of their fellow citizens, as well as to achieve career satisfaction.

The larger context for this is the growing sense of demoralization in legal practice. This trend, and its probable causes, has been analyzed in studies over several decades.[1] Large-scale changes in the conditions of practice have washed away many of the institutional pilings that supported the ideals expressed in the Model Rules. Lawyer professionalism is still importantly defined with reference to ideals first annunciated by leaders of the bar in the early part of the twentieth century—ideals of independent service to the public, requiring and supporting counsel to clients that would also be independent of possible benefit to the attorney or law firm. Over the last several decades, however, the relatively stable and secure relationships that characterized at least the upper levels of the bar in the mid-twentieth century have altered radically. Decades of major economic restructuring, along with social changes that have brought significant numbers of previously underrepresented groups into the legal profession, have disrupted the old patterns beyond recovery. Ours is an era marked by a growing body of lawyers trained by an increasing number of law schools who then enter unstable and highly competitive domains of practice. Under these conditions, it has proven hard to make the old ideals of independent public service the basis of everyday legal practice. The result has been confusion and uncertainty about what goals and values should guide professional judgment in practice, leaving many lawyers "wandering amidst the ruins of those [past] understandings" (Glendon, 1994, p. 37).

Not in spite of but precisely because of these social pressures, legal education needs to attend very seriously to its apprenticeship of professional identity. Professional education is highly formative. The challenge is to deploy this formative power in the authentic interests of the profession and the students as future professionals. Under today's conditions, students' great need is to begin to develop the knowledge and abilities that can enable them to understand and manage these tensions in ways that will sustain their professional commitment and personal integrity over the course of their careers. In a time of professional disorientation, the law schools have an opportunity to provide direction. Law schools can help the profession become smarter and more reflective about strengthening its slipping legitimacy by finding new ways to advance its enduring commitments.

To do this, however, law schools need to further deepen their knowledge of how the apprenticeship of professionalism and purpose works. That is, they must improve their understanding of their own formative capacity, including learning from their own strengths, as well as those of other professions. Further, the schools need to attend more systematically to the pedagogical practices that foster the formation of integrated, responsible lawyers.

Toward that goal, in this chapter we survey what is known about how ethical identity develops and can be fostered. We consider how these educational principles are currently exemplified in educating for lawyer professionalism and how they could better inform that endeavor. We show how virtually all the forms of teaching that take place in law schools, ranging from the academic teaching of the case-dialogue classroom through various approximations of legal practice to clinical training in which students take direct responsibility for clients, are pedagogies that can be used to shape professional identity.

"Doing Justice" to Professional Formation

The term *formation* proved an illuminating lens through which to analyze the effects of different kinds of preparation in the Carnegie Foundation's study of education of Jewish and Christian clergy (Foster, Dahill,

Golemon, and Tolentino, 2005). The core idea is at once simple and profound: the ensemble effect of professional schools' various educational practices is greater than the sum of the particular pedagogies taken in isolation. Seminaries and, we believe, law schools shape the minds and hearts of their graduates in enduring ways. This is true of habits of thinking such as analytical skills, but it is especially salient in the development of professional purpose and identity.

An apprenticeship of professional identity involves two areas that legal education currently tends to treat under separate rubrics. It involves both the area of professional ethics, the rules of conduct for lawyers, often taught as the "law of lawyering," and the wider matters of morality and character. The area of ethics, in the sense of professional responsibility, is the subject of a course mandated by the American Bar Association and of a substantive field that is tested on the bar exam. The wider issues, many of which would be understood as moral or ethical matters in everyday understanding or in philosophical discourse, are usually discussed in law schools under the heading of "professionalism." This is not an area directly tested by the bar and, consequently, perhaps not perceived by students to be as significant as ethics, in the more restricted sense.

Professional ethical engagement, however, spans this distinction. It includes matters of character and of the rules of conduct, but it comes to life most vividly, we think, in matters of responsibility for clients, especially as these are taught and experienced in clinical-legal education. For that reason, we consider law school's clinical programs as part of the teaching for professionalism and professional identity. But in thinking about how they can better provide an apprenticeship of professional identity, law schools face a larger question: How can law schools best teach that sense of public responsibility, indeed, public service that the American Bar Association uses to frame its own discussion of model rules? This question bring us full circle to the question we pose in the opening of this volume: How is legal education best able to combine education in law's formal knowledge and techniques with a spirit of ethical engagement?

The Ethical-Social Values of the Profession

The complexity, as well as the urgency, of these questions is written deeply into the American Bar Association guidelines themselves. According to these guidelines, the ethical-social values of the profession of law, at least in theory, can encompass several distinct concepts. The most familiar set of issues concerns ethical conduct in relation to one's immediate clients, opposing counsel, and the court. Some of the best-known issues in legal ethics involve conflicts between advocacy on behalf of one's client and standards of professional ethics. For example, if an attorney is representing a defendant in a lawsuit, is it ethically permissible to impeach a witness for the plaintiff whom that attorney knows to be telling the truth?

But many aspects of what students learn as part of the apprenticeship of professional purpose and identity are as simple and straightforward as basic honesty and trustworthiness—financial propriety, accurate representation of one's expertise, and the like. Although it may seem obvious that these are essential to professional practice, the reality is that they cannot be taken for granted. Though it is a small percentage, every year finds attorneys disbarred, often for reasons of financial impropriety of some kind. In law school as in practice, competitive pressures tempt students to misrepresent things like grade point average and class rank on their résumés. Clearly, they are not immune from the cheating that is widespread in both secondary and higher education.

Establishing and maintaining trust with one's clients is, of course, essential to the effective practice of law. But as central as honesty is to maintaining trust, it is not the only factor that affects the lawyer-client relationship. Respect and consideration for one's clients are also important contributors to that relationship. It is important, then, for the ethical-social apprenticeship to foster these human qualities, which fall within the scope of professionalism, if not legal ethics per se.

Trust is equally essential in the doctor-patient relationship—for diagnosis, patient compliance, and medical outcomes. Its absence contributes to a well-known intersection between medicine and law—the malpractice case. Research on medical malpractice reveals that what might be called the physician's manner—respect, consideration, even simple courtesy toward the patient—plays a central role in patients' trust in their doctors and in their decisions about whether to pursue malpractice suits when mistakes occur. Training in how to establish and maintain trust in the relationship with one's patients is addressed at many points in medical education and is even beginning to show up in important assessments of competence.

Trust is related to responsibility. Both are integral to professionalism; research in the medical domain is relevant here. In 2006, the Accreditation Council for Graduate Medical Education, which accredits clinical residency training programs, began including professionalism as one of six assessed "core competencies" required for graduation. Recent research on medical students and physicians has found that unprofessional attitudes and behavior were better predictors of later disciplinary action from licensing boards than were either test scores or grades. A large-scale study by Maxine Papadakis of the University of California at San Francisco found a strong statistical relationship between reports of "unprofessional behavior" among students and later serious ethical infractions by physicians. In sum, students who showed a repeated pattern of irresponsibility in attending clinics and failure to follow up on patient care, along with an inability to accept constructive criticism, were found to be three times more likely to receive disciplinary action from licensing boards than other doctors. Immaturity, poor initiative, and poor relationships with other staff were also found to be associated with these students—traits they carried into professional life (Papadakis and others, 2005). As is true for lawyers, only a tiny fraction of doctors—0.3 percent—receive formal disciplinary censure. But the study shows that "professionalism," although its measurement remains controversial, has a far from insignificant effect on both the welfare of patients and the careers of physicians. Understanding better how to develop the qualities of professionalism is rapidly moving closer to the center of attention in medical education. The same logic points toward the need for similar efforts in law schools.

A Central Question of the Profession

In law, however, there is a more controversial issue within the broad scope of the apprenticeship of professionalism and purpose: Does the responsibility to pursue substantive justice in individual cases and to consider the broader impact of one's actions conflict with advocacy on behalf of one's client? This is a matter of considerable debate. In the view of many attorneys and law school faculty, the only justice that can be known with certainty is procedural justice, and the adversary system ensures the greatest possible justice in the long run if lawyers on each side promote their clients' interests in the narrow sense. Others disagree. William Simon of the Stanford University Law School argues that, to the best of their ability, lawyers ought to "take such actions as, considering the relevant circumstances of the particular case, seem likely to promote justice" in a broader sense (Simon, 1998, p. 9). This opposition between roles is further complicated by the lawyer's other role as counselor, with the obligation to not just explain what is within the law but to raise for the client the ramifications and implications of particular courses of legal action.

Although it may be true that many faculty teach what Simon calls the "dominant view" that "the only ethical duty distinctive to the lawyer's role is loyalty to the client" (Simon, 1998, p. 8), the possibilities of what Glendon calls "peacemaking and problem-solving" lawyering also need forceful representation among students' formative experience. Indeed, we spoke with faculty who believe that they should, from the outset, introduce students into the nuances of lawyers' complex roles. One professor put it this way: "There is no one distinct role that is appropriate for lawyers. It all depends on the type of lawyering you do. There are many lawyers who do many things. Torts is basically litigation-oriented. It would focus on questions like 'if you were a judge or in the legislature, how would you resolve or answer the question?' In contract drafting, it would be helping people draft documents to represent the agreement. It is concerned with *avoiding* litigation rather than creating it. So it would be a totally different perspective on what lawyers do." Students at least need to be made aware, not only of the various sorts of lawyer they might become but also of the various kinds of approaches they can take toward lawyering itself.

A Place for the Apprenticeship of Identity and Purpose

All these features of the lawyer's role, including the potential conflicts among them, are the proper subjects for the ethical-social apprenticeship. This apprenticeship of professional identity should encompass issues of both individual and social justice, and it includes the virtues of integrity, consideration, civility, and other aspects of professionalism. The values that lie at the heart of the apprenticeship of professionalism and purpose also include conceptions of the personal meaning that legal work has for practicing attorneys and their sense of responsibility toward the profession. However, in legal education today, most aspects of the ethical-social apprenticeship are subordinate to academic training in case-dialogue method and contested as to their value and appropriateness. It is noteworthy, then, that at the sixteen law schools we visited, we saw faculty who treat ethical understanding and a commitment to the public good as central goals of their teaching, even in courses that are not explicitly identified as courses on professional responsibility or legal ethics. We also saw courses in which content and pedagogies were carefully chosen to support the development of personal and professional virtues for the ethical and socially responsible practice of law.

The Knowledge Base: Law Schools and the Moral Development of Practitioners

It was evident that the commitment to serving society informed and shaped the culture and programs at some of the schools we visited, and we highlight these in examples throughout this volume. Overall, however, we came away from our campus visits with the strong impression that in most law schools, the apprenticeship of professionalism and purpose is subordinated to the cognitive, academic apprenticeship. In fact, in the minds of many faculty, ethical and social values are subjective and indeterminate and, for that reason, can potentially even conflict with the all-important values of the academy—values that underlie the cognitive apprenticeship: rigor, skepticism, intellectual distance, and objectivity.

However, if law schools would take the ethical-social apprenticeship seriously, they could have a significant and lasting impact on many aspects of their students' professionalism. This is not widely understood by faculty, who often argue that by the time students enter law school it is too late to affect their ethical commitment and professional responsibility. Indeed, this common refrain is heard throughout higher education, especially with reference to professional education. Skeptics argue that moral character is the only thing that really matters in determining ethical conduct, and that character is established earlier in life, in the context of the family. As one law school faculty member asked, "Can it really be taught when ethical issues are a matter of right and wrong?"

Many students share the belief that it is too late to develop morally by the time people enter law school. One student remarked, for example, "For the most part, I think our values are set before we get to law school. I've seen some self-centered people here. I've been somewhat shocked. I don't know where they get their values from. I think it comes from your family. Of course you can change, but I don't know if law school could really change or shape your values."

At first glance, social science research may seem to bear out faculty skepticism about the potential for law schools to influence the ethical maturity of their students. In fact, a number of studies have shown that students' moral reasoning does not appear to develop to any significant degree during law school.[2] The same pattern, either flat or slightly declining scores on measures of moral judgment, has been shown in medical, dental, and veterinary school samples (Self and Baldwin, 1994; Bebeau, 1994).

This pattern cannot be explained by entering scores at the top of the measurement scale—what social scientists call a "ceiling effect." Moral judgment scores of entering law students are roughly equivalent to those of entering medical and dental students and somewhat higher than entering veterinary and accounting students; all are well below the maximum on the instruments used.[3] This picture of a lack of growth in moral thinking during law school is borne out by studies of practicing lawyers, which reveal scores for attorneys that are comparable to those of entering law students (Ernest and Bebeau, 2000; Scofield, 1997). It is notable, however, that public-sector attorneys in one study scored significantly higher than private-sector attorneys, whose scores are equivalent to those of first-year law students (Long, 1993).

Although these findings may seem to call into question the potential for ethical growth in professional school, in reality the research shows only that, as presently constituted, legal education and education for several other professions do not support the development of students' moral judgment. They do not show that professional education cannot support that development. As Muriel Bebeau commented in regard to dental education, we cannot expect that the typical, technically oriented dental program will have a positive influence on students' moral development. After implementing a comprehensive dental ethics curriculum, however, Bebeau reports very sizable increases in students' scores (Bebeau, 1994).

Research on legal education shows similar results. Although in 1981 Willging and Dunn reported that a traditional legal ethics course had no effect on students' moral judgment level, in 1995, Hartwell found that teaching legal ethics and professional responsibility in small, highly interactive seminars had a strong positive impact on students' moral judgment scores. Happily, the importance of connecting ethical theory with active learning in context is receiving more attention in legal education—a trend that should be reinforced by the results of studies of how students develop moral judgment in other professional contexts.[4] These results are consistent with those reported in studies of comparable interventions in other fields, which typically show quite sizable effects, as compared with control groups. Overall, then, the research makes quite clear that higher education can promote the development of more mature moral thinking, that specially designed courses in professional responsibility and legal ethics do support that development, but that unless they make an explicit effort to do so, law schools do not contribute to greater sophistication in the moral judgment of most students.

This overall finding of the research is of real practical importance because clarity of moral thinking is not only important in its own right, especially for attorneys, but it has also been shown to play an important role in predicting ethical conduct (Landsman and McNeel, 2004). Naturally, though, sophisticated thinking about ethical issues is not the only factor that shapes individuals' ethical conduct. A key factor mediating the relationship between individuals' ideals and their actual conduct is their sense of moral identity—the moral values, goals, and feelings that are central to their sense of who they are. Like moral judgment, moral identity is not established once and for all in childhood. It can be transformed quite dramatically in adulthood when individuals encounter conditions that are conducive to further growth. A number of studies have shown that moral identity and ethical commitment can change quite dramatically well into adulthood (Colby and Damon, 1992).

Law school experiences, if they are powerfully engaging, have the potential to influence the place of moral values such as integrity and social contribution in students' sense of self. This is especially likely to take place in relation to the students' sense of professional identity, which is, of course, an important part of the individual's identity more broadly. Professional identity is, in essence, the individual's answer to questions such as, Who am I as a member of this profession? What am I like, and what do I want to be like in my professional role? and What place do ethical-social values have in my core sense of professional identity? Because law school represents a critical phase in the transition into the profession, it is inevitable that it will influence students' image of what kind of lawyers they want to be. As far as we know, there is no research on the extent to which this influence results in greater incorporation of the ethical-social values of the profession into students' personal and professional identities. Based on other research, however, we do know that for students to incorporate the profession's ethical-social values into their own, they need to encounter appealing representations of professional ideals, connect in a powerful way with engaging models of ethical commitment within the profession, and reflect on their emerging professional identity in relation to those ideals and models. Our observations make it clear that this incorporation happens for some students but that countervailing influences are likely to be more powerful for many.

The Value of Education for Professional Responsibility

Many faculty who doubt the value of education for professional responsibility in law schools equate efforts to support students' ethical development with inculcation, which they see as illegitimate and ineffective. This is further complicated by their belief that some of their colleagues are pushing ideological agendas. A typical comment comes from a legal ethics professor who teaches ethics in a way that is directly responsive to the bar exam's requirements regarding "law of lawyering" but does not stray far from the effort to convey knowledge of the basic rules. "I don't have an agenda," insisted this professor. "I bristle when people from the profession tell us we have to teach them to be ethical. We're talking about mature people. We should not be trying to push them in a particular direction. Some people here don't agree. They have an agenda."

Another senior faculty member echoed this view: "I want to push students to think by asking them 'what would you do?' but I avoid asking them 'what is good?' or 'what should you be doing?' or 'what role should you have?' or 'what view should you take on this issue?' I consider them to be adults and would prefer them to bring their own values to law school than to try to inculcate them with my values." This perception that it is indoctrination even to ask students to articulate their own normative positions was surprisingly prevalent on the campuses we visited.

In contrast to this kind of skepticism on the part of some faculty and students about the effectiveness and legitimacy of efforts to foster ethical development in law school, the legal profession, as represented by the American Bar Association, has acknowledged both the potential of law schools to contribute to professional responsibility and ethics and the importance of these educational goals. Since the 1970s all students have been required to take a course in professional responsibility and legal ethics. But in the 1990s, the American Bar Association made it clear that, from its point of view, this single course requirement is not sufficient. In two highly visible reports—those of the MacCrate Commission and the American Bar Association Professionalism Committee—the American Bar Association urged law schools to increase their attention to professional-ism and ethics.

The 1992 MacCrate report called not only for the explicit teaching of a wide range of legal skills, it also prominently counted among its prior-ities "four fundamental values of the profession," including "striving to promote justice, fairness, and morality" (American Bar Association, 1992, pp. 140–141). Taking this challenge a step further, the 1996 report from the Professionalism Committee of the American Bar Association Section of Legal Education and Admissions to the Bar concluded, based on liter-ature reviews and surveys, that "lawyer professionalism has declined in recent years and increasing the level of professionalism will require sig-nificant changes in the way professionalism ideals are taught" (p. 5). *Best Practices for Legal Education* makes many of the same recommendations, while providing examples of progress in addressing the challenge of teach-ing values within approaches to context-based education (Stuckey and others, 2006).

Many commentators from within law schools have also pointed to troubling declines in public esteem for the profession and attorneys' apparently growing dissatisfaction with their work, offering empirical evi-dence that these problems are widespread and serious. According to many observers, the "crisis of professionalism" is manifest in a decline of civil-ity and an increase in adversarialism, a decline in the role of the counselor and in lawyers' competence, including ethical competence, and a new sense of the law as a business, subject to greater competitive economic pressures and answerable only to the bottom line. Others note a loss of calling or sense of purpose among lawyers.

Whether these problems represent a change or simply a contemporary situation that is unacceptable, even if it is not new, there are undeniable problems with both the public perception of the legal profession and dissatisfaction from within the profession. In her book *In the Interests of Justice,* Deborah Rhode reviews survey data showing that the public perceives lawyers as greedy, unethical, and arrogant. She also notes that "a majority of lawyers report that they would choose another career if they had the decision to make over, and three-quarters would not want their children to become lawyers" (Rhode, 2000, p. 8). In addition, "An estimated one-third of American attorneys suffer from depression or from alcohol or drug addiction, a rate that is two to three times higher than in the public generally" (p. 8). Of course, there are many reasons for lawyers' dissatisfaction with their work, but lack of a sense of meaning is one central concern. Only one-fifth of attorneys report that their careers have borne out their hope of contributing to the social good (p. 8).

Evidence from the experience of beginning lawyers provides a more qualified and fine-grained analysis of these larger trends. When inquiring about the quality of their working lives, the authors of *After the JD* asked early-career attorneys to evaluate their satisfaction in four distinct areas. The subjects were asked first to rate their satisfaction with "job setting," meaning security of employment, recognition from supervisors, collegial relations in the workplace, and the like. The second category was "work substance," the intrinsic interest of the work. This was distinguished from the third, or "social value" of the work, its relation to broader social purposes and commitments. The fourth area was "power track" satisfaction: compensation, advancement, prestige, and status in the profession. The study found that the first three types of satisfaction are highly correlated with each other. Further, the level of satisfaction in these areas was higher among attorneys in smaller firms and serving in government or public interest organizations than in those working for large firms. By contrast, attorneys in large firms expressed higher "power track" satisfaction—but lower satisfaction about job setting, intrinsic value, and the social value of their work (Dinovitzer and others, 2004).

The study concludes that "there is no evidence of any pervasive unhappiness in the profession," a finding noted as consistent with the American Bar Foundation study of Chicago lawyers (Heinz, Nelson, Sandefur, and Laumann, 2005). But *After the JD* does show an inverse relationship between the achievement of conventionally defined "success" in highly paid, large-firm work and overall professional satisfaction, at least at the law associate level (Dinovitzer and others, 2004). This finding helps concretize the way in which law schools present students with conflicting messages. On the one hand, emphasis on the Model Rules and attention to the intrinsic purposes of legal work that are at the core of the ethical-social apprenticeship are apparent in every law school we visited. On the other, the praise and reverence bestowed on "power track" careers often dominate the lore in the schools. We found such attitudes to be widespread, especially at the more selective schools.

If this conflict among the values and aspirations that law schools promote is not recognized and publicly attended to, "power track" values are likely to trump concern for the other dimensions of job satisfaction among ambitious and competitive students, setting them up for dissatisfaction and soul-searching in their early practice lives. Without serious curricular attention to these concrete tensions and contradictions of professional identity and purpose, law schools are failing to provide the kind of open-eyed preparation needed for today's complicated professional world.

The Potential of Pro Bono Work

Law schools hold another potential for strengthening students' development as moral, as well as legal, reasoners and actors: the legal services provided free *pro bono publico*. Long a defining feature of legal professionalism, analogous to the claim of medicine to provide "charity" care in the days before widespread medical insurance and managed care, free legal work for clients who cannot afford legal services is a vivid enactment of law's professional identity. However great the decay of this aspect of law's profession of service, the vast majority of law schools offer their students some organized opportunity to take part in pro bono work. The results of a recent study of this issue reveal, however, a mixed picture. In *Pro Bono in Principle and in Practice: Public Service and the Professions*, Deborah Rhode (2005) argues that the organized bar has been resistant to focusing on pro bono service, apparently because it seems to conflict with the profession's vigorous efforts to bar specialists from outside the legal profession from providing basic legal support to the unrepresented—in other words, that it is a threat to the profession's monopolies of practice.

For their part, law schools vary considerably in how much importance they give to such service: a few schools, notably Tulane and the University of Pennsylvania, require such service of all students; most are voluntary. The effects of such participation also vary. The study supports the intuition that a good pro bono experience can strongly influence a student's future involvement in pubic service and even become a highlight of law school experience. The key differential factor is how supportive the school's overall culture is of such experience and how well integrated it is into the students' developing understanding of what it is to be a lawyer. Significantly, positive experiences with pro bono work were often part of clinical-legal courses. However, about a fifth of the students surveyed reported negatively on their experiences, frequently noting a lack of faculty supervision or interest in this connection. This is corroborated by the finding that recent graduates ranked pro bono work at the bottom of law school experiences they found useful in their transition to practice (Dinovitzer and others, 2004). Because Rhode believes that it is unrealistic to expect the bar to emphasize such learning through service, the strongest way to enhance such efforts would be to require that schools—and law firms—report publicly their pro bono activities. Such a requirement would exert something like the pressure that schools experience from *U.S. News & World Report* surveys: a new dimension for competition for admissions, as well as external support and prestige.

An Inevitable Apprenticeship

Although some people believe that law school cannot affect students' values or ethical perspectives, in our view law school cannot *help* but affect them. For better or worse, the law school years constitute a powerful moral apprenticeship, whether or not this is intentional. Law schools play an important role in shaping their students' values, habits of mind, perceptions, and interpretations of the legal world, as well as their understanding of their roles and responsibilities as lawyers and the criteria by which they define and evaluate professional success. In these and other ways, the curricular emphasis on analysis and technical competence at the expense of human connection, social context, and social consequences is reinforced by the broader culture in most law schools. Even though the three years of law school represent a relatively brief period in the lifelong development of a lawyer, the law school experience, especially in its early phases, is pivotal for professional development. In effect, students are apprenticing to the whole law school experience, not just to those elements that are intentionally designed to train and socialize them. As noted earlier, the slackening of interest among students in the third year points toward the need to make that year more challenging rather than less so. The findings of the Law School Survey of Student Engagement also suggest that there is plenty of room in the existing curriculum to emphasize the practical and ethical-social, as well as the integration among these.

A critical look at the nature of the encompassing apprenticeship on many law school campuses reveals some important positive messages for professionalism but also many implicit messages that may undermine the development of students' professionalism and commitment to "the central moral tradition of lawyering," as Roger Cramton has called it (Cramton, 1997, p. 18). Insofar as law schools choose not to place ethical-social values within the inner circle of their highest esteem and most central preoccupation, and insofar as they fail to make systematic efforts to educate toward a central moral tradition of lawyering, legal education may inadvertently contribute to the demoralization of the legal profession and its loss of a moral compass, as many observers have charged.

Students are learning not only from the courses they take but also from the moral culture or atmosphere of their classrooms and the law school campus more broadly. They also learn from their relationships with particular faculty and with fellow students, their perceptions of faculty interests and priorities, their experiences in clinics, their pro bono work, externships, summer jobs, and other extracurricular activities. All these experiences have great potential to prepare students to practice law with integrity and a sense of meaning and purpose. But in order to realize this potential, law schools need to take a systematic look at the many experiences that can contribute to students' moral learning, including the curriculum, legal clinics, clubs and other extra-curricular activities, summer jobs and internships, and the moral culture or climate of the institution. If these building blocks are used well and intentionally integrated with each other, they form the basis for a powerful developmental experience during the three years of law school. Unfortunately, this kind of intentionality and integration is evident in very few law schools.

What Their Experience Tells Students

In law school, students learn from both what is said and what is left unsaid. There is a message in what the faculty address and what they do not. When faculty routinely ignore—or even explicitly rule out-of-bounds—the ethical-social issues embedded in the cases under discussion, whether they mean to or not, they are teaching students that ethical-social issues are not important to the way one ought to think about legal practice. This message shapes students' habits of mind, with important long-term effects on how they approach their work. Conversely, when faculty discuss ethical-social issues routinely in courses, clinics, and other settings, they sensitize students to the moral dimensions of legal cases.

These messages, as well as the process of learning what they mean, begin in a powerful way in the very first weeks of law school, when students become immersed in the rigors of case analysis. Despite the undeniable value of intellectual rigor, law schools' imbalance toward the cognitive aspects of professional apprenticeship and the associated emphasis on legal analysis serve to color, and can even undermine, the apprenticeship into professionalism and purposes. As we have seen, a concentrated focus on the details of particular legal cases, disconnected from consideration of the larger purposes of the law, begins very early in law school. In their all-consuming first year, students are told repeatedly to focus on the procedural and formal aspects of legal reasoning, its "hard" edge, with the "soft" sides of law, especially moral concerns or compassion for clients and concerns for substantive justice, either tacitly or explicitly pushed to the sidelines.

This focus is justified on pedagogical grounds, with an implied assumption that law school can flip off the switch of ethical and human concern, teach legal analysis, and later, when students have mastered the central intellectual skill of thinking like a lawyer, flip the switch back on. In earlier chapters, we saw Karl Llewellyn describe the necessity, but also the difficulty, of reconnecting the peculiar kind of "sapiens" formed through the first-year experience with the full humanity of the student (Llewellyn, 1996). No doubt some students do enter law school with misconceptions about how the law works, which can get in the way if they become entangled in initial forays into legal analysis. Students must learn that their intuitive impressions about cases are often misleading, as they attempt to master the precision of legal language and reasoning.

But such a critical transition point in professional development needs to be approached with great care. It is not surprising that students can be quite confused when the professor turns this switch off. Many in our focus groups expressed this sort of confusion about what they feared were the implications of this dispassionate perspective for the nature of their roles as lawyers, diminishing their hopes that they might serve substantive goods in their careers. In its extreme form, the tacit message sent by the current separation among the apprenticeships can provide very distorted notions of what a career in the law is about:

> "It seems like legal thinking can justify anything."

> "When I took criminal law, I started to think of it in technical terms and stopped looking at the human side."

> "Most teachers don't bring in ethical issues. You are supposed to divorce yourself from those concerns."

The danger for second- and third-year students is that the analytic blinders they have laboriously developed may never come off when they deal with the law or with clients. Students often reported that they found substantive and moral concerns seldom reintroduced in advanced courses, even after they had mastered the analytical skills for whose sake these concerns were set aside. Although some students developed fuller and more complex understandings later in law school, others come to take this dichotomy for granted; some become disillusioned with the law because of this experience: "The way law is taught assumes that there is a Truth that's out there. It is taught in a way that assumes the law is neutral. But, in fact, it is not neutral. The way it is taught is devoid of humanity more than it needs to be. You could have a quality of teaching that has more human beings involved in it."

In a more extreme statement of this idea, a student from a highly selective private law school assailed law school's formative effects by declaring that it seemed to him that "law schools create people who are smart without a purpose."

However, we heard from many students how lawyering experiences, especially their participation in clinical work, were able to round out and modify a too-rigid understanding of law. But precisely because these experiences are less common than required courses encountered by all students in the first year, we believe it is especially important that law schools examine the tacit, as well as more overt, education that students receive in their core, doctrinal courses. In fact, a fuller grasp of principles of effective learning would suggest that simply asking students to set aside their inchoate concerns for substantive justice or human welfare does not, in itself, help them learn why their intuitions are misleading or clarify the relationship between moral and legal concerns.

Keeping the Moral and Legal in Dialogue

A more effective way to teach is to keep the analytical and the moral, the procedural and the substantive in dialogue throughout the process of learning the law. This approach is not new to legal education. It is just too infrequently practiced; perhaps the issues are too rarely thought through rigorously. Consider, as a positive example, the well-regarded case book, *Basic Contract Law*, by Lon L. Fuller and Melvin Aaron Eisenberg (1996). Along with others of its type, it exemplifies the potential of an alternative approach—one that confronts directly questions about the relationship of morality and the law. The first section of the volume is titled "What promises should the law enforce?—The doctrine of consideration," thus raising, at the outset of this first-year course, the question of what the law should do (Fuller And Eisenberg, 1996). The very first section of the first chapter is an excerpt from John Rawls's 1971 *A Theory of Justice,* which explicates the social significance and moral basis of promise keeping and contracts—"the principle of fairness." Before moving to the first legal case, students encounter two more philosophical excerpts—one that discusses the breaking of promises as a violation of the promisee's rights (drawing on Melden, 1977), the other making the provocative claim that "a rational society" should require that most but not all promises be kept (drawing on Cohen, 1933).

The case that follows, *Dougherty v. Salt,* concerns a lawsuit by an eight-year-old boy against the estate of the boy's aunt (Fuller and Eisenberg, 1996). The aunt had given a promissory note to the boy for $3,000, payable at her death or before. She gave the note, she told his guardian, because she saw the boy one day and said, "I would like to take care of him now." The note was printed on a form that included the words "value received." At the aunt's death, the note had not been paid, and the boy sued her estate for $3,000. At the trial, the jury returned a verdict for the plaintiff, but the judge set the verdict aside. An appellate court reversed, and, finally, the court of appeals reversed again, holding that the note was a gift and not an enforceable contract. (In legal terms, there was no "consideration" for the aunt's promise.)

The authors follow the case with a number of other commentaries on doctrine, the history of contract law, and other issues raised by the case. It is noteworthy that the final commentary in the section on *Dougherty v. Salt,* written by one of the case book's authors, immediately raises the distinction between moral and legal obligations:

> The question, what promises should the law enforce, must not be confused with its cousin, what kinds of promises should people keep. Withholding legal enforcement from a promise does not license its breach. A promise-breaker may lose business, friends, or self-respect, and the prospect of such losses may be more of an impetus to performance than the prospect of money damages. Correspondingly, the fact that a promise should be kept affects but does not control the issue of enforceability: for reasons of policy the law may refuse to enforce promises that for reasons of morality should not be broken. (Fuller and Eisenberg, 1996, p. 9)

The commentary goes on to discuss the reasons that the law does not and should not enforce every moral obligation.

When law students bring to their first-year courses confusions about moral and legal obligations, as many of them do, the instructor can tell them that their concerns about fairness or other moral issues are not relevant to legal analysis and ask them to set aside those concerns. We know from our discussions with students that this happens frequently and that many students find it bewildering rather than clarifying, besides providing a distorted understanding of the nature of law itself. If, instead, the instructor, by introducing a careful discussion of the distinction and relationship between the moral and the legal, illustrates something of the breadth of law's concerns, this is likely to deepen students' understanding of the law, both the particular legal issues in the case under consideration and the law as a social institution. In this approach, legal considerations are understood in the context of their social purpose, and ethical considerations are not dismissed as naïve and irrelevant. This conveys a very different set of messages to beginning law students than does a too-simplistic exclusion of all but procedural and strategic thinking from legal reasoning. The broader message that law is a vital and significant social institution worth devoting one's professional life to will be strengthened to the extent that the instructor takes time to discuss, for example, whether such promises as the aunt's ought to be enforced as a matter of policy, thus keeping the connection between the substantive and the procedural in play.

This kind of teaching, which is sensitive to the breadth of substantive concerns and the precision of procedural thinking, keeps reminding students of the broader purpose and mission of the law. Without this grounding in the larger purpose of what they are studying, the sheer challenge and satisfaction of achieving intellectual mastery can become a kind of end in itself. Intellectual mastery alone is, indeed, always a possible pathology of schooling—one that can subtly subvert the best efforts of professional schools by displacing the goal of learning the profession with a more self-contained academic aim of technical virtuosity, detached from attention to the ends of legal training. This danger is intensified by the fact that students who go on to become the next generation of law school faculty are drawn from the subset of students who achieve the very highest levels of technical, intellectual mastery. To counter this tendency to treat intellectual virtuosity as an end in itself, there is evident need in all professional schooling, but perhaps especially in law school, to work hard at reconnecting pedagogically the process of formal analysis with the institutional purposes that the teaching is chartered to serve.

Stepping into Professional Roles:
Uniting the Three Apprenticeships

It is clear, then, that law school exerts a powerful formative influence on students. Considered in relation to the goal of promoting students' growth into competent and responsible legal professionals, however, today's law school experience is severely unbalanced. The difficulty, as we see it, lies in the relentless focus, in many law school courses, on the procedural and formal qualities of legal thinking. This focus is sometimes to the deliberate exclusion of the moral and social dimensions and often abstracted from the fuller contexts of actual legal practice. It is this one-sided emphasis on an academic apprenticeship insulated from considerations of ethical engagement or public responsibility that undercuts the principal aims of the ethical-social apprenticeship. A more robust and well-rounded formative experience demands that the parts of legal education must be mutually adjusted in the interests of creating a functional whole. Particularly today, with the general problem of purpose and meaning in legal work looming ever larger, the cognitive apprenticeship, as it now stands, needs to be rethought in light of the overall formative purpose of law school.

As we have seen in earlier chapters, legal education uses the distinctive and powerful case-dialogue method to ensure that students learn how to do legal thinking, as well as learn about the law. It has long been clear to law school faculty that lecturing to students about legal analysis would not provide the scaffolded practice that is key to students' learning to perform this subtle and complex cognitive skill. Other aspects of legal practice are also taught in many kinds of lawyering courses, though far less systematically, through students' active engagement in the practices they are trying to learn, though these experiences do not reach all students, as case-dialogue teaching does. In high-quality legal clinics, expert performance is modeled by supervising faculty, students enact a wide array of skills, and faculty coach them toward improved performance through continuous feedback. Moot court and other simulations provide opportunities for students to observe and practice a range of complex skills, learning to perform them rather than just learning about them. Effective legal writing programs are also grounded in pedagogies of enactment and coaching.

All these pedagogies are based in an understanding that students must perform complex skills in order to gain expertise. They also recognize that students do not get better through practice alone. If their performance is to improve, they need practice accompanied by informative feedback and reflection on their own performance. And their learning will be strengthened further if they develop a habit of ongoing self-assessment. This emphasis on "context-based education" is rightfully the insistent theme of *Best Practices for Legal Education* (Stuckey and others, 2006).

What does this mean for the development of professional responsibility and ethics? If they are to fully grasp the nature of their responsibilities as attorneys, students must achieve a deep understanding of the multiple dimensions of their roles and the arguments for alternative conceptions of the way that meaning should play out in practice. Achieving a firm grasp of these intellectual issues and their implications for legal practice is a challenge but, as challenging as it is, it is not sufficient. Law school graduates who enter legal practice also need the capacity to recognize the ethical questions their cases raise, even when those questions are obscured by other issues and therefore not particularly salient. They need wise judgment when values conflict, as well as the integrity to keep self-interest from clouding their judgment.

Just as when they learn legal reasoning, legal writing, and other lawyering skills, if students are to acquire important ethical capacities, they need opportunities to perform their understanding with ongoing coaching and feedback. How is this accomplished? Teaching for professional responsibility involves many of the same pedagogical strategies used for teaching other skills. These strategies include case analysis and discussion, simulation and role-playing, enactment and coaching, and various mechanisms for stimulating reflection on current experiences and on aspirations for the future. If these ways of teaching are to lead toward the formation of competent and responsible professionals, however, the teacher's commentary, coaching, and feedback must specifically address the ethical-social dimensions of students' experiences in the course.

The kind of personal maturity that graduates need in order to practice law with integrity and a sense of purpose requires not only skills but qualities such as compassion, respectfulness, and commitment. Course work can contribute to the development of moral values, goals, identity, and compassion, as well as ethical understanding and skills. These outcomes depend even more on pedagogies that actively engage the students than do more traditional dimensions of academic understanding. Compassion and concern about injustice become much more intense when students develop personal connections with those who have experienced hardship or injustice. This has been a persistent theme among students in some of the clinical courses we observed. Likewise, when students form relationships with professionals who inspire them, they can internalize new images of what they want to be like more deeply and vividly than they are likely to do through reading. This is one of the important, though rarely documented, benefits of well-designed experiences of pro bono and service work, of good externships, and especially of clinical courses.

Strategies for Uniting the Cognitive, Practical, and Ethical-Social Apprenticeships

A more adequate and properly formative legal education requires a better balance among the cognitive, practical, and ethical-social apprenticeships. To achieve this balance, legal educators will have to do more than shuffle the existing pieces. The problem demands their careful rethinking of both the existing curriculum and the pedagogies that law schools employ to produce a more coherent and integrated initiation into a life in the law.

A Continuum of Teaching and Learning

As legal educators think about how best to develop a coherent and integrated initiation into the law, it is helpful to consider the teaching and learning experiences in use. Drawing on examples of pedagogies as we observed them, it is possible to imagine a continuum of teaching and learning experiences concerned with the apprenticeship of professional identity. At one end of the continuum would be courses in legal ethics, in particular those directly oriented to the "law of lawyering" that students must master in order to pass the bar examination. A bit further along would fall other academic courses, including those of the first year, into which issues concerning the substantive ends of law, the identity and role of lawyers, and questions of equity and purpose are combined with the more formal, technical issues of legal reasoning. Approaches of this sort are often called the pervasive method of teaching ethics. Further along the continuum we encounter courses that directly explore the identity and roles of lawyers, the difficulties of adhering to larger purposes amid the press of practice, and the way professional ideals become manifest in legal careers. Further still fall the lawyering courses that bring into play questions of both competence and responsibility to the client and to the legal system. Finally, at the continuum's other end, we find externships and clinical courses in which direct experience of practice with clients becomes the focus.

From Courses in Legal Ethics to the Pervasive Method

Let us survey this continuum, probing examples of each type that illustrate the creative energy around the ethical-social apprenticeship that is stirring in the legal academy today.

THE LEGAL ETHICS COURSE. Most law school courses that raise issues of professional responsibility do so in the context of the Model Rules or the particular variations followed in the relevant state. This is for good reason. Because students' understanding of these rules and the case law surrounding them are tested in part of the bar examination, such courses are directly oriented toward a pragmatic purpose. In these required courses on legal ethics and professional responsibility, students learn to recognize the ethical issues that are central to the practice of law, such as those that concern the attorney-client relationship, conflict of interest, and the like. Beyond this minimum, however, courses and the texts used in them range widely. In addition to the content of the rules themselves, covering issues such as obligations to clients (the maintenance of confidentiality) and how these conflict with other obligations (the obligation to tell the truth or to inform others of impending consequences), some courses pursue a much broader range of topics, including concepts of the legal profession, issues of advocacy, counseling, negotiation, mediation, and the distribution of legal services in U.S. society.[5]

One virtue of the required course is that students learn the profession's ethical code as represented in the Model Rules, how those rules have been interpreted and applied, and the circumstances under which sanctions have been imposed. The students learn that these rules are taken seriously and violations are punished. Clearly, this kind of knowledge and understanding is critically important if the legal profession is to maintain basic ethical standards.

Often these courses are structured around legal cases that concern alleged violations of the Model Rules. Students apply their analytical skills to these cases, approaching them in much the same way they have learned to approach challenging legal cases in torts or contracts. This approach—the law of lawyering—is valuable in teaching an area of law that should be of immediate concern to every practicing attorney. The care and thoughtfulness with which the field of law has formulated its ethical code and the seriousness with which both the profession and legal education take the code are exemplary. It is perhaps not surprising, then, that teaching ethics through the law of lawyering is appealing to many faculty because, in a sense, it is morally neutral. This kind of legal ethics course may—but does not need to—address questions of moral right and wrong. It teaches what kinds of violations are subject to sanctions and how borderline cases have been resolved.

Because many law teachers are concerned about imposing their own moral beliefs on students, this approach protects them from having to confront questions of moral right and wrong in their teaching. In addition, when legal ethics is treated as a branch of the law, faculty who specialize in this field are recognized as having expertise that gives them authority of a familiar sort. Unfortunately, this perception also leads many faculty whose specialty is not the law of lawyering to consider themselves unqualified to introduce ethical concerns into their courses. This tends to reinforce the segregation of ethical issues from the rest of the curriculum. When legal ethics courses focus exclusively on the law of lawyering, they can convey a sense that attorneys' behavior is bounded only by sanctions such as the threat of malpractice charges and give the impression that most practicing lawyers are motivated primarily by self-interest and will refrain from unethical behavior only when it is in their immediate self-interest to do so. When legal ethics courses focus exclusively on teaching students what a lawyer can and cannot get away with, they can inadvertently convey a sense that knowing this is all there is to ethics. It is no wonder that Deborah Rhode calls these courses "legal ethics without the ethics" (Rhode, 2000, p. 200).

Such a narrow focus misses an important dimension of ethical development—the capacity and inclination to notice moral issues when they are embedded in complex and ambiguous situations, as they usually are in actual legal practice. This capacity is critical because ethical challenges cannot be addressed unless they are noticed and taken seriously. Legal ethics courses almost certainly shape the way law students understand the scope of ethical issues in the law and, thus, what ethical dilemmas or problems will attract their attention in legal practice. By defining "legal ethics" as narrowly as most legal ethics courses do, these courses are likely to limit the scope of what graduates perceive to be ethical issues.

The unintentional messages of legal ethics courses are of serious concern because they may reinforce professionally counterproductive cultural attitudes that are highly salient in many law schools. The experience of law school is often described by students, and some faculty, as a zero-sum game. This impression is generated, in large part, by competitive classroom climates, including the peculiarities of assessment in first-year courses, not least the inexorabilities of grading on a curve. Many of the students we met spoke of the demoralizing effect of the competitive atmosphere:

> "In law schools we are set up to compete—through grades, curves, and job interviews."

> "The whole adversarial system is set up to produce winners and losers, just as the grading curve creates winners and losers—and the losers don't get the jobs they want. It is a winner-take-all system, and for some people that means winning at any cost."

In addition, many students spoke of the ways in which income as an indicator of a lawyer's success is embodied as a central value on their campuses, and recruitment for large law firms and corporate positions seems ubiquitous. Other key professional rewards are also defined in individual rather than social terms, often rewards directly reflecting the values of the academy: how interesting and challenging their future job will be, for example. No one would deny the importance of these personal rewards, but when they are emphasized to the exclusion of the social significance of the work, they contribute to a conception of professional roles that is disconnected from social purpose and meaning.

Students are acutely aware of these individualistic values on their campuses. As one student said, "I wish the faculty had a more diverse idea about what success in the law is. There seems to be one version of success in the law where you go to this big firm and the firm owns your soul for the rest of your life and that's success. It is unlike other professions where you are shown the alternatives." This comment was echoed by students on virtually all the campuses we visited, and many expressed their sense of vulnerability to the pressure. As another student put it, "There is a strong career tide here that happens early for students. They are socialized toward large firms. The wave of suits and discussions of salaries is overwhelming. Will I be able to figure out and sustain what I want in the face of the tide? It is a struggle, because I am in debt."

Students in our focus groups also talked about an atmosphere in which many law students and faculty feel superior to other people, and many of their fellow students seem to care only for self-promotion. Many students express discomfort at the general sense of elitism pervading the law school experience:

> "You definitely get the sense in law school that lawyers are elite, better than other people."

> "There's a sense of elitism and entitlement in law schools. It is disturbing. We are so self-contained in our own buildings and social activities—we do things only with medical students."

Others are disturbed by their fellows' high-handed attitudes toward low-income clients: "I have seen the extraordinary arrogance that some students have in dealing with the clients at the clinic, as if suggesting that if the clients don't act exactly right, 'Well, we don't have to take their case.' I find this astonishing. I think it is part of the way the principles of law are taught, which is problematic. Not everybody teaches this way, but in general, the law is taught as if these principles, like calculus, exist outside of society and political norms." Again, the conflict in students' experience of the cognitive and the ethical-social apprenticeships is striking.

Despite these evident limitations of the apprenticeship of professional identity and purpose, as offered by most law schools, we also saw some excellent teaching. Indeed, we noted significant efforts to promote an apprenticeship of professional identity at every law school we visited. The schools use a number of different strategies to support the development of students' ethical understanding and commitment and their professional responsibility that include but go beyond formal courses in professional responsibility and legal ethics. Some faculty have adopted the pervasive method of teaching ethics, in which ethical issues specific to particular fields of law are incorporated into substantive courses. Some of the schools provide special experiences in the first year that introduce students to the broader context and significance of the law. These first-year programs serve as a counterbalance to the intensive focus on legal analysis that is the heart of the first-year experience.

As we have said, required ethics courses as traditionally taught can support important learning about ethical issues, but they also have some serious limitations. In order to address some of those limitations, many law schools offer courses in ethics or, more often, professional roles and responsibilities, that go beyond the law of lawyering to a deeper consideration of the complexities of lawyers' roles, the context of meaning for legal work, and the kinds of social capacities lawyers need in order to be fully competent, including the capacity to listen carefully, to work collaboratively, and to question their own stereotypes and assumptions.

THE PERVASIVE METHOD. Recognizing that a single, required legal ethics course is insufficient preparation for the ethical practice of law, the 1996 American Bar Association Professionalism Committee report and leaders in legal education (for example, Rhode, 1998) have called for law schools to incorporate ethical issues into the full range of doctrinal courses; this is often called the pervasive method. The value of this approach is now widely acknowledged, case books and other materials for incorporating ethical concerns into many courses have been developed, and most law schools say their faculty do use the pervasive method, at least to some extent. The progress that legal education has made in developing these materials across a wide range of legal fields is a particular strength for legal education. Although some other professions have called for something like the pervasive method of teaching professional ethics, none has made as much progress in formulating what this would really mean in practice or creating high-quality material with which to implement it.

In addition, many of the law students we talked with feel that addressing ethical issues in the context of their regular course work is valuable;
indeed, they often expressed the desire for more attention to these issues.
For example, one student remarked: "Legal ethics raises very complicated
situations. I wish there was more connection of those issues with the content of our courses. As it is, we don't focus on what is right. We just talk
about what is legally feasible." Another student commented: "I know. It
would be better if it were more integrated. It seems artificial to do ethics
separately."

Across legal education, efforts to expand the use of the pervasive
method so that it becomes truly pervasive have continued and, indeed,
increased. Courses that make a serious effort to incorporate broad concerns of professionalism and ethical engagement are no longer rare. An
example is a course on civil litigation taught by Charles Silver, a senior faculty member at the law school of the University of Texas. Silver teaches a
first-year course called The Law and Practice of Federal Civil Procedure,
in which he makes abundant use of materials relating to legal ethics.
Because the course is required for all first-year students, most of whom will
practice in areas other than litigation, Silver focuses on the behavior of
lawyers and the forces that influence lawyers' decisions. The forces include
economic pressures and needs (including the desire for fees), pressure from
ethics rules, procedural rules, judges, and other sources to represent clients
zealously while conforming to conduct norms, and pressure deriving from
lawyers' values and beliefs. Students emerge from the class knowing the
basics about attorneys' fees, solicitation, fiduciary duties, confidentiality,
interest conflicts, and other subjects covered in professional responsibility courses. Silver, who also teaches legal ethics and writes about the subject extensively, thus uses the context of litigation to convey information
and ideas of value to future attorneys, regardless of practice field.

FIRST-YEAR EXPERIENCES. In other professional schools, it is becoming
increasingly common to require entering students to take a course that
provides an introduction to the profession. For example, all entering
engineering students at the University of Michigan take Engineering 100.
The course combines lectures, discussions, and project work to introduce
students to the many dimensions that are entailed in the work of professional engineers. As one faculty member said, "The impetus for this
course came from industry saying 'the students you're turning out are too
one-dimensional. They are expert appliers of technical problem-solving
techniques but not very holistically oriented, not very good at thinking
about the big picture.'" In addition to introducing students to a wide

array of skills, the course is intended to help students understand the nature of engineering work and to generate enthusiasm and a sense that they belong in the field. It is also seen as a way to anchor, from the outset, a number of threads that are supposed to run through the whole curriculum, including the ethical dimension.

Although courses that offer a comparable introduction to the legal profession are not yet common, they have not been unknown in the past, and today some first-year "lawyering" courses serve a similar function. Some law schools, both in the United States and Canada, have been experimenting with first-year courses or programs that provide a broad intellectual perspective on the law. The goal is to give students greater breadth and a sense that there are many ways to look at the law at the same time that their other courses ask them to narrow their perspectives in order to learn the technical thinking and language of legal analysis. We observed parts of the program at the University of British Columbia that all students must take—a course that extends for a semester and a half, called Perspectives on Law. This course was deliberately designed to counterbalance the first-year focus on legal analysis, narrowly construed, by addressing the relationships among law, social forces, and values, analyzing those relationships from a variety of perspectives. The course consists of three six-week segments or modules, each taught by a different instructor. Students choose from an array of modules, which vary from year to year, but typically include topics like comparative law, environmental ethics and law, feminist perspectives on law, First Nations perspectives, obedience to law, and law and economics.

Faculty teaching these Perspectives on Law modules commented that student papers in the course have been impressive, exhibiting a level of integrated understanding that is an excellent foundation for the rest of students' legal education. Although first-year students are not always enthusiastic about the requirement, they generally appreciate its relevance and importance as they move on in law school, coming to see it as an important part of the curriculum. This kind of program is not unusual in Canadian law schools, many of which provide a first-year course that requires students to "step back and think more broadly and deeply." Osgoode Hall at York University in Toronto, for example, has a similar requirement for first-year students, intended to give them "an appreciation of the complexity of the socio-political context in which law operates."

In Chapter One, we described the CUNY law school's lawyering seminar. It is offered in both the first and second years; in the first year of the seminar, students learn about the roles and responsibilities of attorneys, as well as many practice-related activities. The seminar teaches legal reasoning, professional responsibility, legal writing, and other lawyering skills by integrating clinical methodology with substantive, theoretical, and doctrinal material. The course draws on a number of active pedagogies, using simulation exercises and hypothetical cases, among other sources. Students learn to make connections across courses by role-playing lawyers, clients, judges, or legislators confronted by legal issues arising from material in other first-year courses.

Students at CUNY also take a required first-year course called Liberty, Equality, and Due Process. The course provides a legal and historical perspective on the concepts of liberty and equality, looking at how American history has shaped the national consciousness of issues such as racial and gender equality. As the course description points out, students are challenged to "analyze their own experiences through the lens of the law and to understand how the law may have shaped their values and perceptions— or how it might be used to shift society's values and perceptions" (CUNY School of Law, 2006, Required Courses First Year).

Courses like these can provide beginning students a framework within which to understand the psychological forces and social pressures that too often cloud judgment in today's practice contexts, contributing to the problem of demoralization. By learning to recognize and think about these issues early and repeatedly, students can also be encouraged to develop effective coping strategies. A good introduction to the law today, like a good legal ethics course, can also provide needed positive direction by highlighting the possibilities for structural change in legal practice, disciplinary systems, and public policy to better align material rewards with the profession's purposes and values. It is important, we think, that such courses not be limited to the first year alone. A basis in the first year is essential, but this base soil needs cultivation throughout the three years, especially followup in the form of more advanced courses that enable students to continue relating their growing understanding of the law, their developing skills of practice, and their sense of identity and professional commitment.

Probing Professional Responsibility and Modeling Positive Professional Ideals

To see better what this kind of teaching looks like, consider a course at the University of New Mexico.

PROFESSIONAL RESPONSIBILITY. Robert L. Schwartz teaches several interdisciplinary courses in ethics and professional responsibility. His course on ethics in health care professions is taught jointly with a philosopher and draws students from law, public health, and other health care fields. The course involves small-group projects and papers, drawing heavily on legal cases. The course uses an approach to legal case study that is typical of business schools, taking a broader perspective on the cases than a strictly legal analysis and sometimes role-playing the parties in the case.

This course centrally addresses issues concerning the appropriate roles of lawyers in health care settings, posing questions such as, "What is your obligation as legal counsel to the hospital, and what should you do if doing the best for the patient puts the hospital at risk for liability?" Students are asked to answer these questions "as a human being and as part of the hospital administration." This presses students to think about the ways that their obligations as lawyers differ from or intersect with their obligations as human beings. Schwartz would like students to think about how they might act in both these roles, while making it clear to the hospital in which capacity they are speaking. That is, "the doctors need to understand when they are getting risk management information and when they are getting the attorney's judgment as a human being."

Describing both the health care course and his teaching more generally, Schwartz said that the classes he finds most exciting are those in which students learn how to be both good people and good lawyers—"a lot feel they have to give that up." His courses often address the conflict between being a zealous advocate and being concerned about the human consequences of a case, sometimes asking students to think about what it would take to create a legal system that would do justice.

Courses such as Schwartz's speak directly to the often contradictory pressures besetting contemporary legal practice. Such courses enable students to anticipate these problems, developing and debating strategies for resolving them. These courses are reflexive, asking students to look at and analyze their law school experience while it is going on, paying particular attention to the ways that legal education affects their transformation into lawyers. They can also aid students in developing the imagination to conceive various possibilities for legal practice—a theme found in law and literature courses or professional responsibility courses that incorporate significant reflection on literature.

Another example is Advanced Legal Ethics taught by Daisy Floyd, dean of the Mercer University School of Law. This course is unusual in that it directly addresses issues of meaning, professional identity, and quality of life in law school and in legal practice. Its intent is to mitigate law schools' potential negative effects on lawyers' sense of purpose. But it is also typical of the kind of course that has begun to appear in law schools in response to widespread concerns about the negative climates of law schools and the absence of support for students' development of a sense of positive meaning and ideals in relation to their future careers. Students in Floyd's Advanced Legal Ethics read and discuss essays on the history of American legal education, research on legal education, legal practice, and professions more broadly, including the concept of a profession as a calling. Many students also choose to read biographies of notable lawyers. They write several short, reflective papers, conduct a major research project, participate in a Web-based discussion, and attend a retreat. Lawyers and other professionals participate as guest speakers, both in classes and at the retreat.

In a report titled "The Development of Professional Identity in Law Students," Floyd describes the impact of this course on students, noting that students very much welcome the chance for strengthening their capacity for reflection and self-awareness. They experience law school as devaluing this capacity yet understand how important it is to finding meaning and purpose in law practice, as well as for forming and sustaining relationships. Students also value the opportunities the course provides to develop connections with each other and with practicing lawyers and other professionals. Students are reassured by finding that their reactions to law school are similar to those of other students and by hearing lawyers discuss their own successful searches for meaning in their professional lives and for achieving balance and integration of their professional and personal lives. Many students report that the course has helped them reclaim a sense of purpose, giving them renewed confidence in their decision to pursue a career in law (Floyd, 2002).

MODELING POSITIVE PROFESSIONAL IDEALS. On any law school campus, the faculty is influential in conveying what the profession stands for and what qualities are important for a member of that profession. They do this, often inadvertently, not only through explicit and implicit messages in their teaching but also by the values and standards they personally represent, as perceived by their students. An intellectual grasp of the complexity of professional roles, including lawyers' dual professional identity as advocates and officers of justice, is essential. But, as we noted earlier, professional identity concerns not only responses to conceptual questions such as, How should we think about the proper roles of lawyers? but also responses to more personal questions such as, What kind of lawyer do I want to be? What really matters to me in my work? Although answers to these more personal questions are informed by students' conceptions of lawyers' roles, they are also informed by their internalized images of lawyers or others they admire and wish to be like, relationships with people who exemplify professional ideals, and even experience with people who exemplify distasteful values and behavior that it is best to avoid.

The importance of these factors in shaping students' sense of professional identity raises the question of what kind of role models law schools provide. The 1996 report of the American Bar Association's Professionalism Committee called for law schools to focus greater attention on the significance of faculty as role models for law students' perceptions of lawyering, even to give greater weight to this role-model function in decisions about hiring and evaluating faculty. Of course, most law school faculty are not practicing lawyers. The report dealt with this tension by advocating for greater experience in practice among faculty (American Bar Association, 1996).

Thomas Morgan, in a commentary on the report, suggested a different solution. He argued that what is needed is not the modeling of specific legal tasks, or even of specific ways of dealing with practical ethical questions, but the modeling of the ideals of the profession. Morgan called for a focus not on the specific role as practicing attorney but on the faculty member as a model of some basic moral attitudes and values. "Each [faculty member] lives out in a very public way what it means to live a life in the law" (Morgan, 1997, p. 38). Faculty participation in pro bono programs seems a natural way to intensify these positive effects.

Faculty who teach clinics and other courses that are closely connected with practice have perhaps the greatest opportunities to show students what it means to practice law with integrity. Many of these faculty maintain active practices beyond their work in clinical courses. But all faculty in a real sense represent the profession to their students. Perhaps the most significant quality that faculty demonstrate over and over to students is how to use power and authority. From the first day of class onward, law students are vividly aware of the power that faculty wield over their future prospects. There are real analogies here to the attorney-client relationship that faculty ignore to the detriment of law school's formative mission. Inspiration is an important part of moral motivation, and faculty have many opportunities to inspire their students toward ethical and socially responsible practice, beginning at home, so to speak.

For most faculty, this is not a particularly salient part of their work. Some professors, however, do emphasize the importance of serving as exemplars of lawyer professionalism. And a few did mention its importance. A senior faculty member at an elite public law school, for example, said, "We know they aren't going to be law professors so we are not models in that sense. I think we do think of ourselves as being models of civility. I talk to my students about some of the cases I've done. In the course of talking to them I know they understand that I do volunteer work, I am engaged in the community, that I think it is a normal part of life, which is what lawyers do. My students know the work I do on boards or with the disabled."

In addition to faculty models, many law schools enrich the opportunities for positive experiences by inviting practicing attorneys and judges who are known for exceptional integrity and commitment to teach, to visit campus, talk about their work, and meet with students. Some campus speakers may provide inspiration about the value and meaning of law, even if they do not represent careers that most students will be likely to achieve. NYU's law school, for example, has recently hosted several U.S. Supreme Court Justices, as well as justices from the highest courts in several other countries. These visits from members of the profession are also valuable components of the ethical-social apprenticeship.

Engaging Responsibility: From Lawyering Courses to Clinical Education

Moving along the continuum of pedagogies that contribute to the formation of professional identity, we look now to examples of the "context-based education" that was the focus of Chapter Three. There we presented an overview of the pedagogies used in lawyering, moving from simulations that progressively approximate practice into the direct practice experience of clinical-legal courses. These teaching approaches, in principle, integrate the apprenticeship of practice with the apprenticeship of professional identity. The strategies for such integration range from bringing ethical reflection and the concerns of professionalism to bear in the simulation pedagogy of lawyering courses, to engagement with actual cases and clients in supervised externships and, most important, in clinical-legal education.

SIMULATED PRACTICE. While simulated practice can be an important site for developing skills and understandings essential for practice, it can also provide the setting for teaching the ethical demands of practice. Lawyering courses that use simulation of client interviewing and counseling, for example, permit the introduction of ethical as well as technical problems in a setting that mimics for the student the unpredictable challenges of actual practice. Issues of professionalism around client interaction and the establishment of trust and effective communication can become more salient and directly involved in simulation than in typical classroom settings. We observed examples of this use of simulation, in which students were provided first with critique and then with opportunities to try again elements of client interviewing and counseling that were the focus of the particular class.

It is instructive to note that in order to address similar issues of establishing trust and enhancing professionalism, medical education has been moving heavily into the use of simulation. Its effectiveness seems clear enough to justify increasing investment of resources and teaching time in simulation laboratories and like settings—a trend that has also become significant in schools of nursing. Although law schools do not share identical goals with the health professions, their experience is suggestive that increased use of the pedagogy of simulation is likely to prove a boon to teaching both practical skills and ethical-social development. Ethical engagement has practical dimensions that are more fully evident and can be examined and taught in conditions that simulate practice rather than in conventional classrooms. For this reason alone, there is affinity between the aims of the ethical-social apprenticeship and the pedagogies of practice.

LEGAL CLINICS. Beyond simulation, many students with whom we spoke described their experience working in law clinics as one of the highlights of their law school years. The primary aim of law clinics is to help students develop the wide range of skills they will need as practicing attorneys, including interviewing, negotiating, case planning, conducting trial advocacy, and legal drafting. But clinics also provide a human face for the practice of law. Because most clinics serve low-income clients, they provide students experience with populations who usually have little or no access to needed legal services. Students participating in clinics often speak of the satisfaction they get from working closely with underserved groups, as well as the illumination it provides about what is needed in order to realize the substantive ideals of legal practice.

Both faculty and students described clinics as an essential balance for the often abstract and depersonalized nature of legal analysis. As a third-year student remarked, "The model we are taught is intensely dehumanizing. You are taught to think of opinions without the people in them. That tells a lot about the type of lawyers the school creates. The advantage of the clinic is that you interact with real people." A clinical professor said, "When students go out to an unfamiliar environment, theory no longer comes in handy as much as do listening and empathy skills. Clinics try to re-sensitize students after being de-sensitized in law school." Or, as another student told us, "It reinforces my sense that I can serve people who really need my help. It saves my sanity when I want to drop out."

As we saw in the previous chapter, clinics can be key settings in which students learn to integrate not only knowledge and skill but the cognitive, practical, and ethical-social facets of lawyering as well. The experience of clinical-legal education, corroborated by the research of the Dreyfuses and Benner on the acquisition of practical expertise, points toward actual experience with clients as an essential catalyst for the full development of ethical engagement (Dreyfus, Dreyfus, and Athanasiou, 1986; Benner, Tanner, and Chesla, 1996). This position is bolstered by analysis of medical training. There, beyond the inculcation of knowledge and the simulation of skills, it proves to be the assumption of responsibility for patient outcomes that enables the student for the first time to fully enter and grasp the disposition of a physician.[6] In legal education, too, there is much to suggest that ethical engagement provides a pivotal aspect in the formation of lawyers.

A Truly Continuing Education

Seen in this light, a special value of the pedagogies of the ethical-social apprenticeship lies in their emphasis on ethical engagement, particularly responsibility to clients for justice. Through ever-closer approximations to actual practice, in a range of settings, students can be helped to develop insight into the full dimensions of the identity and purposes proper to a lawyer. This insight should propel them back into the cycle, toward an ever-deepening understanding of the law and the values of the profession that are the truest "continuing education" for the bar.

Thus the intentions embodied in the apprenticeship of professional identity and purpose have to precede and interpenetrate the learning of formal analytical knowledge in the first apprenticeship and the development of skilled practice in the second. To neglect formation in the larger public purposes for which the profession stands and their meaning for individual practitioners is to risk educating mere legal technicians for hire in the place of genuine professionals. Therefore, the goal of professional education cannot be analytical knowledge alone or, perhaps, even predominantly. Neither can it be analytical knowledge plus merely skillful performance. Rather, the goal has to be holistic: to advance students toward genuine expertise as practitioners who can enact the profession's highest levels of skill in the service of its defining purposes.

The situational character of practical expertise strongly suggests that one essential goal of professional schools must be to form practitioners who are aware of what it takes to become competent in their chosen domain and to equip them with the reflective capacity and motivation to pursue genuine expertise. They must become "metacognitive" about their own learning, to use the psychologists' term. To accomplish this, the overall educational context must be a formative one that can encourage students toward entering and understanding the meaning and purposes of their particular professional community. To accomplish this ambitious task, law schools need practices of assessment that can give students and faculty regular and reliable assessments of their progress. Assessment adequate to enhancing such a coordinated educational effort is the topic of the chapter that follows.

NOTES

1. Some of the important attempts of the past two decades to analyze the major shifts in legal practice and their bearing on legal professionalism include Galanter and Palay (1991), Nelson, Trubek, and Solomon (1992), Kronman (1993), Glendon (1994), Rhode (2000), and Heinz, Nelson, Sandefur, and Laumann (2005).

2. See, for example, Landsman and McNeel (2004); Hartwell (1990), Willging and Dunn (1981); and Tapp and Levine (1974).

3. See Landsman and McNeel (2004), Willging and Dunn (1981), Husted (1978), Givner and Hynes (1983), Self and Olivarez (1993), Self, Olivarez, and Baldwin (1994), and Bebeau and Brabeck (1987).

4. For example, see Moliterno (2003).

5. See, for example, Rhode and Luban (2004).

6. For a suggestive ethnographic account from the context of the United Kingdom, see Sinclair (1999).

ASSESSMENT AND HOW
TO MAKE IT WORK

EACH DECEMBER AND MAY, a familiar scene unfolds in law schools throughout the country: seventy to eighty students seated in a tiered lecture hall write their name, the name and number of the course, and the professor's name on the front cover of their blue examination book. The professor, without speaking, slowly makes his way up the center aisle, passing out bundles of examinations alternately from right to left. It is the only examination the students will take in the course. The class is mostly silent. The tension is palpable, for the students realize that their grades in this and a few other concurrent first-year courses will play a pivotal role in the course of their future legal careers.

The examination is composed of a series of fact-based hypothetical problems that require students to analyze hypothetical cases by identifying issues, discerning fact patterns, and applying relevant statute and case law. It is the preeminent instrument by which faculty determine whether students have mastered the ability to think like lawyers, and law school professors devote countless hours to creating test questions and grading student responses. When we asked faculty to comment on the nature and purpose of examinations, they had relatively little to say in the way of critical comment. Most lauded the value of case-based essay examinations. Commented one professor, they bring to bear "fundamental perspectives on how you think about the law."

In the first year of law school, the decisive assessment is the set of three-hour essay examinations that conclude each of the doctrinal courses. Even in law schools that have introduced formative and practice examinations during the course, sometimes accompanied by useful feedback, the three-hour analytical essay is still the preferred and predominant mode of assessing students' ability to think like lawyers. In our visits to law schools, we met professors who supplement the problem-based essays with objective questions—the former testing the depth and the latter the breadth of students' knowledge.

We spoke with a number of professors who voiced concern over the relative infrequency with which students are evaluated in the first year, and a small number of schools require that grades of first-year students be based on more than one test. In isolated cases, faculty give graded midterms at their own discretion and offer practice exams or other non-graded assessments, such as in-class quizzes and take-home exercises, to help first-year students become familiar with exam formats and to give them at least some feedback during the fall term. A number of faculty post old exams for students to use as study aids. During our visits, a handful of faculty members noted that "exam-taking skills are learnable skills" and described ways in which they assist students in acquiring these skills. But all of these concerns and practices are exceptional. None is part of a coordinated effort to work out the best use of assessment to improve the learning of law students. So our purpose in this chapter is to address the important issue of assessing law students' development as professionals and to propose ways of improving the process.

The strengths and weaknesses we have noted in law schools' organization of the apprenticeships of conceptual knowledge, practical competence, and professional identity and purpose are directly reflected in the examinations and assessments that law students are required to take throughout their legal training. What teachers value—what they deem important and essential for students to learn—can be ascertained most directly by what they assess—what they require students to know and be able to do. In this sense, a careful examination of the assessments that law students (or any students for that matter) are required to take during their formal preparation reveals what the professors value. Not surprisingly, in looking at these assessments, we found significant slippage between the knowledge and abilities emphasized by the schools and those prized by the profession at large.

The institutional context shows powerful bias in favor of academic values, as we have noted in earlier chapters. In the matter of student assessment, the competitive atmosphere is intensified by the practice of grading first-year examinations on the curve. The danger in using inter-student competition as a primary motivation is that in a situation in which, by deliberate plan, all cannot excel, the school faces an endemic problem of retaining student interest and effort after the first cut, which is decisive, is made at the end of the first year.

Without the significant balance provided by other kinds of motivation, especially the desire to hone one's craft and serve clients responsibly that the practical and the ethical-social apprenticeships emphasize, we fear that much of the pedagogical effort of law professors may be producing less result that one would wish. This culture of competitiveness is driven by more than student motivation, of course. The intense competition among schools for prestige and advantage seems to have led to ever-greater emphasis on standardized testing as the key admission criterion—a trend that may be threatening the law profession's own mission of access to the profession for underrepresented groups.[1]

In this chapter, we look closely at assessment in legal education—how it is done, how it might be done. We look especially closely at the way in which conceptual knowledge—the focus of the first phase of legal education—is assessed. Although we are aware that law schools employ a variety of other methods of assessing legal knowledge, especially beyond the required courses of the first year, we concentrate on this assessment because it directly and indirectly structures so much of the rest of legal education.

We next consider assessment in other professional schools, as well as outstanding efforts within legal education, and we propose a logic of assessment: an integrated process of forming competent professionals. In our proposal, we build on the work of the Best Practices for Legal Education project, which makes valuable suggestions in this area (Stuckey and others, 2006). Then focusing on the practical and ethical-social apprenticeships, respectively, we use the proposal to explore how well-thought-out assessment can and does function to carry out this formative purpose. We conclude with a discussion of the value of institutionalizing a culture of intentional learning throughout the school in order to make legal education a more integrated and effective preparation for entry into the profession.

Assessing Conceptual Knowledge

The end-of-semester essay examination holds a privileged, virtually iconic place in legal education. This most important and uniform practice of assessment used in law school is, in the language of educational theory, entirely summative: although it measures achievement, its after-the-fact character forecloses the possibility of giving meaningful feedback to the student about progress in learning. In contrast, formative assessment provides feedback in order to support opportunities to improve learning as the course proceeds. Heavy reliance on summative assessment also means that, by precluding useful feedback about the students' learning, the instructor loses a basis for midcourse correction in teaching. Reliance on summative evaluation provides no navigational assistance, as it were, until the voyage is over. Neither student nor faculty learning is likely to be optimized by such procedures.

However, as we have noted, law school faculties are heavily invested in this system. Most instructors spend long hours at the end of each semester laboriously grading each of the exams from their large first-year sections. Perhaps not surprisingly then, many law school faculty are deeply convinced of the value of this assessment procedure.

The perspective of many of the students we met in various schools, however, was often quite different. Students' comments about assessment in their first year of law school often expressed puzzlement, frustration, and anguish. A recurring theme in their comments, striking in its frequency, was that they were not being tested on what they studied for and what they knew. Many felt that the testing was unfair, counterproductive, demoralizing, and arbitrary. Students saw little or no relation between their classroom experience and the end-of-semester examinations, or between learning to be a good lawyer and doing well on the exams—a criticism that has been leveled at the cognitive apprenticeship in many professional and graduate schools. As our earlier chapters showed, law schools' heavy emphasis on academic training, in contrast to the education in settings of practice typical of preparation in the health professions, heightens the likelihood of a disparity between learning to be a law student and learning to be a lawyer.

A number of students complained that the quality and quantity of their studying was unrelated to their performance on the final examination. They claim to have had little opportunity to practice and hone the skills that were tested and, in the absence of feedback during the semester, no basis on which to gauge whether they were mastering the material or making adequate progress toward the desired proficiencies. The following comments by students in our focus groups are typical. Regarding feedback, one student said, "We don't get a lot of feedback. The way success is measured is antiquated and irrelevant to the process." Another commented, "There is poor feedback about student learning. Students get their grades at the end of the semester, and there is no way of knowing how they are doing in the course."

Equally aversive to students was the competitive atmosphere engendered by the widespread practice in legal education of grading on the curve. Commented one student at a highly selective school, "Polarization among students rises after grades are released. The intellectual engagement suffered a great deal after grades . . . we lost the most valuable aspect of law school—learning. They do it—try to hurt students—on purpose." Finally, several students bemoaned the negative effects on motivation that grading on the curve engenders: "I study significantly less this semester. If you do a lot of work, you get the same grade as someone who doesn't. It's discouraging that no matter how hard you work, it doesn't seem to count."

These comments suggest a good deal of negative reaction to the way the first year of legal learning is typically structured and assessed. The thrust and pattern of these statements are clear. Students report that they are not provided a chance to practice what will actually be tested, that they do not get feedback during the course of the semester to gauge how they might do when the day of reckoning arrives, that the expected relationship between hard work and reward is absent, and that the intensely competitive atmosphere militates against a cooperative learning environment. The very format of the assessment appears counterproductive and profoundly at variance with what lawyers do on the job. How often, for example, are practicing lawyers required, in three hours, with no access to relevant statute and case law, to analyze a case? The impression is one of considerable frustration, of effort expended to no avail, of talented learners with long histories of academic success trying their hardest, of profound puzzlement without recourse.

It is noteworthy that these and similar statements come not only from marginal students but from students who made the cut at highly selective universities with eminent teaching faculties. One might well argue that this is the students' fault. After all, some of them, at least, know the right things and acquire the relevant knowledge and skills. But such a reaction misses an important message. The point is that these are real perceptions, and we have no reason to believe that they were not arrived at in good faith; conversely, it should not be inferred from this that there is something inherently misguided about either the content or substance of the first-year final exams. In fact, the students directed their criticism not so much at the content of the examination *as* examination but at what preceded—rather, what did not precede—the exam. Because there was only one real test, assessment in the first year neither served to inform students of their progress nor provided feedback to improve instruction.

Although during the past fifteen years, many schools have supplemented the end-of-semester summative assessment with other measurement instruments, the one-shot, high-stakes exam regime is still very much in evidence in most law schools. Moreover, the Internet is now awash with examples of first-year examinations and even graded student responses to virtually any first-year course, so that student complaints, of which we heard many, about the total absence of any sense of what was expected of them are not entirely justified. But surfing the Internet for guidance is no substitute for constructive and critical feedback on a student's own work by the person or persons who will be evaluating that work.

These student observations help fill in the more general findings of the Law School Survey of Student Engagement (LSSE), which found that a significant minority of students "never" receive "prompt written or oral feedback from faculty members" (Center for Postsecondary Research, 2005, p. 7). This suggests that law faculty are not, as a whole, committed to timely feedback with the intensity that the development of student competence demands. The student comments also resonate with much of the legal education literature, where the testing system during the first year has been criticized for privileging speed and an unreflective manipulation of legal doctrine, for providing insufficient practice and feedback, and for undue reliance on a single examination format. As far back as 1924, Ben Wood wrote of growing disenchantment with the three-hour essay exam at the end of the semester:

> The spectacle of a student trying to record an adequate sampling of his gains from a four-hour course of several months' duration in the English prose which he can produce in three hours under the conditions and circumstances of college examination week, and the correlative spectacle of the college professor passing judgment on that student on the sole basis of the product of those three hours of writing, seem, on *a priori* grounds alone, quite incompatible with current ideals of educational measurement and administration. (Wood, 1924, p. 226)

Writing in 1989, Phillip Kissam, in what many consider the best extended essay on the subject, voiced similar objections. But easily the most severe criticism of first-year assessment is that of Talbot D'Alemberte, former president of the American Bar Association, who asked rhetorically, "Is there any education theorist who would endorse a program that has students take a class for a full semester or a full year and get a single examination at the end?" He went on to comment, "People who conduct that kind of educational program are not trying to educate" (D'Alemberte, 1990, p. 52).

Apparently, D'Alemberte did not feel it necessary to spell out the clear implications of his remarks that the purpose of such a configuration of pedagogy and assessment is to sort. This indictment by a respected leader in legal education (D'Alemberte is also former dean of the Florida State University School of Law) provides an easy segue into a discussion of the continually vexing and controversial issue of grading first-year performance.

Grading on the Curve: The First-Year Evaluation

In stark contrast to graduate and professional education in most fields today, first-year performance at the majority of law schools is graded on the curve. In most law schools a predetermined and rigid distribution of A's, B's, C's, and so on, is the norm, regardless of the mean ability of the students. The practice is the source of considerable historical and current debate in legal education.

Other forms of graduate and professional education are more likely to use what is known as criterion-referenced grading—that is, an absolute standard of performance determines who will receive A's and who will receive other grades; this is the polar opposite of the current law school practice of evaluation. There are noteworthy exceptions to this norm. Yale Law School, for example, grades first-year courses on a pass-fail basis. When coupled with the school's encouragement of students to enroll in introductory clinical courses in the second semester, this approach moves away from the typical highly competitive focus on academic grades and promotes a broader exposure to knowledge, skills, and attitudes of the profession. Of course, Yale has the advantage of admitting only the most academically qualified students. But the same is true of all the other leading schools.

Underlying these two approaches to grading—on the curve and criterion-referenced—are two rarely stated but fundamentally opposed philosophies about the purpose of assessment in professional education. Those who champion grading on the curve assume that legal education largely serves a sorting function. The intent is to identify the best and the brightest in legal theory, analysis, and scholarship. On the one hand, the benefits to society, it is argued, in identifying, recognizing, and rewarding those few who will carry on the tradition of legal scholarship as professors, scholars, and jurists are obvious, and to many they outweigh the negatives associated with this grading scheme. On the other hand, the implicit pedagogical philosophy underlying criterion-referenced assessment is that the fundamental purpose of professional education is not sorting but producing as many individuals proficient in legal reasoning and competent practice as possible.

Grading on the curve is often coupled with a tacit belief that there is little possibility of doing much more than sorting in the first place, since there is little possibility of raising the performance of all or most students. The sorting function, in other words, is consistent with what many faculty and some students believe to be the underlying distribution of student ability. Commented one faculty member, "I should have about

10 percent A's. If I don't, then there is something wrong with the exam. The students tend to curve themselves." These oppositions of fundamental perspectives about education explain why rational debate on the merits of assessment can be so difficult to achieve.

As we have noted, like so much else in contemporary legal education, grading on the curve is traceable to a practice begun at Harvard in the 1870s—the use of first-year tests and their resulting rankings to decide editorial positions on its law review (Kissam, 1989). It was not long before assessments, and the student rankings that they facilitate, also came to be used as an essential aid for potential employers in their hiring decisions. This essentially external function of assessment has come to dominate highly selective law schools throughout the country. Like many other areas of legal education, it is a source of considerable disagreement and debate. But so powerful is the underlying belief in the value of sorting that faculty will expend considerable time and effort to calibrate student performance, often making distinctions with decimal-point precision. This precision is illusory, however, because conditions of testing on any given day, individual differences in test-taking skills, and peculiarities of different raters all introduce unreliability into the results, making them less precise than faculty may realize as valid and reliable indicators of knowledge and skill.

In support of the practice, some argue that it is unfair to students and potential employers to gloss over differences in student preparation and proficiency under a criterion-referenced grading system, or even worse, under an ungraded, pass-fail umbrella—two quite different approaches to assessment that many faculty tend to run together. As one administrator at a regional law school commented, "Pass-fail leads students not to work hard. No grades, no standards. When students must make decisions about time allocation, they do what's needed to 'only pass.'" This conflation of pass-fail with criterion-referenced grading sets up an invidious either-or choice that distorts the real range of assessment possibilities.

A second argument is that grading on the curve serves to identify, early in the process, those who will obviously not succeed in law school—a function useful to both the student and the institution, as the cost in faculty time and student frustration is enormous. (It should be noted in passing, however, that an argument can be made that a criterion-referenced approach to assessment could accomplish this purpose better than the present system and without its attendant negative side effects.)

A third argument of those who favor grading on the curve is that any alternative grading scheme may well lead to such undesirable practices as the awarding of blanket A's by some, B's by others, and so on. Or perhaps even more pernicious, abandoning the practice of grading on the curve might well lead to the rampant grade inflation that infects student evaluation in virtually all of higher education. In practice, this third argument seems the most important objection. But it does not stand up to refutation: in other fields, such as medical education, there is no evidence that using criterion-referenced grading instead of grading on the curve harms either student learning or faculty morale.

The Alternative: Criterion-Referenced Assessment

Defenders of criterion-referenced assessment can make a powerful argument in reply to these objections. The criterion-referenced approach to assessment and evaluation specifies certain points on a numerical scale of quality, above which students receive one grade and below which they receive another. So, for example, a 100-point scale might award A's to any student who obtains a score of 94 or above, B's to anyone who scores between 86 and 93, inclusive, and so on. No predetermined distribution of grades is required. If a particular class of students is unusually able, resulting in, for example, 40 percent A's, then those are the grades. Those who support criterion-referenced grading would say that grades should reflect students' absolute level of accomplishment. They would point out that superior performance in legal argument and analysis by an individual student can and should be judged on the inherent quality of what is produced, not on the basis of what other students have produced.

But this eminently sensible argument encounters some serious difficulties of its own. Perhaps the most serious criticism leveled at criterion-referenced assessment is the difficulty in getting faculty to agree on standards of performance. One professor's A is another's B, or even C. Some critics of criterion-referenced grading argue that, although most law school professors can agree, more or less, on the rank ordering of student responses, they will differ markedly on judgments about absolute levels of performance. However, although a long history of assessment research on rank orderings supports the notion that faculty will agree on performance rankings to some reasonable degree, actual data on the contention that faculty cannot agree on standards of performance is less well established. In fact, there has been considerable progress in the art and science of rater calibration. Professional test developers now routinely achieve impressive levels of rater agreement on standards of performance in many different contexts, from standards for high school graduation to standards for professional licensure in a wide variety of occupations.

Writing in the *Bar Examiner,* Susan M. Case (2004), who directs testing for the National Conference of Bar Examiners, noted how much more attention medical education has paid to advances in testing, and indeed to advances in educational knowledge generally, than the legal academy. Case pointed out that "most medical schools in the U.S. and abroad have an office of medical education led by several Ph.D.- and master's-level staff" who routinely help staff curriculum committees, "working with faculty on assessment of their students," while also conducting research that appears in journals and at international conferences. Case went on to note the effectiveness in medical schools of national, standardized exams. These exams are created by the same organization that develops licensure exams—the National Board of Medical Examiners. The system's virtue is that it allows norms to be developed "that allow a professor to compare local student performance with performance in other schools," as well as norms for "identifying students at risk for failing the licensing exam." Because the licensing exams are administered in staged phases, spread through the curriculum, this means that such assessment can play a formative, as well as a summative role, so that it directly strengthens medical schools' ability to develop better student learning outcomes (p. 29).

Using Assessment as Formative Pedagogy

The current practice in assessment of first-year law courses raises a fundamental question: What should be the purpose of assessment in the preparation of legal professionals? From our observations, we believe that assessment should be understood as a coordinated set of formative practices that, by providing important information about the students' progress in learning to both students and faculty, can strengthen law schools' capacity to develop competent and responsible lawyers. As we have seen repeatedly in previous chapters, studies of how expertise develops across a variety of domains are unanimous in emphasizing the importance of feedback as the key means by which teachers and learners can improve performance. The kinds of feedback needed vary with purpose and with the domain and ability being trained. And the tools that prove most effective in conveying information about actual performance vary in similar ways.

Using Assessments Appropriate to Developing Expertise

The research on how expertise develops is highly relevant to legal education. This research implies that the apparatus of grading that is commonly used for summative assessment in academic settings is less effective as a formative tool for training in settings of practice. In these contexts, where formative feedback is all-important and specific information can be more valuable than overall judgments of relative competence, other methods of conveying information about student development prove crucial. For example, in medical training it is common to find schools using standard academic testing for assessing students' knowledge of basic science. In assessing clinical competence, however, a larger variety of methods is employed, emphasizing narrative, specific task analysis, and other approaches. In medical education, the shift in assessment measures is dictated by the change from classroom pedagogy to instruction provided in settings of practice. Effective learning depends on the student's negotiating a fundamental change in perspective. The student must shift from intellectual operations on abstract, context-free concepts, which are familiar from nearly two decades' experience in school-like settings, to the much less familiar role of apprentice physician. The same development is demanded of law students entering lawyering or clinical-legal courses.

As we saw in Chapter Three's discussion of current understanding of how professional expertise is acquired, learning to practice a complex craft follows a documented progression. The movement, however, is the opposite of the common belief that learners simply move from concrete examples toward gradually more abstract conceptions. Instead, the learner acquires mature skill by moving from a distanced manipulation of clearly delineated elements of a situation according to formal rules toward involved behavior based on an accumulation of concrete experience. The evolution here works through a gradually developing ability to see analogies, to recognize new situations as similar to whole remembered patterns.

In learning lawyering skills, rules and procedures are useful scaffolds for enabling beginners to begin to function in a variety of practice situations. Following a set of rules allows for a gradual accumulation of experience. But in order to progress, the student has to attend to features of the context, even events that occur outside the rules. Whereas in the classroom, learning typically places concepts first and their application second, this is not the order in learning to practice. Rather, in practice situations, a good understanding of context is the necessary prerequisite for knowing what knowledge to apply. The rigid rules followed by beginners are simply temporary substitutes—the "training wheels"—taking the place of the competent practitioner's judgment. Expert judgment requires not the separation but the blending of knowledge and skill. In practice, knowledge, skill, and ethical comportment are literally interdependent: a practitioner cannot employ one without involving the others at the same time. The evidence suggests that in effective programs of clinical learning in many professional fields, the key is to use analytical thinking to foster, rather than replace, the cultivation of analogical and practical reasoning.

The interdependence of knowledge, skill, and sense of purpose in professional practical reasoning is difficult to teach or assess through the usual academic techniques, which focus on procedures and techniques out of context. Academic learning proceeds through specialization and the separation of concepts from contexts. Practical judgment depends on complex traditions of living, which can only come alive through apprenticeship experiences with exemplars of inherited judgment and skill. Thus the apprenticeship of skill takes on aspects of the critical apprenticeship of professional identity and ethical meaning. For this reason, professional schools cannot directly teach students to be competent in any and all situations; rather, the essential goal of professional schools must be to form practitioners who are aware of what it takes to become competent in their chosen domain and to equip them with the reflective capacity and motivation to pursue genuine expertise. They must become "metacognitive" about their own learning, to use the psychologists' term. This is why effective means of formative assessment are so crucial for training professionals.

Assessing Lawyering Skills

In law schools, the means of assessing the skills of practice mirror the wide array of pedagogical practices represented in lawyering and clinical courses. This diversity of assessment procedures can be seen as a strength, as reliance on a single assessment format, especially given the inherent complexity and diversity of legal practice, would be both impractical and ill-advised. Assessment of the lawyering apprenticeship in law schools, when it is done well, is closer to good practice as understood by experts in the field of assessment than the summative regime in use for the cognitive apprenticeship. But law schools usually do not give significant academic weight to courses in legal writing, lawyering, or clinical education. This tends to undercut, as does the competitive climate, the seriousness of the assessment that students receive in these courses. Although doctrinal courses in every year count significantly toward students' overall academic scores, the same is rarely true of courses that fall mostly within the apprenticeship of practice.

Although there have been intimations of concern as far back as the early 1920s, the push for assessing the lawyering apprenticeship in legal education and attaching weight to those assessments reached law schools in a quite public way in 1979 with the publication of the American Bar Association-sponsored report on lawyer competency and the role of law schools. With the 1992 MacCrate report, the areas needing attention were given a sort of canonical form. The report highlights the dearth of serious and systematic attention to the assessment of both the lawyering and the identity and purpose apprenticeships of legal education. It delineates in some detail the fundamental lawyering skills that characterize the day-to-day practice of law: problem solving, legal analysis and reasoning, legal research, factual investigation, oral and written communication, client counseling, negotiation, litigation and dispute resolution, and organization and management of legal work (American Bar Association, 1992). A set of skills involving the recognition and resolution of ethical dilemmas pertains more directly to the ethical-social apprenticeship.

Since MacCrate, this complex constellation of competencies has been reflected in the growing number and variety of courses, often using different forms of assessment, that are available to students in the second and third years of law school. In schools that offer or require clinical placements, for example, assessment includes faculty evaluation of student reports of their experience, as well as evaluative reports to the faculty by those in charge of the clinical setting.

This attention to written products of students' clinical work and to the narrative reports on their performance by faculty points to a promising approach to assessing the complex of skills of practice that has been relatively underused in legal education, as compared with other domains of higher education—student portfolios. Virtually all law schools already maintain some elements of student portfolios in the form of student files that typically contain, at a minimum, first-year essays and student grades throughout the three years of formal training. But these summary files are just that: summaries that may conceal more than they reveal. A fuller student portfolio that encompasses students' entire formal program would provide detailed information on student competencies in the form of research papers, briefs, clinical setting reports, clinical supervisory evaluations, various assessments of client counseling and negotiation, and perhaps even videotapes of actual student performance in a variety of lawyering skills.

It should be obvious, however, that with the partial exception of legal writing, assessing lawyering capacities is not amenable to any single assessment format. Proficiency in negotiating and interviewing clients, for example, cannot be adequately gauged by tests or by having students write about these tasks. Sound assessment must include an evaluation of students actually performing such tasks, perhaps in simulated environments. Because for the most part, methods for these evaluations have not been well elaborated or shared across institutions, observations are less standardized and ritualized than other forms of assessment, but this is not a necessary feature of observational assessments.

This possibility is evident in medical training, which provides a bold contrast with legal education, not only in its greater emphasis on clinical teaching but also in the seriousness with which it takes assessment of clinical skills—and even assessment of professionalism. This begins early in medical school, as students learn to take medical histories and perform physical examinations. These skills, along with associated professionalism issues, are assessed using actors serving in the role of "standardized patients" and other forms of simulation. Assessment of skills intensifies during the clerkship years, which represent the last two years of medical school, and continues throughout residency training. Methods at these more advanced levels can include simulations of various kinds but also include direct observation of interactions with patients. At the residency level, the Accreditation Council for Graduate Medical Education has expanded the range and diversity of the skills assessed to include a wide array of technical and interpersonal skills, assessed through observation, standardized patients, rating forms completed by supervisors, cooperating nurses and patients, and various other approaches. This differentiated approach has been evident in the Carnegie Foundation's study of medical education, currently in progress, and is also noted in *Best Practices for Legal Education* (Stuckey and others, 2006).

Medical education's well-elaborated set of assessment approaches has resulted from a trend over the past two decades toward accompanying clinical training with ongoing assessment rather than a year-end, make-or-break evaluation of proficiency. At its best, this kind of clinical education achieves a thorough merging and integration of training and assessment. Some law clinics aim toward comparable integration of assessment with deep learning in role and show considerable success in achieving it. However, significant work is still needed if legal education is to establish widely used, highly valid procedures for assessing the skills and qualities of the practical and ethical-social apprenticeships.

Certainly the possibilities are there; much of the expertise has already been developed for better integrating teaching and assessment in clinical-legal education and lawyering courses in ways that come closer to the integrated pattern of the best clinical medical training. What has been lacking is precisely the institutional intentionality to develop and mandate these approaches.

In all these areas of the practical apprenticeship, the issue of cost is the unspoken obstacle. Compared to the efficiency of the large case-dialogue classroom, the formats that lend themselves to clinical and lawyering activities, including legal writing, are highly labor-intensive. Giving major value to students' performance in these areas through summative evaluations, as well as useful formative measures of learning, would substantially raise the per-student cost of law school. However, it is hard to see how serious efforts to integrate the skills of practice with legal knowledge can go forward without willingness to incur higher student-faculty ratios and, with these, higher unit costs. It is clear that the public and the profession want to see movement in the direction of more serious attention to training-for-practice. For a variety of reasons, movement toward more intensive (and expensive) forms of instruction will pose major challenges to many law schools. However, the pedagogical gains are likely to be significant on both the level of learning and of student motivation.

Assessing Ethical-Social Development

We noted in the chapter on professional responsibility (Chapter Four) that law schools practice two more or less distinct forms of teaching for the apprenticeship of professional identity and purpose. The first comes under the general umbrella of the Model Rules, which govern the ethical issues, such as attorney-client relationship and conflict of interest; these are central to the practice of law (American Bar Association 2004). As such, assessment of students' knowledge of the Model Rules and the circumstances under which they apply is relatively straightforward and is not materially different from the assessment of other standard courses, such as contracts and civil procedure, that make up the cognitive apprenticeship. This is not to imply that the Model Rules are simple and straightforward. Quite the contrary. They require significant skill in interpretation. However, there is near-universal agreement that knowledge of legal ethics and procedural justice, as distinct from larger issues of substantive justice and social good, are entirely proper topics for assessment, both during the first year of law school and beyond. In fact, failure to include these topics as essential components of legal education and assessment would be viewed by most as a serious failure of legal pedagogy. However, as we have noted, this approach to the assessment of the moral apprenticeship can often amount to little more than a variant of the legal reasoning characteristic of the cognitive apprenticeship.

Assessing the more complex goal of students' professionalism or ability to embody good ethical and professional judgment is more difficult to achieve, and the very idea of developing professionalism remains contentious, as we saw in the previous chapter. Significant evidence from medical schools, however, suggests that some basic aspects of professionalism can be assessed and that, moreover, such assessments yield highly significant predictions about which students are likely to exhibit ethically problematic behaviors as practitioners.[2] Part of the problem in legal education is resistance to the idea that it is really possible to assess students' disposition toward matters around the issue of moral character. As we have observed, many faculty and students are deeply skeptical of, if not outright hostile to, the notion of teaching values or moral character. It follows that attempts to assess these attributes would be intensely resisted, even aside from the inherent difficulty in doing so. It should be noted, however, that an informal system for assessing moral conduct and character already exists, not only in law schools but throughout education generally. All of higher education contains codes of conduct such as honor codes that, if transgressed, would be cause for dismissal. The historical prohibitions against plagiarism, cheating, and misrepresentation are all but universal.

These difficulties notwithstanding, healthy debate about how professional responsibility should be formally included and assessed in legal education curricula is a legitimate issue for discussion, as the MacCrate report attests. This report's list of important lawyering skills includes explicit mention of several aspects of the apprenticeship of identity and purpose. It specifies that lawyers should know (1) the nature and sources of ethical standards, (2) the means by which ethical standards are enforced, and (3) the processes for recognizing and resolving ethical dilemmas. But the report does not stop here. It also includes a statement of the "fundamental values of the profession" that encompass "competent representation," "striving to promote justice, fairness, and morality," "striving to improve the profession," and "professional self-development" (American Bar Association, 1992, pp. 140–141). A systematic way of assessing these values has yet to emerge, although the profession itself already has safeguards against violations of competent representation. But attempts to gauge inclination to strive for justice, fairness, and morality and to participate in improving the profession and one's professional development remain highly contested issues.

But perhaps this is to pose the question in the wrong way. Instead of asking how one can be sure a student has the right character and dispositions, we might ask what kinds of pedagogies and assessment procedures are effective in developing professional dispositions and good judgment. As we have seen, critical analysis of students' own experience in both simulated and actual situations of practice, including expert feedback, is a pedagogical process with enormous power—power that in most schools is still only partially tapped. Here again, cross-professional comparison indicates that although difficult, it is not impossible to systematically provide feedback to students about both their understanding of and performance with regard to the ethical norms of the profession. The analogous clinical training in the health professions and for the clergy offers useful models.

Formative education comes about through guided experience or performance—in essence, learning by doing. Ethical formation, as we argued in the previous chapter, comes about in the same way. The key components are close working relationships between students and faculty, opportunity to take responsibility for professional interventions and outcomes, and timely feedback. Unless law schools can provide the proper opportunities, however, little such formation is likely to occur.

We noted earlier that the ways in which faculty assess students reflect, in a very direct way, the knowledge, dispositions, and competencies that the faculty values. So it is with the assessments of learning in the apprenticeship of ethical and professional responsibility. An increased emphasis on instruction in and assessment of professionalism in legal education sends an important message to students. Often this might involve simply maintaining high standards for conscientious and respectful work in clinics—issues that are uncontroversial from an ethical point of view. Even when the questions being confronted are more complex and subject to multiple interpretations, however, teaching for and assessing professionalism need not entail the imposition of individual faculty members' own moral views on their students. Nor must all students agree on what the "right" or ethically defensible behavior is in ambiguous or complicated situations. Rather, the infusion of ethical concerns into teaching and assessment in legal education conveys a profoundly important message that, as future stewards of the profession, students must figure out for themselves an ethically defensible approach to their work. The message is also that, as officers of the court and as citizens, lawyers should not ignore the larger consequences of their professional behavior and conduct.

As we have argued in earlier chapters, the context in which they learn must encourage students to grasp the meaning and purposes of their particular professional community. Thus the apprenticeship of professional responsibility has to precede and interpenetrate the analytical knowledge and the development of skilled practice. Legal analysis alone is only a partial foundation for developing professional competence and identity. It is not enough even to develop analytical knowledge plus merely skillful performance. The goal has to be integration into a whole greater than the sum of its parts. Assessment of students' learning and growth needs to be consistent with the goal of this integration: professional judgment and the ability to continue to learn and develop toward the highest standards of the legal profession. These broader aspects of professional development can be assessed in ways that can help students, but the assessment must take place in role rather than in the more detached mode that law-of-lawyering courses typically foster.

The teaching and learning that make up the practical and ethical-social apprenticeships in law require the same kind of transition in perspective from observer to actor demanded by clinical experiences in medical and nursing schools. These ideas are not foreign to contemporary legal education, as our examination of the "lawyering" curriculum at schools such as CUNY and NYU documented, but they are still not central to students' experience at most schools. The LSSSE, for example, found that even among third-year law students, participation in any kind of clinical or pro bono project for academic credit was confined to about half the sample (Center for Postsecondary Research, 2005).

In the case of NYU, we saw that simulation of legal tasks in context—what the NYU law faculty like to call working in role—is the core pedagogical practice in lawyering courses. Learning goals are made explicit. Students learn to think critically about practice as they develop legal arguments, analyze facts, interview and counsel clients, negotiate a transaction or a dispute, mediate a claim, and plead a motion before a simulated court. Developing professional identity is explicitly involved as well: students are assessed on their adherence to the school's Code of Lawyering Standards and Responsibilities, which is modeled on the American Bar Association's Code of Ethics. Students receive feedback on progress toward each of the learning goals. The feedback takes a number of forms, including videotapes of simulated interviews and extensive coaching on legal writing. Furthermore, the feedback addresses the learning of all three apprenticeships—cognitive, practical, and ethical-social. Doctrinal teaching goes on informally as students engage the simulated cases, so that assignments used to teach practical lawyering skills also reinforce their learning of legal analysis. Students routinely receive feedback about their facility with legal knowledge and reasoning as they try out the complex role of attorney. Students are also taught to work in teams, in part, to offset some of the competitive pressures of the first year and, in part, to emphasize the need to engage standards of client and public service, collectively. Feedback on their performance in these group processes also helps shape the students' understanding of what it means to act as responsible lawyers.

The combination of pedagogies and assessment strategies used in such lawyering courses represents what is called intentional learning. The term *intentional learning* comes from cognitive research on the qualities of effective learners. What is meant are educational practices that help students become self-conscious about and self-directed in their own learning (Bereiter and Scardamalia, 1989). Teaching for intentional learning aims explicitly at enabling students to become aware of what they are doing as they learn the law. Based on research that suggests that students learn more effectively when they become "metacognitive," or aware of what they are trying to accomplish (rather than just trying to pass a test, for example), this kind of teaching adds an important dimension to the usual aims of law school classes. Such pedagogy pays direct attention to student learning through devices such as making goals explicit and coaching toward these goals; formative assessment is then linked to them. Mary Huber and Pat Hutchings point out that, because they have gained a grasp of their own processes and goals, "intentional learners . . . know how to regulate and focus their efforts as learners—how to make the most of study time, to practice new skills, to ask probing questions. They are, if you will, on the road to lifelong learning" (Huber and Hutchings, 2004, p. 6).

Toward Institutional Intentionality

Faculty benefit from understanding how effective their teaching is toward achieving their goals for student learning. When teachers have such self-awareness, educational researchers tell us, it is because they use assessment procedures to promote continuous, intentional learning in students. Indeed, student development toward intentional learning is significantly enhanced when faculty understand this goal and seek to shape their pedagogical practices toward it. As the example of the NYU lawyering course suggests, promoting self-aware student learning requires the combination of explicit learning goals and carefully calibrated assessment strategies. Putting these two kinds of assessment together—linking feedback *to* students with feedback *from* students about how well they are achieving the learning goals of a course—moves assessment to a higher level. We call this level institutional intentionality.

When these two kinds of assessment—of student learning and of course effectiveness—are aligned and supported through the practices of the law school as a whole, the result is that the institution provides a coherent educational experience with many of the features of a well-designed course writ large. Such institution-wide efforts extend the idea of formative assessment beyond the individual student to the faculty and administration. At all levels, people get information that allows them to rethink their approach, practices, and goals. That this is possible (and what it requires) is suggested by Anne Colby, Thomas Ehrlich, and colleagues' research on institutional intentionality in undergraduate education for citizenship. Colby and Ehrlich (2003) call attention to colleges and universities that "are explicit about their goals and actively plan strategies to achieve them" (p. 9). These strategies, in turn, become expressions of institutional commitment to a set of orienting values that define the institution and direct its future development. The institutions Colby and Ehrlich studied were noteworthy for their ability to "remain true to their espoused values while continually rethinking the way these values are made concrete on campus through both programs and cultures" (p. 95).

In the realm of legal education, such practices have received similar attention from Gregory Munro of the University of Montana Law School, who has developed the implications of a more intentional use of assessment practices to promote overall coherence in institutional practice. In *Outcomes Assessment for Law Schools,* Munro (2000) argues that in order to realize the goal of forming lawyers at once learned, competent, and able to satisfy the public's demand for greater responsibility and responsiveness, law schools need to refocus their curricula around the twin goals of student learning and faculty improvement. Within this framework, Munro claims, courses need to make learning outcomes clear and explicit to students so they can orient their activity. This effort needs to be guided by assessment practices that help students learn—and also learn to learn—how to be the kind of legal professional the school wishes to educate. "In designing a course," Munro counsels, "a teacher should consider what knowledge, skills, and values can assist the student in law school (as a prerequisite to other courses, clinical work, competitive teams, or student organizations) and after graduation (as building blocks to becoming an effective, reflective professional)" (p. 141). Course assessment procedures, in Munro's conception, become explicitly concerned with making students metacognitive about their own process of learning. This, of course, is the idea of intentional learning worked out through the assessment of course effectiveness.

Finally, as a context for fostering intentional learning among law students, Munro insists that the faculty and institution as a whole need to be clear about the institution's purpose and mission. To be sure, goal setting in any large educational institution is complex and difficult, and in many law schools, the missions are multiple—promoting research and public service, training litigators as well as transactional lawyers, and so forth. However, Munro argues, goal setting for a law school can help focus the educational mission by bringing into sustained dialogue and argument various members of the faculty and administration. Of course, this places real demands on institutional leadership. But designing and implementing a legal education, he insists, is greatly helped by having a formulation of the "articulated mission of the school" that identifies the "functions that the law school should serve" and then devising an alignment of teaching methods, outcomes, and assessment procedures in light of these functions. Munro further asserts that legal education would benefit from having individual schools seriously take into consideration the views not only of administration, faculty, and influential alumni but also representatives of the law school's constituencies in the bar and bench, even representatives of the larger public.

Although some object to Munro's suggestion that the school's constituencies be invited to provide feedback, this kind of wide consultation is already quite common in other professional schools. Engineering schools have long been highly engaged with industry and the federal government. Seminaries must attend to the views articulated by the employers of their graduates—the denominations and "people in the pews" whom their graduates serve. Medical schools have become increasingly responsive to public, as well as professional and governmental, concerns.

These other professions seem to recognize that achieving a high degree of alignment among the interests of the school's internal and external constituencies and using the process to articulate clearly the institution's goals and priorities contributes significantly to educational quality. This may involve deciding, for example, whether the school aims to produce legal generalists (mostly practitioners or perhaps judges) or scholars and legal specialists. The process can also ask where it would prefer to see its students work or how engaged the school should be with segments of the public or with law firms and government. It can also address the question of what kinds of public values the school should embody and promote (Munro, 2000).

Munro asserts that to succeed fully, intentional learning in the law needs a consciously crafted educational environment. The law school must become intentional about its own aims, educational processes, and identity. Like good students, good law schools should also be constantly learning and assessing their progress. They should be developing greater institutional intentionality. This is an aim we endorse and commend.

The Importance of Institutional Climate

In our study of North American legal education, we saw that the cognitive apprenticeship dominates and that the prevalent use of summative assessment reinforces that dominance. The relative weakness of broader means of assessment also makes it difficult for legal educators to be fully aware of the consequences of their concentration on this single aspect of professional preparation. Unless they examine current practice critically, law schools will likely fail to appreciate the powerful formative consequences that privileging legal analysis has on students' sense of what the vocation of "lawyer" is and requires.

A fuller and more adequate legal education that would provide a broader and, therefore, more realistic and more ethically appealing understanding of the various vocations in the law could not be based solely on most schools' current pedagogical and assessment practices. This fuller and more adequate preparation for the profession would, from the beginning, introduce students to lawyering and clinical work, as well as concern with ethical and professional responsibility; in short, the cognitive, practical, and ethical-social apprenticeships would be integrated.

As law schools contemplate reforming legal education toward such an integrated professional preparation, they may find the experience of other professions enlightening. For example, the preparation of Jewish and Christian clergy makes significant investment in the formation of professional identity.[3] The strategies through which seminaries attempt to shape knowledge, professional skill, and character into a whole are diverse and often rooted in the particularities of the various religious traditions. One thing they share, however, is a recognition of the power of institutional culture and climate, as represented in the daily routines of faculty and students and in the notions of the profession that are the focus of repeated, collective attention. The schools understand the core messages, implicit as well as explicit, that institutional culture conveys about the means and ends of studying for a professional career (Foster, Dahill, Golemon, and Tolentino, 2005). Institutional culture is also powerful in law schools, though rarely as intentionally formative as it is in seminaries.

Attention to the formative effects of pedagogy and assessment is a recognition that institutional intentionality matters for professional education. But the concept of formation also provides a useful language for analyzing and criticizing how various pedagogical and assessment practices contribute—or fail to contribute—to the goal of the particular institution. The combination of the competitive and combative structure of the case-dialogue method with the summative assessments used in law school's first year clearly, forcefully, and quite immediately conveys to students a set of priorities and values that, for many, come to define the profession itself. Although formal courses are not the whole of law school, the overwhelming emphasis on legal analysis, especially in its current form, generally establishes the tone of the educational experience as a whole, so that other aspects of the school, whether individual professors and courses or extracurricular programs, find that they must define their purposes with reference to this tone. So, for example, as the leaders of clinical-legal education or other lawyering programs attempt to make their programs effective, they find they must explicitly define their goals in ways that counter the messages of the dominant pedagogy and assessment approach.

The goal should be to create a campus culture that is a positive force. It is clear that this can be done. In a study of lawyers' attitudes toward pro bono work and other kinds of public service, Deborah Rhode found that many alumni who reported law school experiences that positively influenced their attitudes toward public service referred to a supportive campus culture. The cultures of their schools convey support for public service through positive faculty attitudes and graduation requirements, such as mandatory pro bono work. For example, a disproportionate number of Yale Law School alumni in Rhode's study cited Yale's support:

> [Yale provided support] both "financially and philosophically," through curricular opportunities, public interest placements, and relatively generous loan forgiveness policies. As one attorney noted, "I started thinking more about public interest work because the law school valued it so highly and I loved my public interest job during the first summer." (Rhode, 2005, p. 156)

Without conscious attention to these effects—without institutional intentionality—legal educators are less likely to pay attention to the ways that their teaching and assessment are intertwined with the educational climate in which they live and work, and therefore do not ask themselves whether the messages their students get about the profession are the ones they want to send.

Assessment and Institutional Intentionality: A Call for Further Development

Differentiated forms of assessment are key tools for educators of future professionals. However, law schools, like other professional schools, can use these tools more or less thoughtfully and intentionally. Were legal education to take the idea of formative assessment as integral to its purpose of training future lawyers, this would be a significant move toward greater institutional intentionality. In this light, much of what we have seen in previous chapters can be read as showing such processes already at work. Many faculty, some individual programs and initiatives, and even some law schools are already moving in this direction. One of our hopes for this report is to give more visibility to these disparate efforts. The current need, however, is to become more deliberate about this direction: to discuss it, to clarify the sometimes conflicting purposes and approaches in legal education, to study these issues, to experiment, and to learn from the results.

Notes

1. See Mangan (2006).

2. See Papadakis and others (2005).

3. See Foster, Dahill, Golemon, and Tolentino (2005).

CONCLUSION

WE HAVE TRIED TO CAPTURE the special strengths of legal education, for in our campus visits, reading, and conversations, we were impressed by law schools' distinctive forms of teaching and by the results in student learning. Our hope is that this book can make the virtues of legal education better understood in law schools, other professional schools, and even other areas of higher education.

Our travels, both literal and figurative, through North American legal education also revealed areas where law schools could do better to serve aspiring lawyers and the profession. Our extensive study of education in the professions and our experience with research on learning has given us a special perspective: we see where law schools could benefit from ideas drawn from the education of physicians, teachers, nurses, engineers, and clergy, as well as from research on learning. To conclude, then, we offer a summary of our observations and propose a framework for a bolder, more integrated approach to legal education that addresses our findings and observations about both its strengths and its most serious limitations.

LAW SCHOOL PROVIDES RAPID SOCIALIZATION INTO THE STANDARDS OF LEGAL THINKING.

More than other types of occupation, professions are critically determined by the education of their members. For medicine, engineering, and the clergy, as well as law and virtually all other professions, professional schools have become key switching stations that route their graduates toward their future careers. By providing systematic immersion into a distinctive knowledge base, professional schools set their students apart from lay people, binding them into a shared pattern of thinking and acting. Professional schools thereby provide students with their first, and highly influential, orientation toward the domain they are entering. Professional education teaches both a way of understanding how the world works and a distinctive set of skills for working in the world. But, perhaps most decisively, professional education forms the identity of the future professional, show-ing how to succeed and how to comport oneself as a teacher, a physician, a member of the clergy, or a member of the bar.

From this comparative perspective, law schools are impressive educa-tional institutions. In a relatively short period of time, they are able to impart a distinctive habit of thinking that forms the basis for their stu-dents' development as legal professionals. In our visits to over a dozen schools of different types and geographical locations, our research team found unmistakable evidence of the pedagogical power of the first phase of legal education. Within months of their arrival in law school, students demonstrate new capacities for understanding legal processes, for seeing both sides of legal arguments, for sifting through facts and precedents in search of the more plausible account, for using precise language, and for understanding the applications and conflicts of legal rules. Despite a wide variety of social backgrounds and undergraduate experiences, they were learning, in the parlance of legal education, to "think like a lawyer." This is an accomplishment of the first order that deserves serious consideration from educators of aspirants to other professional fields.

LAW SCHOOLS RELY HEAVILY ON ONE SIGNATURE PEDAGOGY TO ACCOMPLISH THEIR SOCIALIZATION PROCESS.

The process of enabling students to think like lawyers takes place not only in a compressed period of time but primarily through the medium of a single form of teaching—the case-dialogue method. Compared to other professional fields, which often employ multiple forms of teaching through a more prolonged socialization process, legal pedagogy is remarkably uni-form across variations in schools and student bodies. Excepting a few schools, the first-year curriculum is similarly standardized, as is the sys-tem of competitive grading that accompanies the teaching and learning practices associated with case dialogue. The consequence is a striking con-formity in outlook and habits of thought among law school graduates.

In particular, the academic setting of most law school training empha-sizes the priority of analytical thinking in which students learn to catego-rize and discuss persons and events in highly generalized terms. This emphasis on analysis and system has profound effects in shaping a legal frame of mind. It conveys at a deep, largely uncritical level an under-standing of the law as a formal and rational system, however much its doctrines and rules may diverge from the commonsense understandings of the layperson. This preference for the procedural and systematic gives a common tone to legal discourse that students are quick to notice, even if reproducing it consistently is often a major learning challenge.

THE SIGNATURE PEDAGOGY HAS VALUABLE STRENGTHS
BUT ALSO UNINTENDED CONSEQUENCES.

The case-dialogue method challenges students to grasp the law as a subject characterized by a particular way of thinking, a distinctive stance toward the world. And as their signature pedagogies do for other professions, the case-dialogue method offers both an accurate representation of central aspects of legal competence and a deliberate simplification. The simplification consists in the abstraction of the legally relevant aspects of situations and persons from their everyday contexts. In the case-dialogue classroom, students learn to dissect every situation they meet from a distinctive, legal point of view.

By questioning and having argumentative exchanges with faculty, students are led to analyze situations by looking for points of dispute or conflict and considering as "facts" only those details that contribute to someone's staking a legal claim on the basis of precedent. Again, much like the signature pedagogies of other professions, the case-dialogue method drills students, over and over, in first abstracting from natural contexts, then operating on the facts so abstracted, according to specified rules and procedures; they then draw conclusions based on that reasoning. Students discover that thinking like a lawyer means redefining messy situations of actual or potential conflict as opportunities for advancing a client's cause through legal argument before a judge or through negotiation.

By contrast, the task of connecting these conclusions with the rich complexity of actual situations that involve full-dimensional people, let alone the job of thinking through the social consequences or ethical aspects of the conclusions, remains outside the method. Issues such as the social needs or matters of justice involved in cases do get attention in some case-dialogue classrooms, but these issues are almost always treated as addenda. Being told repeatedly that such matters fall, as they do, outside the precise and orderly "legal landscape," students often conclude that they are secondary to what really counts for success in law school—and in legal practice. In their all-consuming first year, students are told to set aside their desire for justice. They are warned not to let their moral concerns or compassion for the people in the cases they discuss cloud their legal analyses.

This warning does help students escape the grip of misconceptions about how the law works in order to hone their analytical skills. But when the misconceptions are not addressed directly, students have no way of learning when and how their moral concerns may be relevant to their work as lawyers and when these concerns could throw them off track. Students often find this confusing and disillusioning. The fact that moral concerns are reintroduced only haphazardly conveys a cynical impression of the law that is rarely intended—one of several unintended consequences.

Another unforeseen consequence results from the near-exclusive focus on systematic abstraction from actual social contexts, which suggests two major limitations of legal education. One limitation is the casual attention that most law schools give to teaching students how to use legal thinking in the complexity of actual law practice. Unlike other professional education, most notably medical school, legal education typically pays relatively little attention to direct training in professional practice. The result is to prolong and reinforce the habits of thinking like a student rather than an apprentice practitioner, thus conveying the impression that lawyers are more like competitive scholars than attorneys engaged with the problems of clients. Neither understanding of the law is exhaustive, of course, but law school's typically unbalanced emphasis on the one perspective can create problems gratuitously for what *After the JD* calls "the transition to practice" (Dinovitzer and others, 2004).

The second limitation is law schools' failure to complement the focus on skill in legal analysis with effective support for developing the ethical and social dimensions of the profession. Students need opportunities to learn about, reflect on, and practice the responsibilities of legal professionals. Despite progress in making legal ethics a part of the curriculum, law schools rarely pay consistent attention to the social and cultural contexts of legal institutions and the varied forms of legal practice. To engage the moral imagination of students as they move toward professional practice, seminaries and medical, business, and engineering schools employ well-elaborated case studies of professional work. Law schools, which pioneered the use of case teaching, only occasionally do so.

Both these drawbacks—lack of attention to practice and the weakness of concern with professional responsibility—are the unintended consequences of reliance on a single, heavily academic pedagogy to provide the crucial initiation into legal education.

ASSESSMENT OF STUDENT LEARNING REMAINS UNDERDEVELOPED.

Assessment is important in all forms of professional education. In law schools, too, assessing students' competence performs several important educational functions. In its familiar summative form, assessment devices such as both standardized and essay tests sort and select students. In legal education, summative assessment plays a major role at the beginning of the process as a filter, as when law schools typically admit only students who are likely to succeed in law school, as judged by performance on the

Law School Admissions Test. High-stakes, summative assessment is also critical at the end of the first year of law school, when essay examinations in each doctrinal course determine students' relative ranking, thus opening and closing academic options for the remainder of students' legal education and legal careers. The bar examination is another form of high-stakes, summative assessment that directly affects law school teaching, but the exam is administered by an independent body.

Law schools give less attention and emphasis in their formal procedures to the second type of assessment, called formative assessment. Here feedback is provided primarily to support students' learning and self-understanding rather than to rank or sort. Contemporary learning theory suggests that efficient application of educational effort is significantly enhanced by the use of formative assessment. For educational purposes, summative devices have their place primarily as devices to protect the public by ensuring basic levels of competence. Formative practices directed toward improved learning ought to be primary forms of assessment.

LEGAL EDUCATION APPROACHES IMPROVEMENT ONLY INCREMENTALLY RATHER THAN COMPREHENSIVELY.

Law schools have been sent stern messages about these issues for decades. Legal theorists such as Karl Llewellyn and Jerome Frank long ago pointed out the need to connect training in legal argument with the fashioning of legal interventions and artifacts in the various milieus of practice. Prestigious commissions of both the American Bar Association and the Association of American Law Schools have issued well-documented and closely argued reports making the same argument. The 1992 MacCrate report concluded that law schools were paying inadequate attention to lawyering skills and professionalism. A few years later, in 1996, the Professionalism Committee of the American Bar Association's Section of Legal Education and Admission to the Bar further articulated the lack of adequate preparation for professionalism and the need for law school programs that would support the development of a stronger sense of ethical integrity, civility, and commitment to the profession's public mission. Since then, through its standards of law school accreditation, the American Bar Association has placed increased emphasis on instruction in practice skills, as well as pro bono work, while urging schools to upgrade the status of clinical faculty members.

And, indeed, over the past decade, important changes have been taking place. Compared to fifty years ago, law schools now provide students with more experience, more context, more choices, and more connection with the larger university world and other disciplines. However, efforts to improve legal education have been more piecemeal than comprehensive. Few schools have made the overall practices and effects of their educational effort a subject for serious study. Too few have attempted to address these inadequacies on a systematic basis. This relative lack of responsiveness by the law schools, taken as a group, to the well-reasoned pleas of the national bar antedates our investigation.

Consider the imbalance among the students' experiences of the three apprenticeships. We believe that the still relatively subordinate place of the practical and ethical-social apprenticeships in many law schools is symptomatic of legal education's approach to addressing problems and framing remedies. To a significant degree, both supporters and opponents of increased coverage for lawyering and professionalism have treated the major components of legal education in an *additive* way, not an integrative way. Even the MacCrate report and the American Bar Association's report on professionalism assume an additive model. To quote the latter:

> Providing additional classroom coverage of professionalism issues will not be an easy task. Law school curriculum reform is a tedious and often frustrating task and seems to work best when modest changes are made at the margin by adding one or two additional courses. If the proponents of the need for increased law school training in ethics and professionalism are right, however, an effort equivalent to that which led to the increase in clinical legal education in the 1970s and the increased emphasis on skills training in the 1990s is required. The aim of this effort should be to elevate the twin concepts of the practice of law as a public service calling and the development of the capacity for reflective moral judgment to the same level as legal knowledge and traditional legal skills. This is indeed an ambitious goal. (American Bar Association, 1996)

Moreover, efforts to add new requirements are almost universally resisted, not only in legal education but in professional education generally, because there is always too much to accomplish in too little time. Sometimes this problem becomes so acute that the only solution is to extend the time allocated to training. In engineering, for example, current debate centers on the question of whether the master's rather than the bachelor's degree should be the entry-level credential for the field. Extending the duration of training is a radical solution, however, and certainly not one that would appeal to law school administrators, faculty, or students.

This additive strategy of educational change assumes that increasing emphasis on the practical and ethical-social apprenticeships will reduce time for and ultimately weaken the cognitive apprenticeship. When academic values and goals are preeminent, as we believe they are in legal education, this assumption implies that each of the apprenticeships is actually freestanding. Thus the practical and ethical-social apprenticeships can be strengthened only to the point at which they might begin to encroach on the first. This is not only a logistical problem (too much to accomplish in a limited amount of time), but it is also a conceptual and pedagogical problem. In essence, the additive strategy assumes that the cognitive apprenticeship of legal education is sufficient in its own terms, only requiring enlargement of the practical and ethical-social without disturbing the existing cognitive emphasis.

An Integrative Strategy for Legal Education

Among the positive findings of our study, however, have been powerful examples of serious efforts to go beyond these limitations of the typical model of legal education. Taken together, these developments suggest ferment in the field. We hope that this activity signals that the time has come for articulation of purpose and organization for action.

We endorse a different strategy, which we call *integrative* rather than *additive*. Something like an integrative strategy has, in fact, begun to emerge recently in discussions of legal education. The core insight behind the integrative strategy is that effective educational efforts must be understood in holistic rather than atomistic terms. For law schools, this means that, far from remaining uncontaminated by each other, each aspect of the legal apprenticeship—the cognitive, the practical, and the ethical-social— takes on part of its character from the kind of relationship it has with the others. In the standard model, in which the cognitive apprenticeship as expressed in the Socratic classroom dominates, the other practical and ethical-social apprenticeships are each tacitly thought of and judged as merely adjuncts to the first. That is why adherents of the additive strategy resist the idea that all experiences are critical, that they are inseparable, and that all three will be strengthened through their integration.

As we have said, all law schools teach lawyering skills and professionalism, and the offerings at many are very rich. But it is extremely rare for the three aspects of legal apprenticeship to be linked so seamlessly that each contributes to the strength of the others, crossing boundaries to infuse each other. And in virtually no law schools do these experiences systematically reach all of the students. Perhaps because of its highly academic character—its strong grounding in legal analysis—the field of legal education has not been inclined to embrace far-reaching reforms on

an institutional level, at least not since the time of Langdell. Legal scholarship has generated a succession of bold, even radical, new ways of understanding the law, but this kind of scholarly innovation has proved entirely
compatible with a stable, even conservative orientation toward educational practice and is part and parcel of an orientation that privileges the
cognitive apprenticeship in its present, stand-alone configuration.

Could it be otherwise? It may appear that a cognitive apprenticeship
unmoored to practical experience must always be the central driving force
for any learned profession whose training is located in institutions of
higher education. But this is not so. For medical education in the United
States, the practical apprenticeship has begun to emerge as the cutting
edge of pedagogical advance.

An Example from Medical Education

Because most medical training occurs not in classrooms but in settings of
practice, notably the teaching hospital and clinic, medical education has
always relied more heavily on the practical apprenticeship than has legal
education. However, it is noteworthy that medical education has for three
decades been steadily enhancing the role of clinical education, bringing
the teaching of skills into increasingly close contact with the teaching of the
basic sciences that underlie medical practice.

Clinical training now begins in the first year of medical school and is
dominant by the third year. The teaching of basic science is still essential,
but the modes of teaching science have shifted in many medical schools,
with greater emphasis on teaching science as it informs and will be used in
the practice of medicine. This does not mean that medical education is con-
sumed with teaching mere techniques. A great deal of both foundational
and cutting-edge knowledge is imparted at every stage in the process. The
difference is the growing recognition that medical science is best taught in
the context of medical practice, with integral connections between the fundamental knowledge base and the complex skills of professional practice.

This intensification of the practical apprenticeship in medical education
has also opened the way to more authentic and powerful means of fostering professionalism. Students grapple with real issues of patient auton-
omy, inter-cultural communication, responsibility for public health, and
the challenge of maintaining compassion in the press of a fast-paced medical environment. When they confront these and related issues, professionalism becomes tangible and visible to them. Their teachers are models,
for better or worse, and opportunities to reflect on what they are experi-

encing take on a new urgency. Although medical educators believe their field still faces serious unresolved problems, particularly because of changes in the settings of patient care that militate against time for teaching, medical education has been receptive to pedagogical and curricular change to advance the goals of a more seamless integration of theory, practice, and professional responsibility.

A Cautionary Tale from Business Education

Business education offers a cautionary tale about the importance of a more integrative approach. A prominent business school professor, economist Robert Shiller, whose well-timed *Irrational Exuberance* (2000) criticized fatuous idolization of the stock market just as the speculative bubble of the 1990s was about to burst, has argued that "education molds not just individuals but also common assumptions and conventional wisdom." In a 2005 op-ed piece in the *New York Times,* Shiller argues that when it comes to "the business world, our universities—and especially their graduate business schools—are powerful shapers of the culture." For this reason, Shiller writes, business education is implicated in the scandals that have weakened global confidence in American business practices. Shiller singles out for indictment the "cornerstone of modern business education"—financial theory (Shiller, 2005,p. A25).

At the heart of that theory Shiller finds the "selfish rational actor." When that theoretical abstraction is presented as the unquestioned truth about human individuals "and we spend the entire semester developing the implications of this assumption," it is little wonder that the (otherwise laudable) addition of courses in business ethics must seem to students "like a side order of some overcooked vegetable." Therefore, Shiller maintains, ethical behavior on the part of many graduates of business school "must involve overcoming their learned biases." Unfortunately, the mistaken learning in question seems an indirect result of a core practice in business education. Thus Shiller's argument is, in effect, a critique of the additive strategy for righting a curricular imbalance created by the business school version of the cognitive apprenticeship. As he sums up his argument, a merely additive strategy of trying to balance a semester (or years) spent "developing the implications of this [strategic actor] assumption" with a course in professional responsibility would seem manifestly inadequate (Shiller, 2005, p. A25). When law schools seek to introduce more formative balance into the curriculum, Shiller's example suggests why a bolder strategy of integration is called for.

A more integrated drawing together of the three apprenticeships could enable students to place their learning of legal reasoning, including its assumptions about legal actors that we examined earlier in this book, within a fuller understanding of law as a moral and social institution. The integrative strategy imagined here would, from the outset, link the learning of legal reasoning more directly with consideration of the historical, social, and philosophical dimensions of law and the legal profession, including some cross-national comparison—a dimension that is sure to become increasingly important in an age of global integration among legal systems. Such a rich intellectual matrix would provide a context within which students could pursue a fuller "theorizing of legal practice," including their own future roles and responsibilities.[1]

Toward an Integrative Model for Law Schools

Law school provides the beginning, not the full development, of students' professional competence and identity. Law school should provide an initiation into all three aspects of that development. Integrating the parts of legal education with a formative intent would help students fit together the various elements of their educational experience, preparing them for the varied demands of professional legal work. When thinking of the law school curriculum as a three-part model, whose parts interact with and influence each other, those elements are

1. The teaching of legal doctrine and analysis, which provides the basis for professional growth
2. Introduction to the several facets of practice included under the rubric of lawyering, leading to acting with responsibility for clients
3. A theoretical and practical emphasis on inculcation of the identity, values, and dispositions consonant with the fundamental purposes of the legal profession

Our model of integration has the most immediate implications for the first-year experience. However, it also addresses the problem of the larger curriculum, particularly what should happen in the third year. In most schools, curriculum lacks clear shape or purpose. The gradual reduction over the years in the number of required courses has opened up lots of elective space. Some of this curricular space is rightfully now given to courses that enable students to concentrate on specific areas of legal knowledge and expertise. Nonetheless, the goal of greater integration means that the common core of legal education needs to be expanded in qualitative terms to encompass substantial experience with practice, as well as opportunities to wrestle with the issues of professionalism.

Both these purposes are importantly affected by students' work experience, especially the summer employment typical of the first and second summers of law school. *After the JD* reports that graduates mostly see these experiences as having the greatest influence on their selection of career paths (Dinovitzer and others, 2004). It is very important, then, to bring these experiences into the educational program in intentional ways. One way would be to give new emphasis to the third year as a kind of "capstone" opportunity for students to develop specialized knowledge, engage in advanced clinical training, and work with faculty and peers in serious, comprehensive reflection on their educational experience and their strategies for career and future professional growth.

As we have repeatedly seen, law school's standard model conditions both the balance among the three aspects of apprenticeship and the way in which each is conceived in relation to the others. We suggest that, building on the work already under way in several law schools, the teaching of legal analysis, while remaining central, does not stand alone. Rather, the teaching of legal doctrine needs to become fully integrated into the curriculum. It should extend beyond case-dialogue courses to become part of learning to think like a lawyer in practice settings. Nor should doctrinal instruction be the exclusive content of the beginner's curriculum. Rather, learning legal doctrine should be seen as prior to practice chiefly in the sense that it provides the essential background assumptions and habits of thought that students need as they find their way into the functions and identity of legal professionals.

Courses focused on the skillful performance of legal knowledge in role extend students' preparation beyond the cognitive apprenticeship, starting with a basic introduction in the first year and continuing thereafter. In the first phase of legal education, well-designed lawyering courses should be taught as intentional complements to doctrinal instruction. Ideally, this experience of complementarity would continue in the second and third years as a gradual development of practice knowledge and skill, beginning in simulation and moving into actual responsibility for clients. This means that lawyering should always be taught in conscious relationship to the students' growing understanding of particular features and areas of legal doctrine. In the work of lawyering, the most significant intellectual skill lies in the development of case theory, about which an impressive body of sophisticated literature continues to grow.

Both doctrinal and practical courses are likely to be most effective if faculty who teach them have some significant experience with the complementary area. In an integrated model, the practical apprenticeship stands not subordinate to but in a complementary relationship with legal analysis. At its best, the relationship between formal knowledge and practical knowing might be thought of as symbiotic. Because all law faculty have experienced the case-dialogue classroom from their own education, doctrinal faculty will probably make the more significant pedagogical discoveries as they observe or participate in the teaching of lawyering courses and clinics. These discoveries, we suggest, are also likely to be taken back into doctrinal teaching. Faculty development programs that consciously aim to increase the mutual understanding of doctrinal and lawyering faculty of each other's work are likely to improve students' efforts to make integrated sense of their developing legal competence. However it is organized, the sustained dialogue among faculty with different strengths and interests united around common educational purpose that is likely to matter most.

Because it directly addresses professional life in all its dimensions, the apprenticeship of identity and purpose is a natural site for integration. The question for law schools is how and to what ends students are to weave together quite different kinds of knowledge and skill: a strong element of formal knowledge, as in the law of lawyering and courses in legal ethics, and professional judgment gained through typical situations of practice. The pedagogies appropriate for professional identity and purpose range from classroom didactics to reflective practice in clinical situations.

The key challenge in supporting students' ethical-social development is to keep each of these emphases in active communication with each other. A purely theoretical approach to professional ethics is unlikely to deeply affect the learner. But important aspects of ethical understanding are lost when students only attend to particular relationships with clients or specific aspects of practice. The aim has to be stereoscopic: the "big picture" of the profession, its history, aims, and context, as well as that of the law itself, must inform micro-level experience. Daily practice makes meaningful this dimension of legal work. Students who lack experience in negotiating the complex issues facing the profession today can hardly be expected to take up active roles as civic professionals, contributing to the public direction of their areas of the law.

We believe that the demands of an integrative approach require *both* attention to how fully issues of the ethical-social apprenticeship "pervade" the doctrinal and lawyering curricula *and* the provision of educational experiences directly concerned with the values and situation of the law and the legal profession. As the example of medical education suggests, these concerns "come alive" most effectively when the ideas are introduced in relationship to students' experience of taking on the responsibilities incumbent on the profession's various roles. As in teaching for legal analysis and lawyering skills, the most powerful effects on student learning are likely to be felt when faculty with different strengths work in a complementary relationship. Students need a dynamic curriculum that moves them back and forth between understanding and enactment, experience and analysis, as they strive to become mature legal professionals.

Getting Practical: Examples from the Field

Some law schools are already addressing the need for a more dynamic, integrated curriculum. The ongoing work of centers such as the Institute for Law School Teaching at the Gonzaga University School of Law and a far-flung network of legal educators that has resulted in *Best Practices for Legal Education* testify to substantial interest in many aspects of the pedagogical project. Indeed, our idea for an integrated approach draws liberally on their inspiration.

In Chapter One, we profiled NYU and CUNY's law schools because they each exemplify, in different ways, ongoing efforts to bring the three aspects of legal apprenticeship into active relation. At CUNY, we discovered close interrelations between doctrinal and lawyering courses, including a resource-intensive investment in small sections in both doctrinal and lawyering seminars in the first year and a heavy use of simulation throughout the curriculum. The school also provides extensive clinical experience linked to the lawyering sequence. At NYU, doctrinal, lawyering, and clinical courses are linked in a variety of intentional ways. There the lawyering curriculum also serves as a connecting point for faculty discussion and theoretical work, as well as a way to encourage students to consider their educational experience as a unified effort.

Other schools have embarked on different experiments. Yale Law School has restructured its first-year curriculum by reducing the number of required doctrinal courses and encouraging students to elect an introductory clinical course in their second semester. This is not full-scale integration of the sort we believe is necessary to legal education, but it and other efforts like it point toward an intermediate strategy: a course of study that encourages students to shift their focus between doctrine and practical experience not once but several times, so as to gradually develop more competence in each area while, it is hoped, making more linkages between them.

Courses and other experiences that develop the practical skills of lawyering are most effective in small-group settings. Of all the obstacles to this reform, the relatively higher cost of the small classes is the most difficult to overcome, especially at institutions without large endowments. In this light, it is encouraging to note the emergence of what may be another, less resource-intensive strategy. Southwestern Law School has instituted a new first-year curriculum in which students take four doctrinal courses in their first semester rather than five, allowing for an intensified two-semester, integrated lawyering course plus an elective course in their second semester. The lawyering course expands a legal writing and research experience to include detailed work in legal methods and reasoning, as well as interviewing and advocacy. Professionalism explicitly grounds the course through the introduction of case studies of lawyers' careers that have been drawn from empirical research, such as the studies done by the American Bar Foundation referred to earlier. In addition, the Southwestern plan provides extensive academic support where needed to enhance student success (Southwestern Law School, 2006).

The Richness of Cases: A Legacy and Renewable Resource for the Future

When legal educators set out to introduce students to the intricacies of legal analysis, they turn to cases. When clinical professors lead students toward addressing clients' needs, they are perforce dealing with cases, though in coaching students struggling to develop a theory of the case, they are also helping to shape the case, as well as analyze it. When law school faculty take up issues of jurisprudence or professionalism, they are again very likely to approach these themes through the medium of case discussion. Clearly, this is deeply related to the nature of the law itself— that legal thinking, even the creation and application of doctrinal principles, proceeds by cases. But could it also reflect more than that? Case teaching may be powerful pedagogy because it distills into a method the distinctive intellectual formation of professionals.

In a historical survey of the evolution of the case method at Harvard, David A. Garvin, who teaches case pedagogy at the Harvard Business School, points out that half a century after Langdell's innovation at the law school, case method migrated to the business school. The second dean of the business school at Harvard was Wallace P. Dunham. A graduate of the law school, Dunham sought to adapt the case-dialogue method to the very different context of preparation for business where there was no analogy to the authoritative weight of precedent or legal doctrine. Instead,

Dunham sought to use case material, extensively researched and carefully developed, to engage students' imaginations through taking on the role of protagonist and making crucial decisions. Dunham wanted to use cases to teach students "to think in the presence of new situations," forming habits of making decisions for action (Garvin, 2003).

The business school use of cases was also tied to small-group study and teamwork. Instructors gave students assignment questions designed to organize their approach to analyzing the particulars of the cases. Not surprisingly, the early emphasis on deliberation and judgment has, over time, often given way to a focus on the application of theory and elaborate data analysis. However, the fundamental pedagogical point has remained: elaborate reconstruction of events and situations—enriched cases we might say—as ways to unite analytical with practical reasoning. The use of cases in law courses outside the case-dialogue format often resembles this business school model, as does the use of ethics cases, both in law school and other professional settings such as engineering schools, education schools, and seminaries.

It was another half century before the case model migrated again, this time into medical schools. Although it only reached Harvard in the 1980s, a form of case teaching, known popularly as "problem-based learning" was pioneered in the 1960s as a new way to initiate medical students to both basic sciences and clinical judgment; problem-based learning was used at a small number of medical schools such as McMaster in Canada and Michigan State in the United States. The interesting upshot of this history is that these latter-day case methods, with their focus on problem solving and decision for action, in principle address the cognitive, the practical, and the ethical-social. In this sense, they represent an enriched and more complex development of the original model. In the process, cases have become far more flexible as teaching occasions, as their adoption by virtually all kinds of professional schools testifies. At Harvard Law School itself, recent curricular discussions have brought this range of possibility to faculty attention, probably for the first time since the innovation migrated from the law school nearly a century ago.

For law schools, a new look at the potential richness of case teaching could be both a way to reinvigorate a heritage and a common focus for renewal of educational mission. Such a new look would involve faculty in probing and appreciating anew their venerable pedagogy of legal analysis. It would also naturally involve a larger conversation with other types and uses of cases—in business, in medicine, in nursing, engineering, and teaching, for example—as well as the case pedagogies of clinical teaching. It is hard to predict the results of such a dialogue on the future of law teaching. However, it may significantly enhance the pedagogical imaginations of law school faculty. This would seem a fitting way to welcome home the prodigal case method. In its wanderings, it has enriched many other forms of professional preparation. Welcoming it back with its various enhancements would be to reclaim a legacy while acquiring new resources for legal education's own renewal. We think a renewed attention to case teaching can serve as a common theme around which legal educators can focus and expand their pedagogical vision.

The Rewards of Innovation

As these examples show, integrating, toward a common formative mission, the long-separated and unequally established forms of law school pedagogy will not be a simple or effortless process. On the part of faculty, it will require both drawing more fully on one's own experience and learning from each other. It will also require creativity. The examples we offer throughout the book are noteworthy for the ingenuity that serious interest in improving the educational effects of law school can spark. Greater coherence and integration in the law school experience is not only a worthy project; it can also incite faculty creativity and cohesion.

Peggy Cooper Davis of NYU's law school has described some of these effects. In a recent paper on experiential legal education, Davis draws on the insights of learning theory to lay out a vision of legal education. In Davis's conception, the cognitive, practical, and ethical-social apprenticeships become intertwined as students' understanding of fundamental concepts is deepened through experience. Using those concepts in practice, questions of professional responsibility come to life for students who "try on the role of lawyer in simulations and clinical settings." The intellectual base of law and legal education is strengthened through efforts to "theorize legal practice" in order to create intellectual tools that help structure students' thinking about key dimensions of legal practice. Davis illustrates this vision with accounts of work at her home institution. She points out not only the positive impact on students' preparation as attorneys but also a reflexive impact on scholarship—the coin of the realm for the cognitive apprenticeship. In this and other ways, the integration of the three apprenticeships is mutually enhancing rather than a zero-sum game. She writes:

> The clinical law professor who aspired to progress from the discredited *ad hoc* apprenticeship model to a clinical model for the systematic study of practice had to fill in, from scratch, vast neglected areas of knowledge and theory . . . [This] required new kinds of legal

research and scholarship in the form of qualitative and quantitative studies, partaking of the tools of other disciplines to probe the elements of inarticulate expertise. And it required recourse to other disciplines within which similar or analogous problems had been theorized and studied. Clinical and lawyering scholars have led the effort to build conceptual ground under experiential legal study, producing a valuable and growing body of scholarship about how law evolves and how it is applied. They have been joined in this effort by scholars from other disciplines, and by legal scholars who . . . [have] learned . . . that the study of law is not comprehensive unless it encompasses the study of law in use. (Davis, 2006, pp. 124–125)

The self-awareness that formative education needs and fosters is thus not only a matter for students. It is also at the core of all renewal of education for the professions. Attending to one's own practice of teaching and learning can improve pedagogical self-awareness. It often results in experiments in teaching. But by making such investigations more available to colleagues and peers, the practice of teaching can become the basis of a community of interest—a community whose interest can sustain attention to issues of teaching and learning.[2] The scholarship of teaching and learning encourages faculty to devise methods for documenting their pedagogical practices publicly and for gathering and presenting evidence that will shed light on the concrete impact of these interventions on student learning. The knowledge produced by these inquiries can then be put to work in the dynamic setting of the individual classroom. Equally important, this knowledge becomes available for public consideration and peer review through publications and conferences. The scholarship of teaching and learning is also about overcoming the pedagogical isolation of faculty from one another, in order to ensure that substantive knowledge produced through pedagogical inquiry can be built on and elaborated publicly over time in the fashion of traditional academic scholarship, rather than being gained and lost anew with each individual teacher.

By making classroom practice the subject of critical scrutiny, law professors are applying to their teaching and their students' learning the kind of skill they routinely bring to their legal scholarship. Doing these things— making teaching explicit, going public with the results, and engaging in discussion with others concerned about the same issues—follows one of the central insights derived from the research on learning that we have already noted. Improvement of practice and movement toward expertise take place best within a community of learners in which more experienced and recognized others can serve as coach and guide but in which mutual teaching provides insight and impetus for further development of legal teaching.

A strategy of curricular integration could also open the opportunity for faculty, particularly new faculty, to develop their careers in novel ways, both directly through practical pedagogy and through the scholarship of teaching and learning. In any innovation, the question is always, Who will teach it? Legal education in its organizational procedures of hiring and promotion has typically given little formal attention to the matter of preparing teachers or their development throughout their careers. Today's advances in pedagogical knowledge, especially in a context of greater attention to preparation for practice, makes new emphasis on faculty preparation and development an essential support for new directions in the larger enterprise.

Developing a more balanced and integrated legal education that can address more of the needs of the legal profession than the current model seems highly desirable on its merits. However, as we have seen, there are major obstacles such a development will have to overcome. A trade-off between higher costs and greater educational effectiveness is one. Resistance to change in a largely successful and comfortable academic enterprise is another. However, in all movements for innovation, champions and leaders are essential factors in determining whether or not a possibility becomes realized. Here the developing network of faculty and deans concerned with improving legal education is a key resource waiting to be developed further and put to good use.

We believe that it is well worth the effort. The calling of legal educators is a high one: to prepare future professionals with enough understanding, skill, and judgment to support the vast and complicated system of the law needed to sustain the United States as a free society worthy of its citizens' loyalty; that is, to uphold the vital values of freedom with equity and extend these values into situations as yet unknown but continuous with the best aspirations of our past. If this report has been able to suggest useful ways to think about meeting the challenges entailed by commitment to this end, it will have repaid the contributions of the many students, faculty, and administrators who gave freely of their time and insight in hopes of fostering such dialogue.

NOTES

1. Shiller (2005) suggests the value of taking a "liberal education" approach to the teaching of core concepts in business schools.

2. See Huber and Hutchings (2005).

REFERENCES

American Bar Association, Center for Professional Responsibility. *Model Rules of Professional Conduct.* (2004 ed.) Chicago: American Bar Association, 2004.

American Bar Association, Section of Legal Education and Admissions to the Bar. *Report on Recommendations of the Task Force on Lawyer Competency: The Role of the Law Schools.* Chicago: American Bar Association, 1979.

American Bar Association, Section of Legal Education and Admissions to the Bar. *Legal Education and Professional Development—An Educational Continuum.* Report of the Task Force on Law Schools and the Profession: Narrowing the Gap. Chicago: American Bar Association, 1992.

American Bar Association, Section of Legal Education and Admissions to the Bar. *Teaching and Learning Professionalism: Report of the Professionalism Committee.* Chicago: American Bar Association, 1996.

American Bar Association, Section of Legal Education and Admissions to the Bar. "2004 Enrollment Statistics." [http:www.abanet.org/legaled/statistics/fall2004enrollment.pdf]. 2005a.

American Bar Association, Section of Legal Education and Admissions to the Bar. *Standards for Approval for Law Schools.* (2005–06 ed.) Chicago: American Bar Association, 2005b.

Amsterdam, A. G., and Bruner, J. S. *Minding the Law.* Cambridge: Harvard University Press, 2000.

Barry, M. M., Dubin, J. C., and Joy, P. A. "Clinical Education for this Millennium: The Third Wave." *Clinical Law Review,* 2000, 7(1), 1–75.

Bebeau, M. J. "Influencing the Moral Dimensions of Dental Practice." In J. Rest and D. Narváez (eds.), *Moral Development in the Professions: Psychology and Applied Ethics.* Hillsdale, N.J.: Erlbaum, 1994.

Bebeau, M. J., and Brabeck, M. M. "Integrating Care and Justice Issues in Professional Moral Education: A Gender Perspective." *Journal of Moral Education,* 1987, 16(3), 189–203.

Benner, P., Tanner, C. A., and Chesla, C. A. *Expertise in Nursing Practice: Caring, Clinical Judgment, and Ethics.* New York: Springer, 1996.

Bereiter C., and Scardamalia, M. *The Psychology of Written Composition.* Hillsdale, N.J.: Erlbaum, 1987.

Bereiter, C., and Scardamalia, M. "Intentional Learning as a Goal of Instruction." In L. B. Resnick (ed.), *Knowing, Learning, and Instruction: Essays in Honor of Robert Glaser.* Hillsdale, N.J.: Erlbaum, 1989.

Binder, D. A., Bergman, P., Price, S. C., and Tremblay, P. R. *Lawyers as Counselors: A Client-Centered Approach.* (2nd ed.) St. Paul: Thomson West Publishers, 2004.

Blasi, G. L. "What Lawyers Know: Lawyering Expertise, Cognitive Science, and the Functions of Theory." *Journal of Legal Education,* 1995, *45*(3), 313–397.

Boyer, E. L. *Scholarship Reconsidered: Priorities of the Professoriate.* Princeton: Carnegie Foundation for the Advancement of Teaching, 1990.

Boyer, E. L., and Mitgang, L. D. *Building Community: A New Future for Architecture Education and Practice.* Princeton, Carnegie Foundation for the Advancement of Teaching, 1996.

Bransford, J. D., Brown, A. L., and Cocking, R. R. (eds.). *How People Learn: Brain, Mind, Experience, and School.* Washington, D.C.: Committee on Developments in the Science of Learning, National Research Council, 1999.

Brown, J. S., Collins, A., and Duguid, P. "Situated Cognition and the Culture of Learning." *Educational Researcher,* 1989, *18*(1), 32–42.

Bruner, J. S. *Actual Minds, Possible Worlds.* Cambridge: Harvard University Press, 1985.

Bruner, J. S. *Making Stories: Law, Literature, Life.* New York: Farrar, Straus & Giroux, 2002.

Case, S. M. "The Testing Column: Musings About Assessment in the Professions." *The Bar Examiner,* 2004, *73*(4), 29–31.

Center for Postsecondary Research. *The Law School Years: Probing Questions, Actionable Data—Law School Survey of Student Engagement 2005 Annual Survey Results.* Bloomington, Ind.: Indiana University, 2005.

The City University of New York School of Law. "Required Courses First Year" [http:www.law.cuny.edu./app/courses/courses_detail.jsp?part=firstyear]. 2006.

Cohen, M. R. "The Basis of Contract." *Harvard Law Review* 1933, *46*(4), 553–592.

Colby, A., and Damon, W. *Some Do Care: Contemporary Lives of Moral Commitment.* New York: Free Press, 1992.

Colby, A., Ehrlich, T., Beaumont, E., and Stephens, J. *Educating Citizens: Preparing America's Undergraduates for Lives of Moral and Civic Responsibility.* San Francisco: Jossey-Bass, 2003.

Collins, A., Brown, J. S., and Newman, S. E., "Cognitive Apprenticeship: Teaching the Crafts of Reading, Writing, and Mathematics." In L. Resnick (ed.), *Knowing, Learning, and Instruction: Essays in Honor of Robert Glaser.* Hillsdale, N.J.: Erlbaum, 1989.

Costello, C. Y. *Professional Identity Crisis: Race, Class, Gender, and Success at Professional Schools.* Nashville: Vanderbilt University Press, 2005.

Cramton, R. "On Giving Meaning to 'Professionalism.'" In *Teaching and Learning Professionalism, Symposium Proceedings.* Chicago: American Bar Association, 1997.

D'Alemberte, T. "Law School in the Nineties: Talbot D'Alemberte on Legal Education." *American Bar Association Journal,* 1990, 76(9), 52–53.

Davis, P. C. "Experiential Legal Education in the United States." In *Can Justice be Taught? Social Responsibility and Legal Education.* Report by the Publications Committee of the Results of the First International Symposium, Kwansei Gakuin University Law School Support Program for Professional Graduate School. Nishinomiya, Japan: Kwansei Gakuin University Press, 2006.

Davis, P. C., and Steinglass, E. E. "A Dialogue About Socratic Teaching" *New York University Review of Law and Social Change,* 1997, 23(2), 249–279.

de Tocqueville, A. *Democracy in America.* (G. Lawrence, trans.). New York: Doubleday Anchor, 1969.

Dinovitzer, R., and others. *After the JD: First Results of a National Study of Legal Careers*: Overland Park, Kans.: The National Association for Law Placement Foundation for Law Career Research and Education and the American Bar Foundation, 2004.

Dreyfus, H. L., Dreyfus, S. E., and Athanasiou, T. *Mind Over Machine: The Power of Human Intuition and Expertise in the Era of the Computer.* New York: Free Press, 1986.

Ernest, M., and Bebeau, M. J. "Use of Defining Issues Test in Leadership Education." Paper presented at the Twenty-Sixth Annual Conference of the Association for Moral Education, University of Glasgow, Scotland, 2000.

Fisher, R., Ury, W. L., and Patton, B. *Getting to Yes: Negotiating an Agreement Without Giving In.* New York: Penguin, 1992.

Flexner, A. *Medical Education in the United States and Canada.* New York: The Carnegie Foundation for the Advancement of Teaching, 1910.

Flower, L. S. *The Construction of Negotiated Meaning: A Social-Cognitive Theory of Writing.* Carbondale: Southern Illinois University Press, 1994.

Floyd, D. H. "The Development of Professional Identity in Law Students." Final report to The Carnegie Academy for the Scholarship of Teaching and Learning. Menlo Park: Carnegie Foundation for the Advancement of Teaching, 2002.

Foster, C. R., Dahill, L., Golemon, L., and Tolentino, B. W. *Educating Clergy.* San Francisco: Jossey-Bass, 2005.

Frank, J. *Courts on Trial: Myth and Reality in American Justice.* New York: Atheneum, 1963 (Originally published 1949.)

Freidson, E. *Professionalism Reborn: Theory, Prophecy, and Policy.* Chicago: University of Chicago Press, 1994.

Fuller, L. L., and Eisenberg, M. A. *Basic Contract Law.* (6th ed.) St Paul: West Group, 1996.

Galanter, M. "The Faces of Mistrust: The Image of Lawyers in Public Opinion, Jokes, and Political Discourse." *University of Cincinnati Law Review,* 1998, *66*(3), 805–845.

Galanter, M., and Palay, T. *Tournament of Lawyers: The Transformation of the Big Law Firm.* Chicago: University of Chicago Press, 1991.

Galbraith, D., and Torrance, M. "Conceptual Processes in Writing: From Problem Solving to Text Production." In M. Torrance and D. Galbraith (eds.), *Knowing What to Write: Conceptual Processes in Text Production.* Amsterdam: Amsterdam University Press, 1999.

Gardner, H. *The Mind's New Science: A History of the Cognitive Revolution.* New York: Basic Books, 1987.

Gardner, H., Csikszentmihalyi, M., and Damon, W. *Good Work: When Excellence and Ethics Meet.* New York: Basic Books, 2001.

Garth, B., and Martin, J. "Law Schools and the Construction of Competence." *Journal of Legal Education,* 1993, *43*(4), 469–509.

Garvin, D. A. "Making the Case: Professional Education for the World of Practice." *Harvard Magazine,* 2003, *106*(1), 56–65, 107.

Givner, N., and Hynes, K. "An Investigation of Change in Medical Students' Ethical Thinking." *Medical Education,* 1983, *17*(1), 3–7.

Glendon, M. A. *A Nation Under Lawyers: How the Crisis in the Legal Profession is Transforming American Society.* Cambridge: Harvard University Press, 1994.

Grossman, G. S. "Clinical Legal Education: History and Diagnosis." *Journal of Legal Education,* 1974, *26*(2), 162–194.

Grossman, P., and others. "Unpacking Practice: The Teaching of Practice in the Preparation of Clergy, Teachers, and Clinical Psychologists." Paper presented at the Annual Meeting of the American Educational Research Association, Montréal, Canada, 2005.

Guinier, L., Fine, M., and Balin, J. *Becoming Gentlemen: Women, Law School, and Institutional Changes.* Boston: Beacon Press, 1997.

Hartwell, S. "Moral Development, Ethical Conduct, and Clinical Education." *New York Law School Law Review,* 1990, *35*(1), 131–167.

Hartwell, S. "Promoting Moral Development Through Experiential Teaching." *Clinical Law Review,* 1995, *1*(3), 505–539.

Hayes, J. R., and Flower, L. "Identifying the Organization of Writing Processes." In L. W. Gregg and E. R. Steinberg (eds.), *Cognitive Processes in Writing.* Hillsdale, N.J.: Erlbaum, 1980.

Heinz, J. P., and Laumann, E. O. *Chicago Lawyers: The Social Structure of the Bar.* (rev. ed.) Chicago: Northwestern University Press and the American Bar Association, 1994.

Heinz, J. P., Nelson, R. L., Sandefur, R. L., and Laumann, E. O. *Urban Lawyers: The New Social Structure of the Bar.* Chicago: University of Chicago Press, 2005.

Huber, M. T., and Hutchings, P. *Integrative Learning: Mapping the Terrain.* Washington, D.C.: Association of American Colleges and Universities and The Carnegie Foundation for the Advancement of Teaching, 2004.

Huber, M. T., and Hutchings, P. *The Advancement of Learning: Building the Teaching Commons.* San Francisco: Jossey-Bass, 2005.

Huber, M. T., and Morreale, S. P. "Situating the Scholarship of Teaching and Learning: A Cross-Disciplinary Conversation." In M. T. Huber and S. P. Morreale (eds.), *Disciplinary Styles in the Scholarship of Teaching and Learning: Exploring Common Ground.* Washington, D.C.: American Association for Higher Education and The Carnegie Foundation for the Advancement of Teaching, 2002.

Husted, S.D.R. "Assessment of Moral Reasoning in Pediatric Faculty, House Officers and Medical Students." In *Proceedings of the Seventeenth Annual Conference on Research in Medical Education.* Washington, D.C.: Association of American Medical Colleges, 1978.

Hutchings, P. "Approaching the Scholarship of Teaching and Learning." In P. Hutchings (ed.), *Opening Lines: Approaches to the Scholarship of Teaching and Learning.* Menlo Park, Calif.: The Carnegie Foundation for the Advancement of Teaching, 2000.

Kissam, P. C. "Law School Examinations." *Vanderbilt Law Review,* 1989, *42*(2), 433–504.

Kronman, A. *The Lost Lawyer: Failing Ideals of the Legal Profession.* Cambridge: Belknap Press, 1993.

Lagemann, E. C. *Private Power for the Public Good: A History of the Carnegie Foundation for the Advancement of Teaching.* New York: College Examination Board, 1999.

Landsman, M., and McNeel, S. P. "Moral Judgment of Law Students Across Three Years: Influences of Gender, Political Ideology and Interest in Altruistic Law Practice." *South Texas Law Review,* 2004, *45*(4), 891–919.

Lauer, J., and others. *Four Worlds of Writing: Inquiry and Action in Context.* New York: Longman and Pearson Custom Publishing, 2000.

Lemann, N. "Liberal Education and Professionals." *Liberal Education,* 2004, 90(2), 12–17.

Llewellyn, K. "The Normative, the Legal, and the Law-Jobs: The Problem of Juristic Method." *Yale Law Journal,* 1940, 49(8), 1355–1400.

Llewellyn, K. *The Bramble Bush.* New York: Oceana Publications, 1996.

Long, V. A. "The Moral Judgment of Attorneys: Employment in the Public or the Private Sector and Courses in Legal Ethics." *Dissertation Abstracts International,* 1993.

Mangan, K. S. "Law Schools' Emphasis on LSAT Scores Hurts Black Applicants, Report Says." *The Chronicle of Higher Education.* [http://chronicle.com/daily/2006/02/2006022102n.htm]. Feb. 21, 2006.

Melden, A. I. *Rights and Persons.* Berkeley: University of California Press, 1977.

Menkel-Meadow, C. "Legal Negotiation: A Study of Strategies in Search of a Theory." *American Bar Foundation Research Journal,* 1983, 8(4), 905–937.

Mertz, E. *The Language of Law School: Learning to "Think" Like a Lawyer.* New York: Oxford University Press, forthcoming.

Miller, B. "Teaching Case Theory." *Clinical Law Review,* 2002, 9(1), 293–336.

Minnich, E. K. "Some Reflections on Civic Education and the Curriculum." In B. Murchland (ed.), *Higher Education and the Practice of Democratic Politics: A Political Education Reader.* Dayton: The Kettering Foundation, 1991.

Moliterno, J. *Ethics of the Lawyer's Work.* (2nd ed.) St. Paul: Thomson/West Publishing Company, 2003.

Morgan, T. "Law Faculty as Role Models." In *Teaching and Learning Professionalism, Symposium Proceedings.* Chicago: American Bar Association, 1997.

Munro, G. S. *Outcomes Assessment for Law Schools.* Spokane: Institute for Law School Teaching, Gonzaga University School of Law, 2000.

Nelson, R. L., Trubek, D. M., and Solomon, R. L. (eds.). *Lawyers' Ideals/Lawyers' Practices: Transformations in the American Legal Profession.* Ithaca: Cornell University Press, 1992.

Noonan, J. T. *Persons and Masks of the Law: Cardoza, Holmes, Jefferson, and Wythe as Makers of the Masks.* New York: Farrar, Straus & Giroux, 1976.

Osborn, J. J., Jr. *The Paper Chase.* Albany, NY: Whitson. (Originally published 1971.)

Packer, H. L., Ehrlich, T., with Pepper, S. (eds.). *New Directions in Legal Education: A Report Prepared for the Carnegie Commission on Higher Education.* New York: McGraw-Hill, 1972.

Papadakis, M. A., and others. "Disciplinary Action by Medical Boards and Prior Behavior in Medical School." *New England Journal of Medicine,* 2005, *353*(25), 2673–2682.

Putnam, R. D. *Bowling Alone: The Collapse and Revival of American Community.* New York: Simon & Schuster, 2000.

Rawls, J. *A Theory of Justice.* Cambridge, Mass.: Belknap Press of Harvard University Press, 1971.

Redlich, J. *The Common Law and the Case Method in American University Law Schools.* Carnegie Bulletin No. 8. New York: The Carnegie Foundation for the Advancement of Teaching, 1914.

Reed, A. Z. *Training for the Public Profession of the Law.* Carnegie Bulletin No. 15. New York: The Carnegie Foundation for the Advancement of Teaching, 1921.

Rhode, D. L. *Professional Responsibility: Ethics by the Pervasive Method.* (2nd ed.) New York: Aspen Law & Business, 1998.

Rhode, D. L. *In the Interests of Justice: Reforming the Legal Profession.* New York: Oxford University Press, 2000.

Rhode, D. L. *Pro Bono in Principle and in Practice: Public Service and the Professions.* Stanford: Stanford University Press, 2005.

Rhode, D. L., and Luban, D. *Legal Ethics.* (4th ed.) New York: Foundation Press, 2004.

Rose, M. "Our Hands Will Know: The Development of Tactile Diagnostic Skill—Teaching, Learning, and Situated Cognition in a Physical Therapy Program." *Anthropology and Education Quarterly,* 1999, *30*(2), 133–160.

Sacks, A. M. "Legal Education and the Changing Role of Lawyers in Dispute Resolution." *Journal of Legal Education,* 1984, *34*(2), 237–244.

Sander, R. H., and Williams, E. D. "Why Are There So Many Lawyers? Perspective on a Turbulent Market." *Law and Social Inquiry,* 1989, *14*(3), 431–479.

Scofield, S. B. "Re-Examination of the Application of Cognitive Developmental Theory to the Study of Ethics and Socialization in the Accounting Profession." *Dissertation Abstracts International,* 1997.

Self, D. J., and Baldwin, D. C. "Moral Reasoning in Medicine." In J. Rest and D. Narváez (eds.), *Moral Development in the Professions: Psychology and Applied Ethics.* Hillsdale, N.J: Erlbaum, 1994.

Self, D. J., and Olivarez, M. "The Influence of Gender on Conflicts of Interest in the Allocation of Limited Critical Care Resources: Justice Versus Care." *Journal of Critical Care,* 1993, *8*(1), 64–74.

Self, D. J., Olivarez, M., and Baldwin, D. C. "Moral Reasoning in Veterinary Medicine." In J. Rest and D. Narváez (eds.), *Moral Development in the*

Professions: Psychology and Applied Ethics. Hillsdale, N.J: Erlbaum, 1994.

Sheppard, S. *Educating Engineers.* San Francisco: Jossey-Bass, forthcoming.

Shiller, R. J. *Irrational Exuberance.* Princeton: Princeton University Press, 2000.

Shiller, R. J. "How Wall Street Learns to Look the Other Way." *New York Times,* Feb. 8, 2005, A25.

Shulman, L. S. *The Wisdom of Practice: Essays on Teaching, Learning, and Learning to Teach.* San Francisco: Jossey-Bass, 2004.

Shulman, L. S. "Searching for Signature Pedagogies: Teaching and Learning in the Professions." *Dædalus,* 2005, *134*(3), 52–59.

Simon, W. H. *The Practice of Justice: A Theory of Lawyers' Ethics.* Cambridge: Harvard University Press, 1998.

Sinclair, S. *Making Doctors: An Institutional Apprenticeship.* London: Oxford University Press, 1999.

Southwestern Law School. "Southwestern Launches New First-Year Curriculum." [http://www.swlaw.edu/news/overview/newsr.7fXnfV1a8V]. March 10, 2006.

Stevens, R. B. *Law School: Legal Education in America from the 1850s to the 1980s.* Chapel Hill: University of North Carolina Press, 1983.

Stuckey, R., and others. "Best Practices for Legal Education." Nelson Mullins Riley & Scarborough Center on Professionalism at the University of South Carolina School of Law. [http://professionalism.law.sc.edu/news.html#CLEA]. March 2006.

Sullivan, W. M. *Work and Integrity: The Crisis and Promise of Professionalism in America.* San Francisco: Jossey-Bass, 2005.

Tapp, J. L., and Levine, F. J. "Legal Socialization: Strategies for an Ethical Legality." *Stanford Law Review,* 1974, *27*(1), 1–72.

Tomain, J. P., and Solimine, M. E. "Skills Skepticism in the Postclinic World." *Journal of Legal Education,* 1990, *40*(3), 307–320.

Turow, S. *One L.* New York: Warner Books, 1977.

U.S. Bureau of Labor Statistics, Office of Occupational Statistics and Employment Projections. *Occupational Outlook Handbook.* (2006–07 ed.) Washington, D.C.: U.S. Bureau of Labor Statistics, 2006. [http://www.bls.gov/oco/ocos053.htm].

Valler, B. "Compositional Practice: A Comment on 'A Liberal Education in Law.'" *Journal of the Association of Legal Writing Directors,* 2002, *1*(1), 148–152.

Velmahos, G. C., and others. "Cognitive Task Analysis for Teaching Technical Skills in an Inanimate Surgical Skills Laboratory." *The American Journal of Surgery,* 2004, *187*(1), 114–119.

Weber, M., "Science as Vocation." In H. H. Gerth and C. W. Mills (trans. and eds.), *From Max Weber: Essays in Sociology.* New York: Oxford University Press, 1977.

Willging, T., and Dunn, T. "The Moral Development of the Law Student: Theory and Data on Legal Education." *Journal of Legal Education,* 1981, *31*(3–5), 306–358.

Williams, G. R. "Using Simulation Exercises for Negotiation and Other Dispute Resolution Courses." *Journal of Legal Education,* 1984, *34*(2), 307–314.

Wood, B. D. "The Measurement of Law School Work." *Columbia Law Review,* 1924, *24*(3), 224–265.

INDEX

A

Accreditation Council for Graduate Medical Education, 130

Actual Minds, Possible Worlds (Bruner), 96

ADR (Alternative Dispute Resolution), 105–106, 112, 113–114

Advance Legal Ethics course (Mercer University School of Law), 155–156

Advocacy vs. justice debate, 131–132

After the JD study, 76, 87, 106, 137, 188

American Association of Law Schools, 93

American Bar Association: Code of Ethics of, 179; ethnical-social values promoted by, 129; externships promoted by, 88; JD degree and bar exam requirements of the, 3; legal education accreditation standards of, 91; MacCrate report (1992) by, 93, 113, 136, 173–174, 177, 189, 190; *Model Rules* of, 126, 127, 138, 148, 176; Professionalism Committee of the, 126, 136, 189; reporting on legal competencies, 111; single standard promoted by, 45; on value of negotiation training, 112

American Bar Association Professionalism Committee, 136, 151, 157

American Bar Foundation, 51, 76, 189

American Medical Association, 94

Amsterdam, A., 41, 42, 43, 97, 103

Analytical thinking: case theory use of, 123; definition of, 96

Apprenticeships: definition of, 25; ethical-social, 145–161, 193; expert practice, 28; of identity and purpose, 28; moral development through, 139–140; of professional identity, 129, 132; reappraising learning benefits of, 25–27; three types of professional, 27–29; transmission of expert knowledge through, 98. *See also* Cognitive (or intellectual) apprenticeship; Students

Apprenticeships of practice: application to legal practice, 98–99; challenges of providing, 95; ethical-social, 145–161, 193; forming professional expertise through, 96–97; as heart of education, 97; using iteration mode for, 99–100; learning sciences used to facilitate, 95–96; legal writing for connecting, 104–106; understanding profession's defining practices through, 100. *See also* Clinical-legal education; Lawyering curriculum; Theory for practice

"Artificial trust," 1

Assessment: appropriate to developing expertise, 171–173; case-based essay examinations used for, 162–163, 167; conceptual knowledge, 164–171; criterion-referenced grading, 168, 170–171; of ethical-social development,